Energy Exercises

Energy Exercises

**Easy Exercises
for Health and Vitality
based on
Dr. Randolph Stone's Polarity Therapy**

**By
John Chitty
and
Mary Louise Muller**

**Illustrations by
Mark Allison**

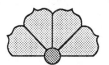

Polarity Press

Contributing Editors:
Mark Allison
Eileen Bach-y-Rita
Anna Chitty
Gail Dennison
Gloria Kamler
Will Leichnitz
Kathleen Morrow
Gary Peterson
Kathleen Petryshyn
Sharon Porter
James Z. Said
Tom Strathairn

Polarity Press
2410 Jasper Ct.
Boulder, CO 80304

ISBN: 994173208-3
Library of Congress Catalogue Number: 90-062289

Printed in the United States of America
First Printing, July, 1990
Second Printing, September, 1992
Third Printing, October 1996

TABLE OF CONTENTS

Table of Contents: Exercises Listed in Order of Appearance

Table of Contents: Illustrations Listed in Order of Appearance

Dedication

This book is dedicated to Dr. Randolph Stone (1890-1981), father of Polarity Therapy.

"Is it not possible for man to keep well by doing a few simple things daily and by living less strenuously? The answer is yes."
--Stone, <u>Health Building</u>, p. 101.

"May this work reach the seekers who are looking for a deeper perspective of a common denominator in the healing art, to push it along in keeping with all the other atomic discoveries of today. The health and well-being of the people should not be neglected. It should really be the first concern of the scientists, doctors and educators. Without health and happiness, all our modern conveniences are of little comfort to us."
--Stone, <u>Polarity Therapy, Vol. II</u>, p. 77.

"Happiness is the consciousness of growth."
--Lowen, <u>Bioenergetics</u>, p. 33.

ACKNOWLEDGEMENTS

There must be pioneers for every new idea, or our world would stagnate and become utterly uninteresting.
--Stone, <u>Polarity Therapy, Vol. II</u>, p. 103.

This book presents a unique exercise system which is effective for health maintenance and stress relief. The postures are easy to do, requiring little time or effort, and yet they provide great benefits for all ages. These benefits have been proven over many years, with thousands of people, in the practice of Polarity Therapy.

The postures and exercises have many sources. They represent a synthesis of understanding and practice from modern and ancient times, and from West and East. The primary source is the pioneering work of Randolph Stone, D.O., D.C. (1890-1981), father of Polarity Therapy, to whom this book is respectfully dedicated. His pamphlet "Easy Stretching Postures" was published in 1954 as a way for Westerners to experience some of the benefits of the Eastern health concept of "Energy Balancing."

Polarity Therapy is a uniquely comprehensive model for understanding health. It has a theoretical foundation strong enough to accommodate a wide range of knowledge, old and new, and from East and West.

The deeper sources for these exercises are the ancient traditions of Yoga and Ayurveda in India and T'ai Chi and other Martial Arts in the Far East. These venerable traditions are not necessarily fully accessible to the busy modern Westerner: the considerable discipline, commitment, study time, and supervision associated with these systems make them unavailable for many. "Energy Exercises" extract simple basic movements and postures that anyone can do safely and easily, with little training. Dr. Stone's frequent use of the term "Polarity Yoga"[1] indicates the extent of his intention of a linkage between the ancient practice and the modern adaptation.

Dr. Stone's work has been supplemented by many people in the field of Polarity Therapy, including Pierre Pannetier (1914-1984), the numerous practitioners of Polarity Therapy throughout the world, and the staff of the Murrieta Foundation. The American Polarity Therapy Association is the primary organization for Polarity in America today, setting Standards for Practice and registering Polarity Practitioners.

A major new source of material for this book comes from a branch of the new field of Kinesiology. These applications,

---

1. Stone, <u>Health Building</u>, pp. 164 ff. Use of the title "Dr." Stone repeatedly in this book reflects the common practice in Polarity literature, an unusual honorific which has become standard.

Randolph Stone, D.O., D.C.

Born in Austria in 1890, Dr. Stone had a medical practice in Chicago for over fifty years. He was an open-minded and vigorous seeker of knowledge, travelling widely to collect health ideas from around the world. He named his collection of theories and techniques "Polarity Therapy." The word Polarity was chosen to describe electromagnetic energy, the idea underlying the ancient health systems of the Orient. Dr. Stone wrote five books and numerous pamphlets, and taught widely until his retirement in 1973. He died in 1981, at the age of 91.

especially Edu-K (for Educational Kinesiology), have opened dramatic new doors in the therapeutic use of energy concepts. Kinesiology seems to complement Polarity Therapy, while adding significant new material and techniques for energy understanding and balancing.

Similarly, the theories, research and techniques known as Cranio-Sacral Therapy are a further advance. These therapies based on the subtle movements of the cranium and spinal system echo and confirm central themes in Polarity Therapy, and open broad new possibilities for the field. Dr. Stone was familiar with the basis for these techniques, being a Doctor of Osteopathy, a personal acquaintance of leading craniopathy practitioners of his day, and having written a significant contribution to the field, Mysterious Sacrum (1954). The incorporation of recent advances in Cranio-Sacral Therapy is a natural area of growth for today's Polarity Therapy practitioner.

A fourth major source for this material is the Murrieta Foundation's staff and students. This organization offered Polarity courses between the years 1978 and 1989 and benefited from the involvement of thousands of people at various times, all of whom shared in its vision of making the ideas of Polarity Therapy and natural health better known to the general public. Without this chain of sincere people, this book would not have been created.

There are many other influences at work in this book, as represented by the footnotes.[2] To these and others we are grateful for contributing to our growth, and to the expansion of the understanding of "Energy in the Healing Arts."

It was Dr. Stone's wish that his work not come to an end with his retirement in 1972, and we feel quite certain that he would approve of and participate in new advances. It is in this spirit that this volume is offered, with the hope that it will prove valuable both to those who are familiar with the underlying ideas and their history, and newcomers to the field of wholistic health.

The Authors & Editors

---

2. We quote widely from many of these sources for several reasons. We hope to give the reader a direct experience of the words of these teachers, and to integrate Polarity with the larger wholistic health movement and with scientific research findings. We believe that Polarity Therapy as described by Dr. Stone is remarkable in its ability to encompass a wide range of subject matter, unifying numerous schools of therapeutic thought in a single comprehensive system. Additionally the wide usage of quotes from related fields is intended to give teachers of Polarity Therapy a good supply of quotable references to use in the presentation of Dr. Stone's work.

INTRODUCTION

Exercises in this book are based on the idea of Energy. Practitioners of traditional Eastern medical systems believe that health is a function of a subtle energy which flows in the body. In this book, we describe easy exercises for enhancing, balancing and facilitating this natural energy flow. These are simple postures and movements which give tangible results. Thousands of people have enjoyed these benefits, changing tension and stress to calm, dynamic power.

The idea of energy is a new concept: most people who will read this book have inherited the world view of Descartes and Newton. Our school training was based on mechanistic, objective, hard scientific assumptions, while the idea of "Energy" requires a subjective, intuitive attitude.[3] It is a new approach with wonderfully broad and powerful implications.

To make this new idea easy for newcomers, the start of this book is purposefully light on theory and esoteric terminology. We want you to experience the benefits first; if later you want to know why it works, the way is clearly marked. As a start, just enjoy and make good use of the exercises and let them speak for themselves. We believe the words of Dr. Stone:

> The Energy Principle is atomic in its concept and is a science of the future...The mechanical approach is totally obsolete in comparison with it."[4]

When you understand "the Energy Principle," you will understand why the exercises are so effective. In these activities, we "work smarter" rather than "work harder."

> This new principle of exercise (energy-current-release by posture-stretch-relaxation) is a more natural aid to health than all the forceful muscle straining used in many other methods.[5]

"No force is ever used."[6] Instead we use an "effortless effort." The effectiveness is due to the use of deeper dimensions of the total person, activating the subtle energy currents, fields and pathways which precede tissues, muscles and organs.

> The postures are given in easy steps, so the process is a natural, progressive approach without force. The postures are designed and used as an easy way of effortless effort, to move the deeper energy currents of the body by a process called "Wu-Wei" in the East. This literally means 'doing by not doing.' Let Mother Nature do it by cooperating with her and resting on her bosom. Thus let the Universal Currents take over the job. It is literally riding the River of Life's energy waves and tuning into them.[7]

---

3. Here is a selection of comments on the interaction between the old and the new outlooks, from writers in the fields of physics, psychology and medicine.

"...the classical ideal of an objective description of nature is no longer valid. The Cartesian partition between the I and the world, between the observer and the observed, cannot be made when dealing with atomic matter."

Capra, The Tao of Physics, pp. 68-69)

"...the question [is] whether an objective scientific view could fully comprehend the functioning... of a human being... Students of personality cannot afford this narrow view."

Lowen, Bioenergetics, pp. 279-280

"Modern medicine is still dominated by the notion that disease is caused by objective agents. A sophisticated analysis shows that this is only partly true."

-Chopra, Quantum Healing, p. 211

---

4. Stone, Polarity Therapy, Vol. I, p. 4.

5. Stone, Health Building, p. 100.

6. *Ibid.*, p. 100.

7. *Ibid.*, p. 105.

The basic pulse of life builds and animates all the systems, functions and tissues. These exercises are designed to affect the subtle core energy, and thereby create improvement all the way "downstream" in the denser systems, functions and tissues. Energy exercises affect the entire body through the interrelationship of all systems.

Energy flow feels good! People describe it as warmth, tingling, buzzing or vibration. Tension is released and the mind relaxes.

Benefits that you may experience include release of physical or emotional tension, weight loss, relief from pain, broadening of mental perspective, elimination of waste solids, liquids, and gases, intake of new oxygen, restructuring of posture, improved digestion and blood circulation, enhancement of job or athletic performance, and more. Because the system is based on the whole person, benefits arise on levels and in areas which may have seemed unrelated. "Touch one strand and the whole web trembles;"[8] Energy is the common thread uniting every aspect of our lives.

---

8. Chopra, Quantum Healing, p. 73.

Energy: More Than Just Exercise

Energy is affected by one's entire lifestyle. The whole Polarity Therapy system incorporates diet, exercise, bodywork, health information, resolution of emotional issues and realistic thinking. We believe in working with the whole person. Therefore these exercises are just one part of a whole way of life.

Dr. Stone compared the body to a house with plumbing, heat, light, drainage, etc. This "house" has three levels (mental, emotional and physical) and five phases (space, gas, heat, liquids, solids). An effective health system must incorporate and address the issues of all parts of the whole.

It is up to the tenant (the consciousness, soul, or spirit) to keep the house (mind, feelings, body) in good condition, and different tools and specialties are used for different parts of the house. Energy Exercises is one major tool, but the others are also very significant.

Ultimately it is up to each individual to work toward a continual state of balance; harmonizing of structural, chemical, emotional, spiritual and environmental factors into a life style which enhances health.[9]

9. Thie, Touch for Health, p. 112.

Part One

A quick introductory tour
of energy exercises and theories

"Energy is the real substance behind the
appearance of matter and form."
--Stone, Polarity Therapy Vol. II, p. 207.

A typical beginning routine for Energy Exercises might include an introduction to the idea of energy, Scissors kicks, Foot Reflexology, the Pyramid, the Squat, and a closing Light Rocking Perineal. This sequence would engage and energize the major current pathways in the body, and comprise a tour of some of the landmarks in Dr. Stone's energy exercise system.

For the introduction to theory, a simple question is asked. Of what are we made? High school science told us the answer is atoms, which we think are the primary building blocks of all matter. But the words "building blocks" and "matter," which sound so concrete, can be deceptive.

Far from being the hard and solid particles they were believed to be since antiquity, the atoms turned out to consist of vast regions of space... It is not easy to get a feeling for the... magnitude of atoms... In order to visualize this diminutive size, imagine an orange blown up to the size of the Earth. The atoms of the orange will then have the size of cherries.... In our picture of cherry-sized atoms, the nucleus of an atom will be so small that we will not be able to see it... To see the nucleus, we would have to blow up the size of the atom [the cherry] to the size of the biggest dome in the world, the dome of St. Peter's in Rome [138 feet across]... In an atom of that size, the nucleus would have the size of a grain of salt! A grain of salt in the middle of the vast dome of St. Peter's, and specks of dust whirling around it in the vast space of the dome-- this is how we can picture the nucleus and electrons of an atom.[10]

With this image in mind, the seeming solidity of the body is less definite. It is a small step further to envision the body as a whirling combination of these spacious "events" called atoms. The most "real" part of the system is not the grains and specks of dust, but rather the awesome force of attraction and repulsion which keeps them in place in extremely complex functions. "Energy," the potential or actual expression of this force, is the primary "glue" of the universe.

Energy is always there, whether we are aware of it or not. Usually we are not, but we can actually feel energy. Rub the hands together briskly.[11] Continue with firm pressure back and forth for at least a minute, or until the arms are tired, whichever comes first. Now, take a deep breath in through the nose and blow it out fully, stopping the hand-rubbing and semi-closing the eyes when exhalation is complete. Place the hands palms together, not quite touching. Concentrate on the sensation of the palms. Naturally there will be a warm tingling, coming from the stimulation of neurosensors on the palms.

---

10. Capra, The Tao of Physics, pp. 65-66. Also:

"When you get to the level of atoms, the landscape is not one of solid objects moving around each other like a dance, following predictable steps. Subatomic particles are separated by huge gaps, making every atom more than 99.999 percent empty space."

-Chopra, Quantum Healing, p. 96.

11. Gordon, Your Healing Hands, p. 20.

But there is another sensation here also. Experiment with moving the hands further apart, then closer together, then slightly up and down across each other. That light sensation, which rises and ebbs as the hands move closer and further, and feels like corduroy ridges as the fingers pass each other, is energy![12]

Feeling energy is the first step toward appreciating what energy exercises can offer. Learning increased sensitivity is a theme in Energy Exercise classes: when you're sensitive, energy in the hands can be felt without rubbing. We have suffered a gradual loss of awareness of our feelings and our bodies. We accumulate our tensions gradually so we don't notice the difference from day to day. We could add one small pebble each day to our load (in the form of a frustrating experience or unresolved conflict) and end up years later under a crushing burden which we never really perceive.

> It is... true that most people are unaware of the bodily handicaps under which they labor-- they have become second nature.[13]

This is especially true if we habitually de-sensitize ourselves with painkillers, drugs, alcohol, coffee and other stimulants or depressants. Our everyday state may be tension which feels "normal" to us. Unfortunately as we get more tense we also get more numb. We value sensi-tivity less, and become less likely to know what "good" can really feel like.

Energy is flowing through the body in specific pathways, like busy roads carrying traffic through a city. Our goal is smooth traffic flow throughout the system. Unfortunately, there are always interruptions: accidents, flat tires, bad weather, rush hour congestion, etc. reduce or slow the flow of traffic. In the body, lack of love, stressful living, bad food, lack of movement, etc., have a similar effect, slowing energy flow.

We experience energy blockage as pain and disease. These blockages follow a certain sequence, from subtle to dense manifestation:[14] thoughts affect feelings which affect the physical body. Inefficient or negative attitudes, unrealistic expectations or traumas generate emotionally-charged destructive habits or painful, unresolved, repressed feelings, which lead to physical problems.

Our next activity will start to open traffic up and add to our experience of energy. Move down to the floor, on the stomach, head resting on hands. Lift the feet so that the lower leg is perpendicular to the floor. Start the "Scissors Kick" by gently rocking the feet out, then in, back and forth like windshield wipers. The easy, rhythmic movement emphasizes the out kick. Continue for a few minutes, rocking the legs back and forth, alternat-

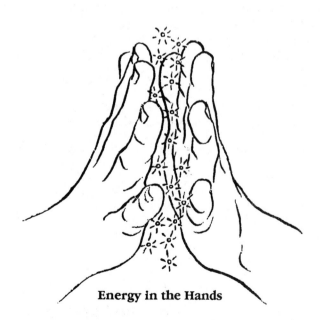

Energy in the Hands

12. Lowen uses a different hand position to get the effect all the way into the arms. Place the fingers together, in a "praying" pose. Then turn the hands (heels and palms always continuing to touch), so that the fingers point at the chest. This hyper-extends the fingers. Hold this position for at least a minute, or as long as you can. Then lightly rest, eyes closed, knees bent, arms hanging loosely. That tingling feeling is also energy! (Lowen, Bioenergetics, p. 63).

13. *Ibid.*, p. 43.

14. This sequence, "the path to illness," is described by many teachers. For examples, see Sills, The Polarity Process, p. 85, and Robbins, Unlimited Power, p. 40.

ing either foot crossing on top. Then roll over and rest, arms either flat to the sides or right hand on the belly and left hand on the forehead. Feel for the tingling, or wavelike movement across the body. That's energy again, and "traffic" is starting to move.

Next, roll to the side to a sitting position for a foot reflexology massage. With one leg drawn up, press and stretch the foot in every part and direction. Give each toe a pull. With the toes flexed, press deeply with the thumb on all parts of the sole of the foot. Find the tender areas: these are reflexes to places where the "traffic" is blocked elsewhere. As you read this book, you will learn what these areas mean. Hold the tender spot until the tension eases. Use the thumb and fingers of the other hand to grasp and press the

Achilles tendon and calves. A good foot massage in the evening is effective first aid for tension accumulated during the day.

After a short rest, stand up for the "Pyramid." Open the stance so that the feet are directly below the knees. The feet should be parallel to the thighs. Lean forward and place the hands just above the knees. Now transfer the weight from the legs and hips to the shoulders and arms. The arms should be straight, the back straight, and the neck relaxed and somewhat retracted into the shoulders like a turtle. Keep moving slightly from side to side with full breathing, concentrating on the exhalation. Feel the arms pressing the knees wider, the suspension of the lower back, and the energizing of the shoulder blades. After a few moments, before it starts to be a strain, come up to standing.

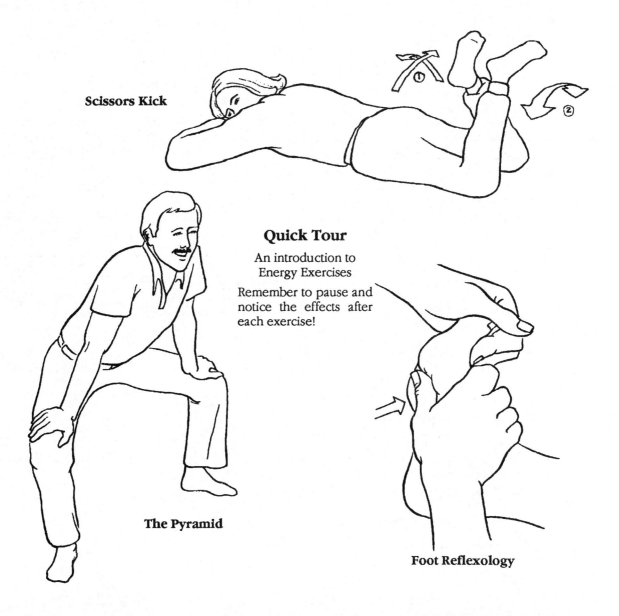

Scissors Kick

Quick Tour

An introduction to
Energy Exercises

Remember to pause and
notice the effects after
each exercise!

The Pyramid

Foot Reflexology

Take another moment of rest, breathing normally, eyes partly closed, knees slightly bent.

Next, lift the hands, arms outstretched in front, and cautiously do some light knee bends. Move up and down, each time a little lower, and see how far down you can go. If it's hard to get down to the haunches, put something (a board or a book) under the heels; if balance is a problem, find something to hold for steadiness. Shift slightly from side to side to add to the movement. When ready, stay in the down position, armpits near the knees, resting in the "Squat." Rock slightly, back and forth and side to side, for as long as you can in comfort. Then put the hands on the floor in front and slowly come back to standing. Finish with a few moments of silent rest, knees bent, eyes partly closed.

Now back to the floor. To finish, lie back down, on the left side. "Curl up" partially, knees up a little. Place the left hand across the chest and up to the right neck/shoulder junction, and the right hand on the right hip. This is the "Light Rocking Perineal." Rock very slightly, using the balance of the body so little effort is needed. After a few moments of rocking, rest quietly, eyes closed. If you like, roll over to the back for further rest. Then, rise back to standing and "take inventory" of the whole system. Attempt to compare the "flow of traffic" now to the flow at the beginning. You'll find a feeling of ease and relaxation, of vitality and calm power. Welcome to the wonderful world of Energy Exercise!

Now that we have an idea of energy and what it feels like, let's discuss the basic details of how it works. This is the topic of "Energy Anatomy."

3 Principles & 5 Elements

The study of anatomy takes on a new meaning in the Energy approach to health. Instead of tissues, muscles, bones and organs, the "energy anatomy" describes pathways, vibratory frequencies and energy functions.

Combining Eastern health theory with his practical experience, Dr. Stone gave thorough descriptions of a "Wireless Anatomy," or the movement of energy through the body. He offered two basic considerations for the mapping of pathways, each with numerous supporting

The Squat

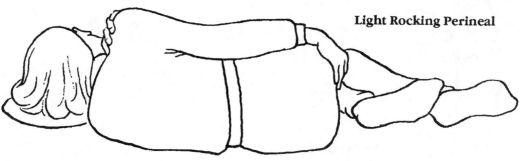

Light Rocking Perineal

details and features. These two levels of differentiation are called "Energy Principles" and "Energy Elements." The Three Principles and Five Elements are the main concepts in understanding energy anatomy and the theory of energy.

The Three Principles

The Three Principles describe the way energy moves. It pulses out, pulses in, and rests, in a constant cycle. In the body, energy moves out to the extremities and back to the core in rhythmic pulsations. Blood, breath, nerves: all systems follow this basic pattern of going out, coming back, and stillness.[15] Many names have been given to these. The best known are from China: *Yang* for going out, *Yin* for coming back, and Neutral for the middle transition. In Polarity Therapy, the terms are Fire Principle for going out, Water Principle for coming back and Air Principle for neutral stillness.

The Five Elements

The world unfolds in stages of increasing density, from light and subtle to heavy and dense. These layers or phases are space, gas, heat, liquids, and solids. In Polarity Therapy they are called Ether (space), Air (gas), Fire (heat), Water (liquids) and Earth (solids). In the body, five centers called *Chakras* transform energy, adjusting its density and speed as it moves up and down the body.

How Energy Exercises Work

These exercises open energy pathways. Energy "blockages," the result of trauma and tension, are "cleared out" by the combination of methods used in this system. The goal is to affect the Three Principles and Five Elements so that there is an ease and balance of expansion and contraction in all fields of action, from subtle to dense. Thus energy flows with optimum ease on physical, emotional and mental levels. Energy movement, feeling well, and health improvement are directly linked: these exercises can lead to all three, often in a way which can be felt immediately.

The energy that forms and operates the body has a great inner "intelligence." It fights germs, heals bumps and bruises, processes emotional experiences, thinks of solutions to complex problems, all far better than could ever be done from outside. In doing Energy Exercises, learn to tune in to this innate intelligence and assist it in its natural healing work. Therefore these exercises should be done "mindfully." Be sensitive to your body's natural biofeedback, and let it guide your choices. The body is a natural self-

---

15. A sampling of comments on the essential pulsation of life:

"We are a sea of liquids making a structure and shape,... a pattern of pulsation leading to certain patterns of experienced life, feeling and thinking both within ourselves and with others...One of the fundamental elements seen in living material is its pulsatory organization, its ability to expand and contract, to lengthen and shorten, to swell and shrink... [Man's] pattern of expansion and contraction organizes basic cognition and perception-- empty, full; slow, fast; expand, withdraw; engulf, disgorge. All feeling and thinking is based on this pumping action... Expansion and contraction are the essential pumps of existence."

-Keleman, (Emotional Anatomy, p. 57, 62

"Modern physics has shown that the rhythm of creation and destruction is not only manifest in the turn of the seasons and in the birth and death of all living creatures, but is also the very essence of inorganic matter... the dance of creation and destruction is the basis of the very existence of matter... Modern physics has thus revealed that every sub-atomic particle not only performs an energy dance, but also is an energy dance; a pulsating process of creation and destruction."

Capra, The Tao of Physics, p. 244.

"This dance of attraction and repulsion between charged particles is called the electro-magnetic force. It enables atoms to join together to form molecules and it keeps negatively charged electrons in orbit around positively charged nuclei. At the atomic and molecular level it is the fundamental glue of the universe."

Zukav, The Dancing Wu Li Masters, p. 206

correcting system; these exercises enhance that self-healing power.

How To Choose Effective Exercises with the Principles and Elements

The Three Principles have basic qualities which are reflected in three types of movement: active for Yang Fire, peaceful for Neutral Air, and dramatically changing for Yin Water. Intuition can tell when to employ exercises in each category (exercises are categorized by Principles on page 142). Perhaps you need to calm down and re-center yourself; the quiet stilling postures of the Neutral Air Principle would be appropriate. Perhaps you feel a need for greater action and self-expression: for this use exercises that activate the Fire Principle. When you feel heavy and sluggish, exercises of the Yin Water Principle will promote a change.

To use the Five Elements to plan exercises, consider their main location and secondary connections as shown below. If you have tension or pain in one of the areas listed in the second column, Energy Exercises based on that element are recommended (exercises are indexed by element on page 140). If emotional stress is causing a problem, find the closest approximate term for the feeling in the far right column, and use exercises relating to that element.

This approach can be simple or very sophisticated. An example of a simple use would be using Fire Element exercises when anger is being experienced: this "vents" the pent-up energy in that center and gives relief. As a more complex example, an Earth Element exercise would be beneficial for a person with chronic Air stress in the chest or problems with excessive desires: it would give an earthy "grounding" of practicality to balance the lofty ambitions. Thus Energy Exercises become a form of "Energy Balancing," a self-given and self-regulated way to create and maintain inner harmony. These have been proven to be effective at both beginning and advanced levels.

Get to "know" the various exercises from both an inner, intuitive sense and an outer, intellectual knowledge of their benefits. You will then be able to use them as your own form of self-help and growth. Many students have said they feel newly empowered in self care through these exercises, enabling them to work with issues of many kinds, from headaches and indigestion to emotional processing.

Listen to Yourself First

The highest authority on what is going on in your body is you. Others may have knowledge of anatomy or exercise physiology or general rules that work for most people, but your perspective is unique.

Get to know your body and listen to its limitations as well as needs. Health comes from within. In Energy Exercises, we work with the body, not on it.

Be especially sensitive to pain. Pain can mean several things: that energy is blocked, that the exercise is being done improperly, that you are not ready for it, or that it is just not a good exercise for you. Furthermore, there are "good" pains, like a deep massage, and "bad" pains, indicating undue stress. You are the judge: your body knows the difference and will tell you if you listen.

Five Elements: Locations, Related Areas, and Emotional Qualities

Element	Main Location	Yang (+)	Neutral (0)	Yin (-)	Related Emotions
Ether	Throat				Grief, Expression
Air	Chest	Shoulders	Kidneys	Ankles	Desire, Hope
Fire	Solar Plexus	Head	Solar Plexus	Thighs	Anger, Frustration
Water	Abdomen, Pelvis	Chest	Genitals	Feet	Enmeshment, Clinging
Earth	Pelvic Floor	Neck	Bowels	Knees	Fear, Anxiety

Ancient Symbols show how Energy Works

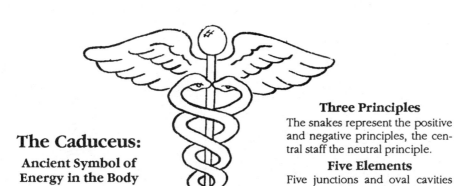

The Caduceus:

Ancient Symbol of Energy in the Body

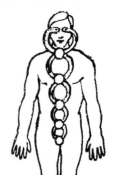

Dr. Stone's placement of the Caduceus in the body.

Three Principles

The snakes represent the positive and negative principles, the central staff the neutral principle.

Five Elements

Five junctions and oval cavities are created as energy is transformed from subtle to dense levels of vibration.

As Dr. Stone developed Polarity Therapy, he sought an understanding of the truths at the heart of the world's great cultures and religions. His books refer to a wide variety of sources, old and new and from East and West.

He was fascinated by ancient symbols. "All these cryptic designs bear a hidden message to thinkers. By knowing them, man can gain intelligent direction and knowledge..." (Polarity Therapy Vol. I., p. 33).

The Caduceus, an Egyptian and Greek symbol also known as the Staff of Hermes or Staff of Life, attracted Dr. Stone's attention. In Roman mythology, the Caduceus was the "magic wand" of mercury (called Hermes by the Greeks), son of Jupiter and messenger of the Gods. A gift from Apollo, the Caduceus was used to guide souls in their travels after death. As in ancient times, the Caduceus is the symbol of the medical profession.

Dr. Stone saw the Caduceus as an esoteric representation of energy fields in the body. As he explained (p. 33):

"MAN KNOW THYSELF is the admonition contained in the symbolism of the Staff of Hermes.

"The wings of the Caduceus represent the two hemispheres of the brain. The knob in the center is the pineal body. The upright staff is the path of the finer energy of the brain and the spinal chord below it.

"The two serpents represent the Mind Principle in its dual aspect. The fiery breath of the sun is the positive pole as the vital energy on the right side of the body. It was called *Yang* by the Chinese... On the left side of the body flows the cooling energy of the Moon essence of nature. It was called *Yin* by the Chinese...

"These two currents cross over in each oval cavity [five in number] and change their polarity. Thus they flow in and out of each other constantly and produce alternating currents in their action...

"The knowledge of these currents [the Three Principles], and the relationship of these ovals [the Five Elements]... was the understanding of the physicians of old. It is concealed and revealed in this symbol of the Caduceus."

The Tao
Emblem of the Three Principles

At least as old as the Caduceus is the Oriental symbol of Yang and Yin, which also conveys the wisdom of the Three Principles concept. "Going out" and "Coming back" are represented as a dynamic interdependent cycle of opposites which are constantly becoming each other. The third principle of neutral stillness is expressed by the balance of the two polarized forces. The small dots mean that in the fullness of one is the seed of the other.

Babbit's Atom

"Congealed energy pathways" are often seen in nature

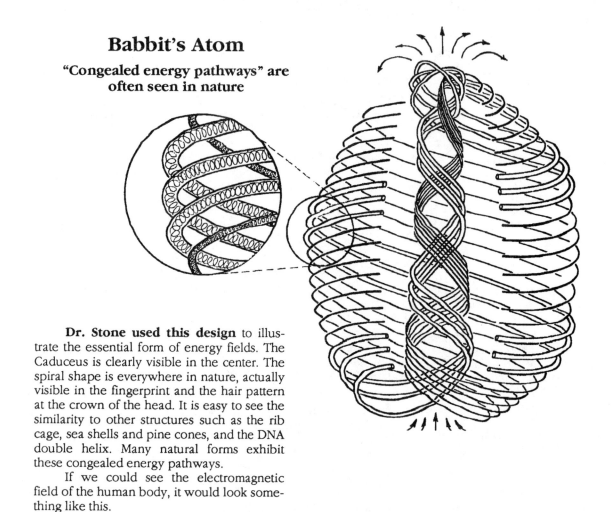

Dr. Stone used this design to illustrate the essential form of energy fields. The Caduceus is clearly visible in the center. The spiral shape is everywhere in nature, actually visible in the fingerprint and the hair pattern at the crown of the head. It is easy to see the similarity to other structures such as the rib cage, sea shells and pine cones, and the DNA double helix. Many natural forms exhibit these congealed energy pathways.

If we could see the electromagnetic field of the human body, it would look something like this.

Cycles of Attraction and Repulsion
"The fundamental glue of the Universe"

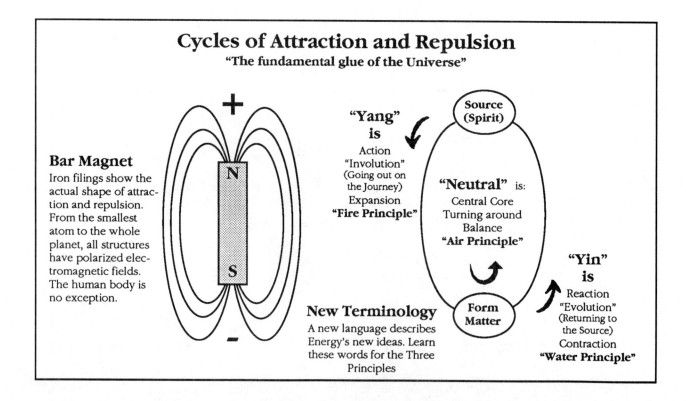

Bar Magnet
Iron filings show the actual shape of attraction and repulsion. From the smallest atom to the whole planet, all structures have polarized electromagnetic fields. The human body is no exception.

"Yang" is
Action "Involution" (Going out on the Journey) Expansion **"Fire Principle"**

Source (Spirit)

"Neutral" is:
Central Core Turning around Balance **"Air Principle"**

Form Matter

"Yin" is
Reaction "Evolution" (Returning to the Source) Contraction **"Water Principle"**

New Terminology
A new language describes Energy's new ideas. Learn these words for the Three Principles

Wireless Anatomy
The Shape of Energy in Man

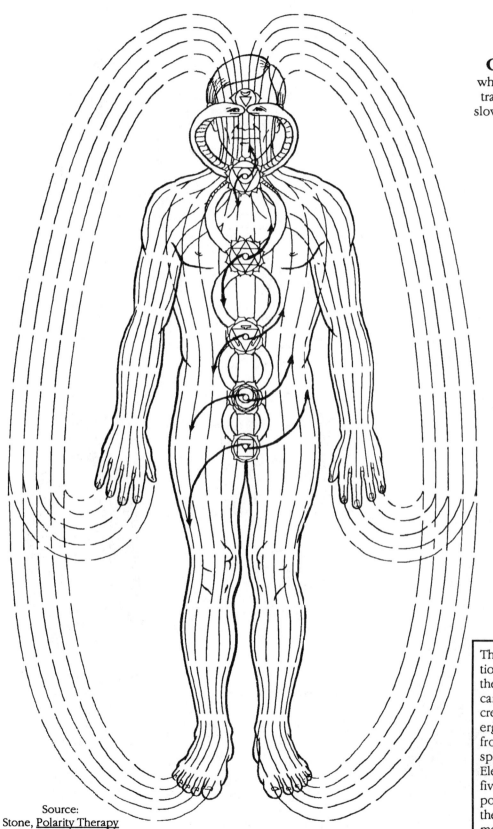

Chakras
where Energy is
transformed to
slower vibrations

Ether

Air

Fire

Water

Earth

Source:
Stone, <u>Polarity Therapy</u>
<u>Vol. I</u>, Book 2, p. 10.

This is Dr. Stone's illustration for the energy field of the body. The Caduceus can be seen in the center, creating the Chakras or energy centers. Radiating out from each Chakra are the spiral circuits of each Element, expressed in the five fingers and toes. All points along lines like these are linked by electromagnetic connection.

The Ways Energy Moves

From the core pattern of the caduceus, energy becomes a radiant, pulsing field of spirals which define the body in three dimensions: side to side, back to front and top to bottom.

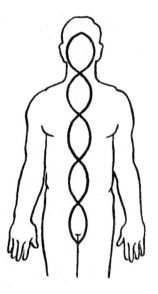

The Caduceus locates the centers of energy transformation moving from subtle to dense and back in five specific steps.

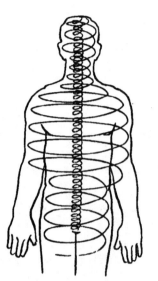

Air Principle
Side to Side
Neutral Balance
Satva
Stillness

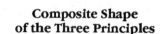

Fire Principle
Back/Front
(+) Action
Rajas
Expansion

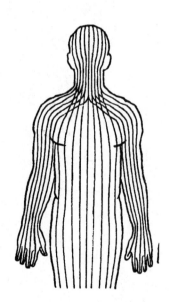

Water Principle
Top/Bottom
(-) Reaction
Tamas
Contraction

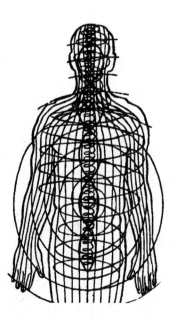

**Composite Shape
of the Three Principles**

This composite drawing shows the weaving effect created by the Three Principles in their continual pulsation of dynamic movement. Babbit's Atom can be seen in the combination. Notice the congestion of lines at the neck. A natural tendency for tension exists at this major crossroads.

Energy Zones
Repeating Patterns
of the Energy Anatomy

Source: Stone, <u>Polarity Therapy Vol. I,</u>
Book 2, p. 11.

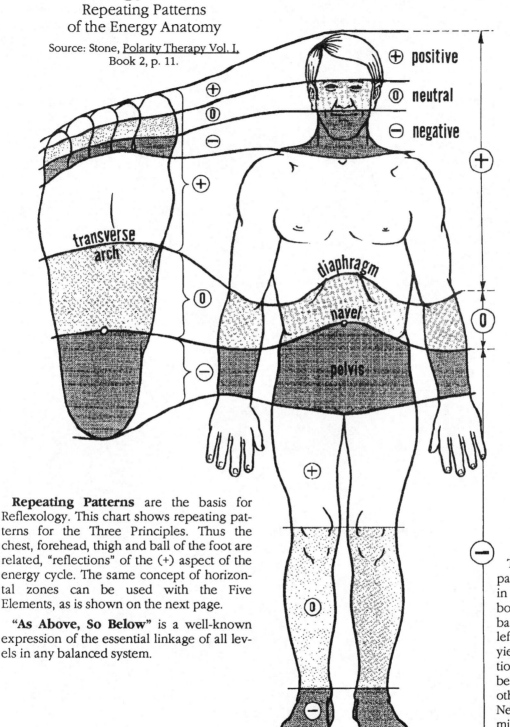

Repeating Patterns are the basis for Reflexology. This chart shows repeating patterns for the Three Principles. Thus the chest, forehead, thigh and ball of the foot are related, "reflections" of the (+) aspect of the energy cycle. The same concept of horizontal zones can be used with the Five Elements, as is shown on the next page.

"As Above, So Below" is a well-known expression of the essential linkage of all levels in any balanced system.

Three Dimensions
The body or any body part may be subdivided in three ways: top/bottom as shown here, back/front, and right/left. Each subdivision yields a polarized relationship, one dimension being (+) Yang and the other (-) Yin, with (0) Neutral always in the middle

Polarization follows this form:

(+) YANG	(-) YIN
TOP	BOTTOM
RIGHT	LEFT
BACK	FRONT

Zones of the Five Elements

The Five Elements also form repeating patterns: Notice the similarity of shape between areas. The jaw fits perfectly in the pelvis, the diaphragm matches the middle of the face, etc.

ETHER

The Ether Element is centered in the neck, and its main reflexes are the thumbs and big toes, the "neck" of each finger and toe, and the center line of the body.

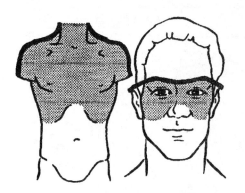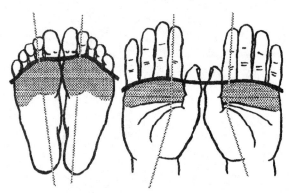

AIR

These areas are related to each other as reflections of the Air Chakra in the chest. Lungs and heart, and feelings of desire and hope are centered here.

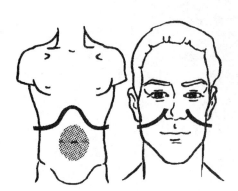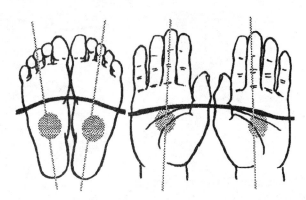

FIRE

The diaphragm line and umbilicus are linked as shown here. Organs located here are Liver and Gall Bladder, Stomach, spleen and intestines; emotions here are anger and frustration.

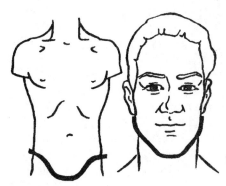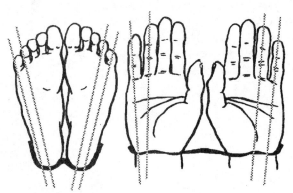

WATER & EARTH

Feelings of enmeshment, sexuality and caring are centered in the Water area, which includes genitals and lower abdomen.

The Earth area is at the base of the pelvis. Fear and anxiety are centered here, as are the rectum and bowels.

Eight Methods of Exercise

In Energy Exercises, we use eight techniques:

•**Lengthening** refers to a gentle increase of the length a muscle can have. It can be as simple as reaching out with the arms, or moving the head from side to side. Many of the exercises in this book make use of natural leverage to create lengthening in specific areas of the body. Properly done, lengthening prompts the muscle to "reset" at a new longer length.

Lengthening does not mean strain or stretch beyond the limit of range of motion, which tends only to cause reactive tightening afterward. The term lengthening is offered to the exercise world as an alternative to the word "stretch." Stretch suggests a rubber band reaction which "snaps back" and nullifies the benefit of the exercise.

•**Pressure** refers to direct touch on the body. Pressure can be light, moderate, or deep, and it can be moving or still. Pressure has two main uses: for energy balancing (as discussed below) and for tissue release.

Firm pressure can be painful. If the pain is an indicator of blocked energy, continued contact will facilitate release. Release can be felt in the hands and the body as a tingling, pulsation and warmth replace the pain.

For tissue release, pressure can be used strategically in a number of ways. Within each muscle are mechanisms to monitor the tension which that muscle exerts on tissues and bones. The spindle cell mechanism in the belly of the muscle monitors length. To relax a muscle that is tight, first push into the belly of the muscle above and below its center, then direct the pressure of the fingers toward each other. The muscle gets a message that there is too much contraction and the brain sends a "lighten up" message, causing relaxation.

A second mechanism regulating tension is the Golgi apparatus. Muscles are attached to bones by tendons. At the end of the muscle in the tendon area, the Golgi apparatus sends messages to protect the muscles from exerting too much pressure, which could break the bone or tear the tendon. Applying sensitive pressure to the areas where muscles originate or insert in the bone resets the Golgi apparatus and thus relaxes the muscle.

•**Activation** means using a muscle lightly against resistance, followed by release. Muscles work in "extension" (opened as long as possible) and "flexion" (contracted as short as possible). Activation techniques consist of extending as far as is comfortable, then lightly flexing in the opposite direction against resistance with an exhalation. This is repeated: each time the flexing/exhaling is finished, further extension becomes possible, and muscles which were very tight are dramatically lengthened. The body uses force in the flexing direction and as it relaxes from that, further extension happens naturally. Thus a "lengthening" is achieved with no force.

Lightness of touch and sensitivity are essential: this is not like isometric resistance used in muscle building, but rather a gentle and sensitive way to increase flexibility and range of movement. It is an excellent companion to bodywork, creating relaxation much more efficiently than mechanical stretching.

•**Breathing** refers to conscious inhalation and exhalation, often timed with specific movements, sometimes combined with sound. One group of exercises in this book (page 92) deals with breathing only. In other exercises breath is coordinated with the exercise. Breathing contributes physical, emotional and esoteric benefits to Energy Exercises. Conscious breathing is so important that some therapies have achieved great success using breath-oriented practices exclusively.

The physical benefits of conscious breathing, especially oxygenation, are well known. Dr. Stone also described a less familiar idea:

> When the breath is used in a posture, it is for a general stretch of the tissues from within, outward, in order to reverse the day-long pressures from without pushing inward.[16]

A more esoteric dimension of breath is found in the concept of "Prana" or Life Force. This subtle cosmic energy is considered to be conducted in the air (also, on sunlight and in flowing water). In esoteric philosophy, breathing means absorbing Prana, nourishing the most subtle functions of consciousness and life.

•**Energy Balancing** can mean a number of techniques. "Energy" refers to energy currents and fields in the body, and "balance" describes reducing surplus or increasing deficiency to achieve an equality of force.

Energy balancing usually involves the use of hands to contact specific key spots on the body. The hands are like jumper cables for a car battery. Energy flowing between the hands supplements the existing current along particular pathways. The increased circulation has a balancing effect. The pathways may be compared to water streams, which are washed free of sediment by increased flow. Polarity, Reflexology, Shiatsu, Touch for Health, Do-in, Acupressure, Ayurveda, and many other health systems are based on the concept of energy balancing.

"Bodywork" is a generic term for energy-balancing contact. More information on the how and why of bodywork is

given under "Balancing Touches" (page 71).

•**Differentiation** consists of consciously moving the body in a way that "differentiates" the various parts that are involved in the motion. This approach was developed by Dr. Moshe Feldenkrais. The movement sequences are executed gently and slowly with great "mindfulness." Moving slowly while noticing the details, such as the quality and level of comfort, gives the brain a certain kind of stimulation. This is the type of sensory-motor stimulation present in the successful learning of all motor skills, beginning at birth. Under these conditions the brain has the time and freedom to make adjustments and to alter habitual limitations in movement. Slowly, body movements become easy, pain-free and efficient; the mind becomes calm and thinking becomes more clear.

•**Movement** means easy motion, either according to specific instructions or free and without specific form. Movement increases circulation, fires neurons, exercises muscles. It can be used to bring life to an area of the body that has become tense and blocked. Stretching, rocking, bending, unbending and rotating are movements used to release and energize. Dr. Milton Trager has artfully demonstrated the value of movement in his bodywork and self-help exercise systems.

•**Sound** is an important part of this system and refers to the several ways the voice and other sources are used to create relaxation and energy balancing. As with breathing, sound has many esoteric dimensions and implications. In addition to its use with many exercises, sound has its own section, on page 84.

---

16. Stone, Health Building, p. 101.

Caution

Certain exercises have this mark. These are exercises which require special caution. LISTEN TO YOUR BODY FIRST. All exercises are to be done with care and consciousness. You are the best judge in choosing exercises and doing them in a way that works best for you.

Part Two

Exercises Listed by Body Area

Neck and Shoulders

The Neck and Shoulders area is the "positive pole" of the torso's electromagnetic field. The neck is the location of the Ether Element center, and the chest is the location of the Air center.

The neck is affected by experiences relating to self-expression and making choices. Pride, shame and longing for worldly or spiritual motives manifest here. Sound is an important part of Energy Exercises for the neck area, so the neck will benefit by all postures which employ sound; this includes many of the exercises in this book.

The shoulders are affected by experiences relating to desire, hope and ambition. Tension here comes from "carrying the weight of the world," from the pressure of unfulfilled wants for ourselves or others.

The interrelationship of body areas is a theme which will be found over and over in this book. Imagine a playground seesaw, with one end directly moving the other. Similarly, the pelvis and shoulders affect each other across the "fulcrum" of the diaphragm.

The superior acts on the inferior and the inferior supports and reacts on the superior pole.[17]

Note: These exercises are presented for the purpose of education and personal growth, and are not a substitute for medical care. Consult with your doctor before using specific exercises for specific health conditions.

Thus the organization of this book by body areas must be approached with a major caution, the understanding that no body area or posture has an isolated existence or effect.

1. Shoulder Reflexes

"A few seconds on the right reflex does wonders."[18]

Reflexology means making use of the energy links which exist between seemingly unrelated parts of the body. Beginners are advised just to get started and let the technique speak for itself: reflexology and its benefits are easier to experience than to explain.

Method

For the neck and shoulders, important reflexes are found where the toes join the foot. In classes, we often have participants take a shoulder-lengthening pose such as the Cliffhanger (page 23) or the

17. Stone, Polarity Therapy Vol. II, p. 21.
18. *Ibid.*, p. 85.

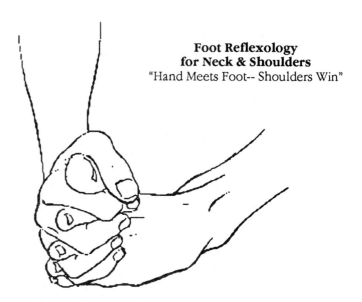

**Foot Reflexology
for Neck & Shoulders**
"Hand Meets Foot-- Shoulders Win"

Pyramid (page 52) for a few seconds first, to gauge the degree of flexibility and to give a standard for comparison. This is a way to give participants a direct experience of the power of reflexology.

Assume one of these poses "cold" (without prior warm-up), do the foot reflexology techniques in the next paragraph, then immediately go back to the test posture. Typically, the Cliffhanger or Pyramid will be difficult before foot reflexology, and noticeably easier after.

Reflexes to the neck are located in the "neck" of each toe, especially the big toe. Massage these areas, feeling for tender spots. When you find areas that are sore, gently push in and hold for a count of at least eight, with full breathing and emphasized exhalation.

For foot reflexology to benefit the

Reflexology for the Toes

For the neck, press the "neck" of each toe, and on the big toe. For shoulder release, press where the toe joins the foot, on top and bottom, and on the second toe.

NECK
Press in this shaded zone

Element

Ether Neck & Throat	
Air Shoulders & Chest	
Fire Solar Plexus	
Water Pelvis	
Earth	

SHOULDER ZONE

NECK ZONE

SHOULDERS
Press in this shaded zone

shoulders, flex the foot (toes pulled up as close to the leg as possible), then stretch the toes either up or down, and press the areas at the bases of the toes.

The main point here is the discovery that the foot must be flexed under a little tension so the areas involved are brought out for all foot therapy applications.[19]

Be creative: using your feelings and intuition as a guide, stretch and press all around the horizontal zone relating to the air element, on top and bottom. This pressure can be quite deep, stimulating with movement, or light. On the top, press around each tendon going to the toes. On the bottom, concentrate on the area around the ball of the foot. Also on the bottom, lift the second toe up and use your thumb to find its tendon underneath. Each toe corresponds to an energy center, and pressure along this tendon affects the chest/shoulders area. Follow this tendon down the foot with pressure and movement. Similar tendon pressure is useful for each of the other energy centers: big toe for the neck, second toe for chest, third for solar plexus, fourth for pelvis, and fifth for pelvic floor.

After pressing on the reflex area, hold the reflex spot on the foot with one hand while the other hand firmly grasps the tissue at the top of the shoulder Hold this "energy balancing" pose quietly for a minute or so, and observe the effect.

An activation technique can be used with the toe stretch to facilitate release. To do this, take one toe and bend it back to its comfortable limit. Now inhale. Relax. As you exhale, push the toe into the fingers as if unbending it into the resistance of the fingers. Inhale, relax and with your hand take up any slack, gently bending the toe further back. Repeat as many times as you feel continued easy release.

---

19. Stone, Polarity Therapy Vol. II, p. 72.

Toe activation has many uses in body-work and exercise therapy. Activating the corresponding toe can be valuable as a specific treatment for an energy center. This technique is highly recommended to bodyworkers.

Next is an efficient shoulder reflex technique in which the fingers are inter-twined with the toes. Our artist calls this "Hand Meets Foot- Shoulders Win." This will be easy for some, difficult for others, who will have to pull the toes apart one by one to make spaces for the fingers. The fingers should be as close to the base of the toes as possible. Once you have the position, wait for at least one full minute, breathing fully and emphasizing exhalation. Then stretch the toes forward and back and rotate.

A second useful reflex to the junction of the neck and shoulders is where the nose meets the eyebrow line, "where the bridge meets the ridge." The entire eyebrow line is a reflex to the shoulders and may be gently pressed with small circular movements. Concentrate on tender spots just to either side of the nose.

A third reflex, described more fully later because it is commonly used to affect the diaphragm, is the web of the hand, between the thumb and first finger. Firm pressure here is a specific energizer for the throat and neck area.

Benefits
•Release of shoulder and neck tension.
•Increased foot flexibility.
•Good for overall relaxation.

References
Stone, <u>Polarity Therapy Vol I</u> Book 2, pp. 11, 37, 40, 44, 80.
Stone, <u>Polarity Therapy Vol II</u>, p. 105 ff., pp. 183-184.
Berkson, <u>The Foot Book: Healing the Body through Foot Reflexology</u>, pp. 46-53.
Gach, <u>Acu-Yoga,</u> p. 136.
Mahoney, <u>Hyperton-X</u>, p.57

2. Rocking Cliff

This exercise is called the "Rocking Cliff" because it is a warm-up for the more strenuous "Cliffhanger" which follows next in this chapter. Leverage is used to release tension in the shoulders and related areas, and movement is used to influence energy circuits.

Method
The original version of the Rocking Cliff is very simple. Sit comfortably in a chair. With straight arms, support some of the weight of the body by pushing down on the chair and suspending the torso from the shoulders. Now rock back and forth, backward and foreword, feeling a gentle movement in the brachial plexus. The shoulder blades start to move and the upper back is relaxed.

A second, better known version has been developed over the years. In this version, the chest is thrust forward and arched back with each rocking move-

**"Ridge meets Bridge"
Shoulder Reflexes**

ment, as shown in the illustration. Inhale and rock back, rounding the back and feeling a lengthening across the shoulders as you expand the chest with a full breath. Exhale and rock forward, pulling the shoulders back and keeping the chin tucked in.

This version of the posture is valuable for its action on the geometric postures of involution and evolution, curving the torso inward and outward. Inward and outward poses are found in many sources, with many variations: in Hatha Yoga, they are recognizable in several forms, including the Cat, Cow, Bow, Leaf, Cobra and other postures. Involution[20] and Evolution[21] are especially emphasized in Polarity Therapy. The concept of Involution/Evolution, an advanced but very important use of the Three Principles idea, is discussed in several places later in this book. The

breathing pattern matches the posture's movement, with the Yang inhalation coinciding with the involutionary, inward rear position, and the Yin exhalation coinciding with the evolutionary, outward forward position.

Benefits
- Releases tension from the shoulders, neck and upper back.
- Opens breathing: beneficial for people with bronchial and asthmatic conditions.
- Integrates and balances top/bottom (Yin) and front/back (Yang) energy currents.

References
Stone, Health Building, p. 180. This comes from Sam Busa's "Health Building Yoga," a South African magazine article published in the early 1970's and reprinted in the CRCS edition of Health Building.
Berkson, Healing the Body through Foot Reflexology, pp. 81-83. Berkson presents traditional hatha yoga poses for curving the back outward (the bow), then inward (the leaf), and adds: "This is the most important exercise in this book!" She calls it the "Reflexology Wake Up Exercise."

---

20. Stone, Polarity Therapy Vol. II, p. 113.
21. Stone, Polarity Therapy Vol. I, Book 1, p. 49.

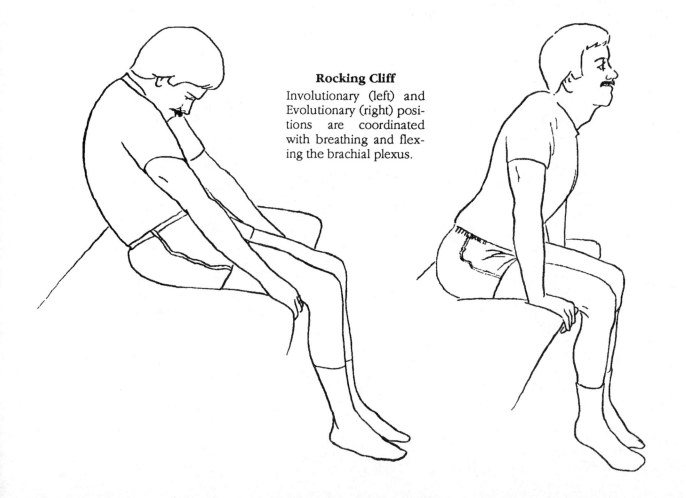

Rocking Cliff
Involutionary (left) and Evolutionary (right) positions are coordinated with breathing and flexing the brachial plexus.

3. Cliffhanger

The Cliffhanger is one of Dr. Stone's best known and most dramatic postures, but it must be used with caution by beginners. Many people need to use the variations first (see next page) to avoid over-straining. Instructors are advised to be alert for those who may have difficulty with the Cliffhanger, and to carefully use warm-up exercises, including reflexology and lengthening, to prepare.

The use of strategic leverage is the key to this exercise, and sound and breath are emphasized. The shoulder-hip energy link is dramatically used:

> The shoulder level base and the hip level base must be engaged simultaneously in the one stretching posture to move the gross energy blocks by means of the subtle energy in the united action on both levels.[22]

Method

For the Cliffhanger, a table or surface is needed, about as high as the thigh or hip. It needs to be quite stable and sturdy:

---

22. Stone, Health Building, p. 172.

a picnic table, sofa arm, kitchen counter, massage table, or an office desk are a few possibilities. Stand with your sacrum and heels of the hands resting on the edge of the table and your feet shoulder-width or slightly more apart. Place your hands on the table edge to either side of your body, with the elbows over the wrists. Take a test run by lowering your body. Your back maintains very light contact with the table as you drop down with knees bent as shown in the illustration.

In this lowered position, most of the body weight is on the hands, with the torso "suspended" from the edge of the table. The pelvis should "hang" from the spine: avoid tightened buttocks or stomach muscles. Feel the opening in the arms and chest and experiment with different pelvic and foot positions. Seek a posture of relaxation, breathing easily, head down. Bring yourself up, using the legs to take the pressure off the arms. The simplest version of the Cliffhanger is just a few repetitions of this up-and-down action.

For a more advanced version, stay in the lower position longer and add conscious breathing. Start with a "cleansing breath." Take a deep breath in through the nose, and give a full, complete exhalation through the mouth. Then inhale again, and as you exhale with a deep "a-a-a-h-h" sound, glide your back down the table edge. Lower the body down until you feel resistance in the shoulders.

Support your body weight with your legs only as much as necessary to avoid straining (having the feet close in gives more support, having the feet further

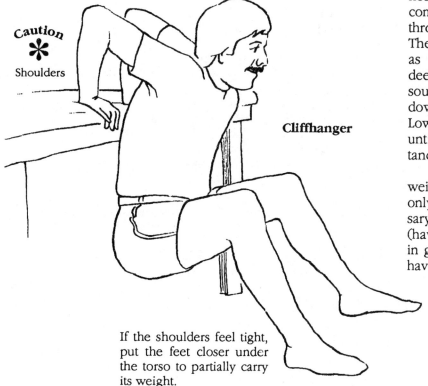

Caution
✳
Shoulders

Cliffhanger

If the shoulders feel tight, put the feet closer under the torso to partially carry its weight.

out gives less support). If your shoulders are loose, let the body's entire weight hang on the arms. If they are tight, use the legs for partial support.

Push the sound out with the diaphragm until all air is out. <u>Come up empty</u>, wait a moment, stand away from the table, then inhale. Remain in a relaxed standing pose for at least 30 seconds, with a sensitive attitude, to experience results.

If this is easy for you, you are ready to do a series of releases (if this is not easy, go back to reflexology for the shoulders). Inhale, and as you exhale with an "aah" sound, go down again to the point of resistance. Stay there after exhaling (blowing all the air out through the mouth) fully and then inhale again, allowing the internal pressure of the full breath to press in to areas of tension in the chest and shoulders. Then exhale and relax down even further. On the next inhale, either come up or continue with one or two more inhale-exhale cycles. As you exhale you may push the shoulder blades together in the back to increase the release. Experiment with slowly moving the hips, legs, head and elbows in this fully-lowered position.

When you are finished with the last exhale, make sure to blow all the air out and then stand up <u>with lungs empty</u>. This is difficult to do since we tend to want to fill up again right away. Allow yourself to stay empty for a moment. Stand empty and blow out any more air that might be left. By making the emptiness as complete as possible, we create more potential for intake of fresh air. Then, take a breath through the nose. Feel how full, satisfying and refreshing that first breath is. Notice any new sensation.

A full series for an advanced session can be three or more up-and-down cycles, with three or more "aah" breaths each.

Variations

For a less difficult Cliffhanger, use a ledge that is close to the floor. The floor supports the buttocks in the down position. A low couch or coffee table can work

well, or a chair using the back as the ledge. This way you can enjoy the opening of the chest and shoulders without the suspension. In a "seated" position with the arms reaching up and back as shown in the illustration, do the same inhale-and-"aah" exhale sequence. Experiment with rotating the shoulder blades toward each other, or up and down. Remember to keep the head down and neck relaxed, and to take a moment afterwards to experience the results.

An easier possibility is illustrated on page 179 of <u>Health Building</u>, which is a cross between the cliffhanger and the pyramid. An armchair is used for support in this variation. From a seated position, place the arms on the side armrests. Lift the body by pressing down with the arms, and follow the same breathing sequence described above.

Benefits

- Release of tension in the chest, neck, shoulders, diaphragm and pelvic areas.
- Opens the Brachial Plexus, which Dr. Stone called "the Governor of the Breath," regulating whether the breath is deep or just enough to keep alive.
- Increases the capacity to breathe deeply, to feel, and to give and take fully with the world around us. This has significant emotional and mental implications.
- Opens the chest for breathing and inspiration. Ventilates unused lung areas, increasing elimination of carbon dioxide and intake of oxygen.
- Opens rounded shoulders or a concave chest.
- Unbinds over-developed or over-muscular brachial plexus areas.
- Preventative for heart conditions; opens heart area.
- Reflexology effects include hyperextension of wrist (pelvic reflex-- see chart, p. 15).

References

Stone, <u>Health Building</u>, pp. 170, 172-173, 180.
Stone, <u>Polarity Therapy Vol</u> I Book 3, pp. 18-19.
Seidman, <u>Polarity Therapy</u>, p. 138.
Seigel, <u>Polarity Therapy</u>, p. 78.
Francis, <u>Polarity Self-Help Exercises</u>, pp. 35-36.
Lowens, <u>The Way to Vibrant Health</u>, p. 95.

4. Shoulder Shrug Neck Roll

This exercise uses dynamic shoulder-neck action to release hard-to-get areas. It is one of those movements that people do spontaneously for stress relief, without knowing why it works. Baseball players spontaneously do a version of this just before stepping up to the plate, and golfers just before an important shot.

Method

Stand or sit in a relaxed position. For part one, shrug the shoulders up, bringing them toward the neck area, so the neck seems to disappear and you look a bit like a penguin. Hold this shrug and lift your chin up. Now begin to make slow "upward arches," arcing the chin left and then right. Inhale one direction, exhale the other. Do this four or five times, or until release feels complete, and then return to the middle position. Keep the shoulders up and now bring the chin down.

Next, with the chin down, begin to make a similar movement in a downward direction. Arc the chin left and then right. Inhale one direction and exhale the other. When done, return to the middle position and allow your shoulders to relax down. Give the arms a shake-out, shrug the shoulders once or twice, and check how they feel. Also, check how your neck feels when you rotate it.

For part two, repeat this same process with the shoulders down. Pretend you are carrying big pails of water which are weighing your arms and shoulders down. Keep the shoulders down and repeat the same movements, first "upward arches" upward, then "downward arcs" downward. Again shake-out, shrug the shoulders, and check the range of motion in the shoulders and neck.

Variations

Place your finger on your nose to mark center position. Now while keeping your finger still, and your nose touching the finger, slowly rotate the chin left and then right while keeping the shoulders

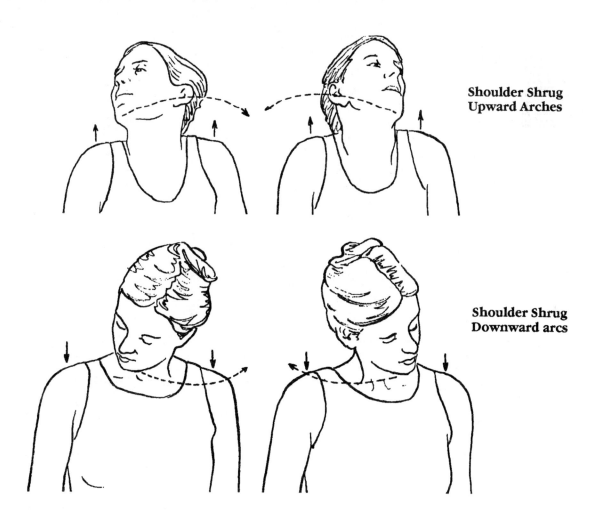

**Shoulder Shrug
Upward Arches**

**Shoulder Shrug
Downward arcs**

pulled down. The head movement "hinges" on the unmoving finger. Hold and feel for the release and lengthening of neck and shoulder muscles.

Benefits

- Release of shoulder and neck tension.
- Lengthening of muscles, helping the neck area to self-correct and adjust itself.

References

Dennisons, Brain Gym, pp. 9-10.

5. Neck & Shoulder Tapping

Hamilton and Elizabeth Barhydt's exercise system is based on Chinese acupuncture and Kinesiology. For a discussion of the link between Polarity (primarily from India) and acupuncture (from China), see page 126. The tapping technique is used in many other energy-balancing techniques, and in traditional massage. Tapping is found in the Thymus Thump and Fountain of Love (pages 83 and 84), and it can be done anywhere on the body for stimulating benefit.

Method

For shoulders, tap with the fingertips in the hollow of the shoulder. For the neck, tap an acupressure point in the stomach midway between the navel and the xiphoid process (the cartilage tip at the bottom of the sternum). These points are on the appropriate acupuncture meridians. When finished, take a quiet moment to feel the results on neck and shoulder areas.

Benefits

- Stimulates energy flow in reflex areas, assisting relaxation of muscles.

Reference

Barhydts, Self-Help for Stress and Pain, p. 32.

6. The Owl

This exercise releases the shoulder and neck area, especially the trapezius and brachial plexus.

Method

Grasp the fleshy area on the top of your shoulder and maintain a firm yet sensitive grip. Inhale and turn your head toward that shoulder until you can look back over it. Exhale and turn your head toward the other shoulder. Repeat this several times and then return the head to the middle. Now inhale and lift your chin up. Exhale and lower the chin toward your chest. After doing this several times, return the head to the middle, relax your grip and feel the change in the shoulder area. Then, repeat the sequence with the other shoulder.

Variations

Grasp the shoulder and again rotate the head toward the shoulder you are gripping. Continuing this firm grasp, lift the arm out on that side with the thumb up and move the arm back behind you. Then turn the head back the other way,

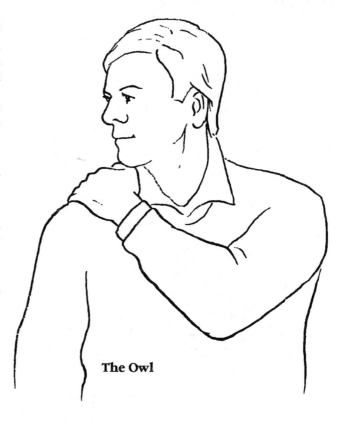

The Owl

while keeping the arm back. As you again turn toward the gripped shoulder allow your arm to float back further if it can. Repeat this several times and then do the other shoulder and arm.

Dr. Stone presents a related treatment which affects the neck a little higher in the same general area. Instead of reaching across to hold the shoulder, reach up and over the head. For most people, the fingertips will reach down to the top or middle of the neck. Give a light pull once or twice, breathing deeply with an emphasis on the exhalation.

A combination of this variation with an activation technique is very good for shoulder relaxation. Reach the right hand across the head, holding above the ear on the left side. Put the left hand on the left shoulder, middle and index fingers pressing into the spot where neck and shoulder meet.

Lengthen the head to the right as you inhale, then activate by pressing the head into the right hand, toward the left side as you exhale. Inhale and relax, allowing the head and neck to lengthen further toward the right. Repeat this three times, then do

the other side. This can be an excellent break from concentrated office or computer work.

Benefits

• Release of shoulder and neck tension. The Owl is especially good during concentrated reading, computer work, telephoning, or other desk work.

• Encourages full breathing.

References

Dennisons, <u>Brain Gym</u>, p. 17.
Stone, <u>Health Building</u>, p. 147.
Stokes and Whiteside, <u>One Brain</u>, chapter 8, p. 30.

7. Arm Activation

This activity is an excellent release for the arm muscles which originate in the chest and shoulders. Releasing them releases neck and shoulder tension and energizes the muscles of the chest and back. This exercise also enhances communication between the brain and hands.

Method

Start with the right arm, by raising it straight up. Wrap the left hand around it, as shown in the illustration. The left hand creates an isometric resistance with the right arm, pushing against it in an activation movement. Activate the arm in four different directions: to the side, back, toward the head, and forward. For each direction, the left hand will be moved and relocated so that it provides resistance for each direction.

First, place the left hand so it wraps around the outside of the right arm. Inhale and as you exhale through pursed lips, push the right arm

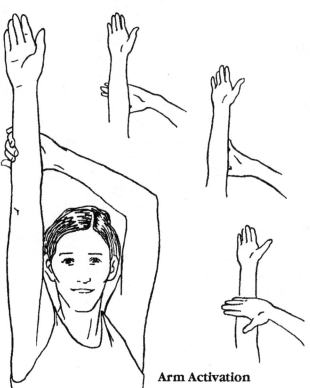

Arm Activation

out using approximately 25% of your full muscle strength. As with most activation techniques, the arm will not really move: the two arms counterbalance each other. As you inhale, relax and allow the arm to lengthen. You may repeat this several times, do the other arm, or move to the next hand position.

In step two, place the left hand so it creates a flat surface behind the right arm. Now activate, pushing back on the exhale and relaxing/lengthening on the inhale.

For step three, place the left hand so it pushes the right arm away from the head. Activate by pushing the arm in on the exhale and relaxing and lengthening on the inhale.

For step four, place the left hand in front of the right arm, using either the palm or back of the hand, whichever is easier. Activate by pushing forward on the exhale and releasing-lengthening on the inhale. Once familiar with this exercise, you can do the complete series easily and quickly by activating on the exhale and moving to a new hand position as you lengthen and relax on the inhale.

Notice that pressing forward and inward affects the chest muscles, while pressing back and outward uses the back muscles.

Repeat the whole sequence for the opposite side.

Variations

This activation of the arm can be used in any direction, any part of the arm (upper or lower), and any posture. Experiment with different muscles to experience its value.

Activation for the neck and head is similar to arm activation, an isometric release for the neck. It can be done in any direction: experiment to feel what is best for you. A detailed variation is given with the Owl posture on the preceding pages.

The technique is familiar: place one hand against the head, and press against it with 25% of neck strength as you exhale through pursed lips. Release pressure as you inhale, and allow the neck to lengthen before repeating or going to a new position. Do one side, then the other, then front and back.

For bodyworkers, massage therapists and physical therapists, we recommend activation techniques such as these for any area of the body as a safer, easier alternative to conventional mechanical stretching. With creativity, most muscles can be opened and relaxed through activation, including such important but sometimes difficult muscles as the hamstring.

Benefits

• Good for desk workers who need an open flexible link between the brain and the hands. A good office break, it opens the energy links and pathways across the shoulders.

References

Dennisons, Brain Gym, p. 18.

8. Head Lift

Neck muscles are often tense and contracted. This postural exercise is a gentle reminder to elevate the head and hold the shoulders back. It is a good discipline to add to walking. The erect posture which this develops reminds us of the dignified upright pose seen in Egyptian art, with the head held high and the back straight.

Method

Imagine having a string attached to the back of your head. As you stand or walk, lift the head up from the back as if pulled by the string from above, tucking the chin down in front slightly. Drop the shoulders allowing the neck to hang from the head. You may be able to feel relaxation as far down as the upper back. The shoulders, diaphragm and pelvis are all affected by this "re-structuring" posture.

9. Rocking V

Dr. Stone called this "Polarity Exercise for the Release of the Brachial Plexus and Neck Tension." It has also been called the Spinal Roll. The contacts on the inner thighs are reflexes for the throat area. The contacts on the outer thighs release the back of the neck and the sides. The shoulder muscles tense and relax during the rocking movement and Dr. Stone says:

> The exercise not only releases all the chest muscles involved in breathing and in heart trouble, but also the trapezius muscles which are supplied by the spinal accessory nerves which are the eleventh pair of cranial nerves and the only ones which innervate a muscle. The psoas magnus and the iliacus muscles are also exercised.[23]

The posture is specifically recommended for rebuilding after heart trouble.

---

23. Stone, <u>Polarity Therapy Vol II</u>, pp. 47-48.

Method

Begin with a reflexology evaluation of the neck. Feel the outer neck and then the throat areas for tender spots. The outer neck area is related to the outer sides of the thigh, and the throat to the inner thighs. The thigh area near the knee is a reflex to the top of the neck near the occiput, while the thigh area near the hip

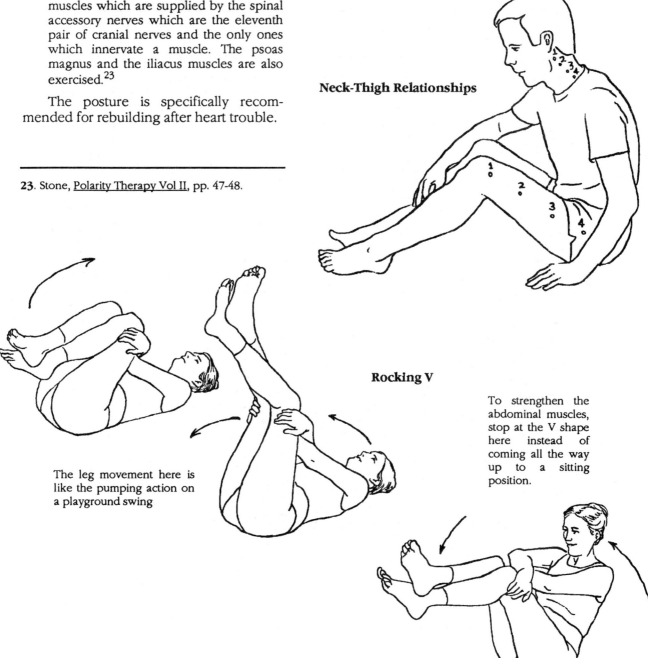

Neck-Thigh Relationships

Rocking V

The leg movement here is like the pumping action on a playground swing

To strengthen the abdominal muscles, stop at the V shape here instead of coming all the way up to a sitting position.

relates to the bottom of the neck near the shoulder. Midway on the thigh relates to midway up the neck.

With this general mapping in mind, see what correspondence you can feel between soreness above and below. Place the hands on the sore spot on the thigh that corresponds to the sore area of the neck and hold these spots firmly. The arms can be crossed or uncrossed, according to which position is more comfortable.

Next is a rocking motion. The movement is continuous and smooth and takes some practice. Sit on the floor with knees bent and legs crossed at the ankles. Rock back and pull the legs up, knees coming closer to the chest. Let the head rest on the floor for a moment, neck relaxed, while the legs finish their movement toward the chest. Then extend the legs to rock the body up and forward again, ready to rock back again. Repeat for twenty or more cycles, until you feel a release of tension on the sore spots on the thighs. The legs are in a continuous smooth circular motion throughout the exercise.

Develop these movements into a smooth self-perpetuating cycle, circling the legs to bring yourself back and up. Continue to firmly grasp the thighs on the sore spots, with arms either uncrossed or crossed, depending on which is easiest for your preferred contact location. Feel how the movement releases the tight spots in the thighs. When complete, take a few moments of rest. Then check the areas on the neck to feel the changes.

Variations

The Rocking V may also be done with an emphasis on the hands pulling the thighs up, rather than the legs lifting with abdominal and back muscles. This gives a more stimulating friction-touch to the thighs and activates the brachial plexus muscles.

Benefits
- Tension in the neck and throat area is released, affecting expression.
- The chest is expanded, breathing improved, and the pelvic area is exercised.
- Colon function is stimulated by contact on colon reflex areas on the thighs.
- Tones abdominal muscles; good as a gradual strengthener in ongoing exercise programs.
- Develops heart stability and rhythm.
- Tones the muscles of the back.
- Stimulates energy circulation in the cranial/sacral pathway.

References

Stone, Polarity Therapy Vol. II, pp. 57-58.
Francis, Polarity Self-Help Exercises, pp. 24-25.
Seidman, A Guide to Polarity Therapy, p. 139.

Related Exercises

Other exercises influence the neck and shoulders, but have been located elsewhere based on their primary action. To make full use of the book, skip around to note these others and remember them in planning your exercise routine.

Pierre Ha Breath (p.43)
Woodchopper (p. 46)
Pyramid (p. 52)
Light Rocking Perineal (p. 61)
Rowing (p. 64)
Sympathetic Balance (p. 80)

Chest & Heart

The chest and heart area has a special significance in energy exercises. Dr. Stone depicted "the tree of life" with its roots in the chest and branches in the head. The chest is described as:

> ...the sensory root system of feeling through the heart center condensing the finer life currents of sound energy and beating it out in rhythmic pulsations.[24]

A gateway to the powers of comprehension above, the heart center is the collector of feelings from below. It is the central conductor of love, expressed in the voice above, the arms to the side, and the pelvis below.

> I have discussed the heart at some length because it is central to all therapy. People come to therapy with various complaints: depression, anxiety, a feeling of inadequacy, a sense of failure, etc. But behind each complaint is a lack of joy and satisfaction in living. It is popular today to talk of self-realization and the human potential, but such terms are meaningless unless one asks-- potential for what? If one wants to live more fully and more richly, it is possible only if one opens one's heart to life and to love... The goal of all therapy is to help a person increase his capacity to give and receive love-- to expand his heart, not just his mind.[25]

The thymus gland near the heart plays an important role. Diamond describes the thymus as a "control room" for the meridians, monitoring the body's flow of Life Force:

> ...the thymus is the first organ of the body to be affected by stress. It is also the first organ to be affected at an energy level by an emotional state. The thymus gland may therefore be thought of as the link between mind and body.[26]

Emotional and psychological difficulties are immediately reflected in the muscles and connective tissue of the chest and heart area. Hardness, rigidity, a concave or slumping posture, over-expansion and other indicators are valuable clues to inner conditions. Emotions relating to desire are centered here, including hope, ambition and greed.

10. Taoist Arch

Versions of this pose are found in many sources. We have adopted Lowen's title from Bioenergetics. The position is taken naturally when we arise and have a good stretch in the morning, another example of Energy Exercises often being the conscious practice of natural, everyday positions. Young children naturally reach out with both arms as an expression of love. For exercise classes or walking groups, this is a great way to begin, with a joyful reach out to the world.

The posture embodies the attitude of the evolutionary Yin side of the energy cycle. In the first part of the cycle (Yang) the body folds inward as it becomes involved (as embodied in the fetal position or the Squat), looking for expression and materialization. Then, as consciousness

---

25. Lowen, Bioenergetics, pp. 88-89. While we quote frequently and respectfully from Lowen, we also note that there are significant differences between his system and the Polarity model upon which this book is primarily based. Lowen's valuable work has roots in the pioneering psychoanalytical teachings of Wilhelm Reich. From a Polarity framework, Bioenergetics seems to emphasize the involutionary, Yang half of human experience. "The capacity for pleasure and joy of living," sexual fulfillment, and grounding are frequently-cited goals of therapy; these are all functions of the involutionary side of the "Journey of the Soul."

In Polarity, equal concern is accorded the Yin, evolutionary force. Expressions of caution against the common excesses of Yang (irresponsible sex, over-expression of anger, etc.) are more likely to be found in Polarity, and a larger, spiritual context is emphasized. Nevertheless, Lowen's pioneering books are eloquent expressions of important ideas in the energy field, based on long experience, and are a valuable resource for the Polarity practitioner.

26. Diamond, Your Body Doesn't Lie, p. 62.

24. Stone, Polarity Therapy Vol. I Book 2, p. 19.

progresses in the second part of the cycle (Yin), the attention turns back out. The body unfolds in a outward reach as it looks to heaven for greater understanding. Dr. Stone describes this turning outward as the most important event in the "Journey of the Soul" (see page 123).

Method

Stand with feet shoulder width apart, or any comfortable pose. Bend the torso back, looking upward, without excessive strain. Reach the arms out fully to the front, the sides and behind the lower back. Breathe fully, exhaling with a deep sigh of satisfaction or a warm expression of greeting and enthusiasm.

Benefits

• A general toning posture for all dimensions: physical, emotional and mental.

• One of the easiest ways to activate the receptive, evolutionary Yin energy of the Water Principle.

• Excellent for emotional processing, especially for people with a collapsed chest or slumping shoulders. This can be dramatic and forceful when the pose is held for a minute or more.

References

Lowen, <u>Bioenergetics</u>, p. 72.
Berkson, <u>The Foot Book</u>, p. 136.
Diamond, <u>Your Body Doesn't Lie</u>, p. 57.
Gach, <u>Acu-Yoga</u>, pp. 53, 69, 166.

Related Exercises

Pierre Ha Breath (p.43)
Thymus Thump (p.87)
Cliffhanger (p. 23)
Foot Reflexology
Lion Roar (p. 38)
Exercises in these groups:
   Shoulders (p. 19),
   Diaphragm (p. 32)
   Breathing (p. 94)

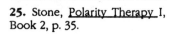

Taoist Arch

Diaphragm

The diaphragm is a large dome-shaped muscle in the center of the torso, at the edge of the rib cage, separating the thoracic and abdominal body cavities.

While it is relatively unknown to many beginners, the diaphragm has great importance in energy movement. With the brachial plexus (the nerve plexus which starts between the shoulder blades and extends up into the neck), it supplies the force necessary for breathing, while also supporting the heart from below.

Dr. Stone considered the diaphragm to be especially important because it represents the neutral, transitional link between Yang (above) and Yin (below).

On a physical level, hardness and rigidity of the diaphragm is associated with shallow breathing and reduced vitality.

> The diaphragm is the main respiratory muscle doing the most important work in life. Every cell needs the life energy contained in the breath... Truly the diaphragm is the firmament which divides the energy above and below... It is the bridge where mind and life cross into the emotional vital field.[25]

> The diaphragm is the elastic, functioning firmament which divides the waters or energies, above from below. It divides the two rivers above (one the 'fire' and the other the 'air' element) from the two riv-

---

25. Stone, <u>Polarity Therapy</u> I, Book 2, p. 35.

ers (the 'earth' element and the 'water' element) below. It is upon this important inter-action that life depends. Without diaphragmatic function, there can be no respiration nor heart beat, no proper assimilation nor elimination, nor motion. It is a fixed stabilizer of bodily function.[26]

From its central position in the torso, the diaphragm supports and massages the internal organs, moves the lymph, and aids digestion.

On an emotional level, diaphragm therapies have been valuable for those experiencing an inability to "give and take" freely, communicate deeply and sincerely, take bold action, or fully engage in relationships.

> When the diaphragm is free, the heart is free to act without fear or apprehension.[27]

---

26. *Ibid.*, Book 1, p. 25.

27. Stone, Polarity Therapy Vol. II, p. 46.

A sample of comments on the diaphragm:

"...the diaphragm is the gateway through which feelings generated in the lower three chakras pass as they move to the upper portions of the bodymind."

--Dychtwald, Bodymind, p. 141.

"Diaphragm: This muscle comes up approximately 95% of the time as the priority muscle in body/mind integration."

-- Mahoney, Hyperton-x, p. 38.

"It is the thorax [which is centered on the diaphragm] which connects the source of power, our pelvis, with our head, the source of orientation and intentional movement. The link doesn't work, and the reason is that we never did actually try to do what we wanted. We always did what somebody found right for us... Ida Rolf understood this. For she made her first lesson, not on the head, nor on the pelvis, but here at the link, and if you ask why... [it is because] she felt she had been trying to find the most effective way to start."

--Feldenkrais, The Master Moves, p. 78.

Tightness of the diaphragm is an indication of a tendency to implode or explode, rather than be able to communicate successfully, when a person is under emotional stress.

The diaphragm is also considered a gateway to the solar plexus, center of power in the body. Thus diaphragm exercises are ideal for developing the ability to manifest power in a balanced (neither tyrant nor wimp) way. It is associated with the fire element and its functions of action, authority, digestion, and force.

11. Diaphragm Reflexes

The web of the hand, the top edge of the foot's long arch, just below the ball of the foot, and the front part of the forearm just below the elbow are the most commonly used reflexes for the diaphragm. Additionally, all joints (ankle, knee, hip, wrist, elbow, shoulder) are diaphragm reflexes often used in Polarity Therapy, and are incorporated in many exercises. As we did with shoulders, it is useful to first press on the diaphragm with the fingertips, to get a feeling for its tension, then do some reflexology, then repeat the test. Typically, the diaphragm muscle will be dramatically relaxed after the reflexology.

A secondary area for the diaphragm is along the lines which form between the corners of the mouth and outsides of the nose, below the cheek bones. Nearby reflex points slightly higher, in the cheeks below the eyes, are linked to the thymus gland. These areas are naturally stimulated by smiling and laughing, perhaps a factor in the benefits of laughter in therapy, as popularized by Norman Cousins.

Method

Use your fingers to find tense or sore spots in any of the reflex areas described above. Press in lightly or deeply, depending on your personal preference and the circumstances: a light touch will be soothing and balancing, while a deeper pressure will create change. Push in and hold for a count of at least 8, waiting for a softening of tissues signaling release. You can also use a circular moving pressure with the fingertips or thumb for a more stimulating effect.

After pressure on a reflex, experiment with a balancing contact. Place one hand on the reflex and the other on the diaphragm area and hold lightly. Often the energy balancing effect can be perceived

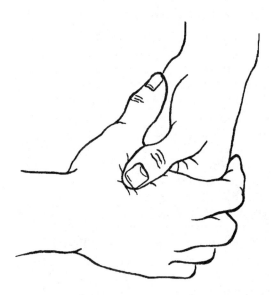

as a pulse in the fingertips or a wavelike sensation of relaxation.

Benefits

- Release of the diaphragm without direct contact. In bodywork, reflex techniques are often used to prepare the target area for direct contact.
- Useful for digestive pains, gas and hiccoughs. For hiccoughs, the web of the hand is particularly useful; it can take deep pressure and require several minutes.
- Useful to facilitate communication and overcome anxiety.
- Facilitates processing of emotions relating to anger and authority.

References

Stone, <u>Polarity Therapy Vol. I</u> Book 2, p. 11.
Stone, <u>Polarity Therapy Vol II</u>, pp. 35-42, 183-184.
Diamond, <u>Your Body Doesn't Lie</u>, p. 89-94.

12. Calf Reflex

A multiple reflex is found in the calves. The calves are the neutral zone in the lower part of the body just as the diaphragm area is the neutral zone in the middle part (see chart on page 15). The calves also have specific reflex relationships with the chest (linked by the Air Principle) and the colon (linked by the Earth Element). Dr. Stone discusses contacts on the calves in relation to elimination of waste gas from the body, and improved digestive function. The same concept appears in the Dennisons' "Foot Flex" contact found on page 62.

Method

Take a kneeling position, resting the buttocks back on the calves. Make the hand into a fist, lift up for a moment, and place the fist on the calf muscle. Now lower the buttocks

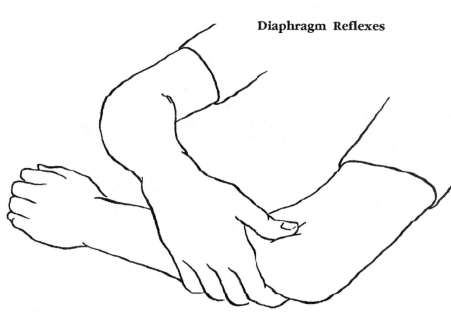

Diaphragm Reflexes

back down, creating pressure on the calf from the knuckles of the fist. Make a strong "a-a-a-h-h-h" sound as you exhale. Hold for a moment, then lift and move the hands to a new spot. The sorest spots offer the most benefit.

In addition to the calves, this same kneeling position is a good stance for reflex treatment of the feet. Continue down from the calves, pressing the Achilles, then ankle, then down the bottom of the foot. This is a good general treatment, and very enjoyable in a class setting, with lots of good-natured moaning and groaning.

References
Seigel, <u>Polarity Therapy</u>, pp. 100-101.
Francis, <u>Polarity Self-Help Exercises</u>, p. 39.

13. Diaphragm Press

This exercise combines conscious breathing with direct pressure of the fingers on the diaphragm. It is effective for opening the diaphragm, and also affects the pelvic area. The diaphragm and pelvis are linked physiologically by the psoas muscle (the muscle we use to lift the legs when we walk), which attaches to the spine at the diaphragm level.

This posture is an easier variation of the Diaphragm Press-Leg Lift, which is described next. It was devised to give diaphragm contact without strenuous leg lifting, which is to be avoided by people with back weaknesses.

Method

Kneel on a soft surface or sit in a chair. Place the backs of the fingers of both hands together, fingers straight, to make a "wedge." With the fingers, push up and in lightly about one and one half inches below the ribs. In the very middle of the rib cage and below the sternum is the xiphoid process, a cartilage structure: make sure that you are well below or to the side of this projection, as it should not be stressed. Check for tense areas. Once you have a sense of the current state of tension, begin the release process.

Pick a tight spot and place your fingertips there. Inhale and as you exhale, lean forward, allowing the fingers to sink in. Keep the fingers at that level of penetration and inhale into them to create more pressure. As you exhale, lean forward again, and allow them to sink in further. This process can continue for some time, gradually going deeper with each breath.

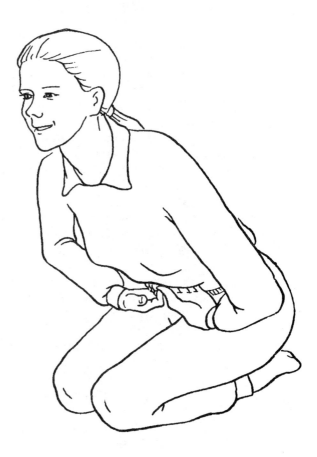

Diaphragm Press

This kneeling position is also used for calf reflexes (make fists and sandwich them between calf and thigh as you sit back), and for the self-organ drain (next page). The hand position is used again in the standing variation of the diaphragm press.

This may be stressful if the knees are weak. All these exercises can be done sitting or standing if needed for knee comfort.

Benefits

- The diaphragm relaxes, facilitating a wider range of expansion and contraction.
- Breathing, digestion, and heart functions are supported and enhanced.
- The torso, from shoulders above to pelvis below, is lengthened and relaxed.
- Beneficial as a part of bodywork therapies dealing with disassociation of mind and body, or self and feelings.
- Enhances communication.
- Primary energy circuits passing through the diaphragm area are opened.
- Assists in the movement of gas.
- Eases problems of fear or low confidence.
- Balances left/right, front/back and top/bottom energy dimensions.

Reference

Stone, <u>Polarity Therapy Vol II</u>, pp. 47-49.

14. Diaphragm Activation

The activation technique is quite useful for the diaphragm, accessing the deeper connections of the diaphragm to the spine and ribs. This activation helps the breath and diaphragm to reset at a wider range of motion, restoring ease to the breathing cycle.

Method

Place both hands flat on the stomach area, with the thumbs just high enough to touch the lowest ribs. Inhale and exhale a few times to experience and become familiar with your breathing pattern. Then inhale fully and hold your breath. As you hold, push gently against the upper belly with your fingertips, and push your belly against your hands. The muscle is internal so the activation of it is largely through holding the breath. When you feel that you need to press the belly out as you exhale. Pause and experience how your breathing cycle feels now. This can be repeated several times.

Benefits

- Provides relief when breathing has become shallow and restricted.

References

Mahoney, <u>Hyperton-x</u>, p. 40.
Dennisons, <u>Brain Gym</u>, p. 10.
Barhydts, <u>Self-Help for Stress and Pain</u>, p. 43.

15. Diaphragm Press Leg Lift

This is a continuation of the diaphragm press described above. The purpose of lifting the legs is to stimulate the diaphragm by flexing the psoas muscle, which attaches at the diaphragm level.

The original exercise described by Dr. Stone is now rarely used: leg lifts have been found to be stressful for the back. The original is described under "Variations" for those whose back fitness is excellent. Instructors are advised to be very sensitive to the fitness level of all students in the class before using an old-fashioned straight leg lift posture.

Method

Lie on the back and again use the fingertips to check under the ribs for tension. As before, be careful not to press directly on the xiphoid process. Place the fingertips on the spot of your choice, or wherever feels most tense along the diaphragm.

Leg lifting movements are combined with a specific sequence of breathing. First, inhale fully with the legs resting. Then, as you exhale, lift one straight leg and allow the fingers to press into the diaphragm area. Inhale again, maintaining that fingertip pressure on the diaphragm. As you exhale, bend the leg, allowing the knee to come toward the chest while the fingers sink in. Inhale, maintaining that same level of penetration with the fingertips into the diaphragm, and breathe into the fingers. Exhale again and allow the fingers to sink in further. Relax in this position, and repeat the inhale/rest-without-backing-off, and exhale/press-in-deeper sequences until you are ready to stop.

When you feel ready to complete this

When you feel ready to complete this leg lift, inhale while straightening the leg; exhale while lowering the leg and allowing the fingers to sink in. Relax and keep your hands at that level of pressure for a while.

To finish, take the fingertips out and let them rest gently on the diaphragm area for a short time, at least one third of the time that was spent doing the posture.

After this rest, go on to repeat the procedure for the other leg.

Variations

This leg lift may also be done from a starting position of feet resting on the floor and both knees bent. Inhale. Exhale and lift both bent legs at once, allowing the fingers to sink into the diaphragm area. Continue as above.

A person with strong abdominal muscles and a strong back can lift both straight legs at once as shown below. This is the way the exercise was originally presented by Dr. Stone. However, this is now considered unsafe for the average person.

In addition, a standing position variation is offered by John Francis. In this posture, the fingertips are placed in the diaphragm area and the torso is lowered, head to the knees, with a slow "ahhh" sound. In the collapsed position, the fingertips can press in more deeply.

Benefits
Same as Diaphragm Press.

References
Stone, Polarity Therapy Vol. II, pp. 55-56
Francis, Polarity Self-Help Exercises, pp. 40-41.

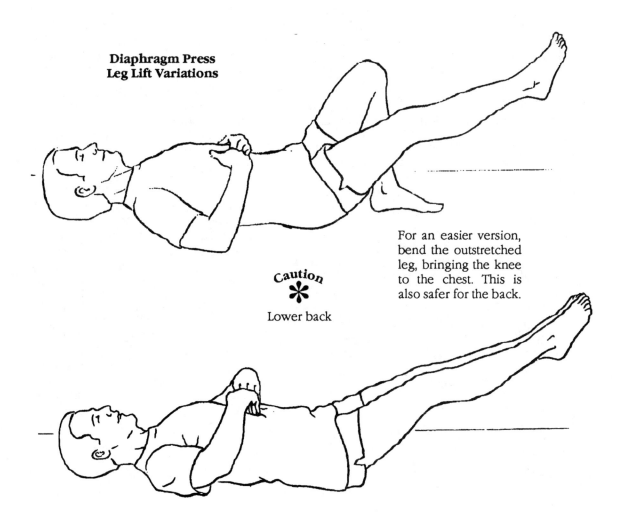

**Diaphragm Press
Leg Lift Variations**

Caution
✳
Lower back

For an easier version, bend the outstretched leg, bringing the knee to the chest. This is also safer for the back.

16. Organ Drain

This is an easy way to activate and "massage" the organs of the abdominal cavity, especially the intestines and colon. It is grouped with diaphragm exercises because they have a common effect in digestive function, and because it can be used for relaxation after a strenuous diaphragm press exercise. It also helps deal with difficulties in the lower back (often lower back problems originate with emotional or digestive tension in front) or pelvis (problems in support of the abdominal area create problems in the area itself).

Method

In a kneeling position, leaning over the knees (as shown in the illustration for the Diaphragm Press on p. 35), use the fingertips to gently explore the abdominal area. Press in with small circular motions. Start on the lower right corner above the hip, and gradually work up and across, then down the left side, repeating as desired. If a particular spot is painful, reduce the pressure.

This can also be done by holding in one place in the abdomen, exhaling, and then inhaling into the spot being held. Gentle rotational pressure can then be used.

This exercise is based on Dr. Stone's "Gas Releasing Technique."

Benefits
- Gives relief from gas pains.
- Tones the internal connective tissues.
- Can be helpful with sluggish bowels.

References
Stone, <u>Polarity Therapy Vol. I</u>, Book 3, p. 93-94.
Stone, <u>Health Building</u>, p. 178.

17. Lion Roar

The Lion Roar uses sound to expand and project the heat of the solar plexus. The roaring sound is a deep, full, continuous emptying of the lungs, which vibrates the body from the inside out and opens the diaphragm. The rich, loud sound is quite exhilarating, giving the same therapeutic warmth we feel when singing in a choral group or yelling at a sports event. The Lion Roar is a specific therapy for those wishing to strengthen or activate the ability to express feelings, safely expel pent-up frustration, or strengthen Yang qualities such as creativity, responsibility and assertiveness.

Method

Take a position in which you can comfortably place your elbows between your knees with hands clasped in the middle. Make sure your chest is open. There are several possibilities for this position, the best being the Squat (page 54).

First, take one or more "cleansing breaths." Inhale deeply through the nose and exhale fully. Now you are ready for the "roar." Inhale, expanding the chest, and as you exhale, let the breath out with a roaring sound that is full and rich.

Make a deep, low, relaxed

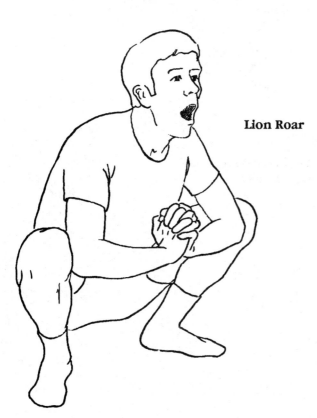

Lion Roar

sound for maximum volume with minimal strain. If there is strain, reduce the loudness. Once there is an easy, steady tone, increase the volume again. Be aware of and avoid the tendency to pinch or constrict the throat. While you roar, push the hands together and the knees into the elbows (a double diaphragm reflex connection), and focus the eyes (the positive pole of the Fire Principle) on a specific spot. Expel the breath to the last drop. This may be followed with more deep breaths and roars (three roars is a good total for most people) until you feel that frustrations are exhausted and warmth is shining through.

After the roars, move into a balancing posture by placing both thumbs between the eyebrows. This pose is Dr. Stone's "Youth Posture" depicted on p. 138 of Health Building. Take a few moments to feel the inner energy level, the heat of the solar plexus, tingling in the hands and face, increased ability to express feelings and deeper breathing ability.

Variations

When you are in a situation in which it is not appropriate to be noisy, this posture may be done with a muted long deep forceful exhalation.

Also in this posture, a general toning exercise for the face may be added by "making faces" in all directions, activating the facial muscles. Stick out the tongue as far as possible, open the jaw as wide as possible, raise the eyebrows, purse the lips, etc. The face is a complex field of reflexes for the whole body (see the section on face reading starting on page 111) and this expression-making is both relaxing and fun.

Benefits

- Multiple reflex connections facilitate general energy balancing: Hands clasped and squeezing relates to shoulders and brachial plexus, elbows touching knees makes a diaphragm reflex connection, and belly touching thighs connects neutral and negative poles of the Fire Element.
- Stimulates the body's heat or fire.
- Releases pent-up frustrations and aids digestion.This can be very useful in emotional processing during therapy.
- Improves the free flow of expression.

References

The Lion Roar originates in Hatha Yoga; its energy theories are described by Dr. Stone in discussing the Squat (pp. 138, 163 in Health Building).

Francis, Polarity Self-Help Exercises, p. 22.

Berkson, The Foot Book, pp. 180-181.

Lion Roar Variations

Ha Breath

There are a number of exercises in which Dr. Stone used a sound called the "Ha" breath. To introduce these exercises, we first introduce the sound itself. The "Ha" sound (page 86) takes a little practice for beginners. The sound is full and forceful and comes from deep in the belly, vibrating the whole torso as it comes out.

Begin to develop this sound by placing your hands on the belly just below the diaphragm. If you are making the sound properly, you will feel your hands move as the "ha" comes out. A Santa Claus "ho ho ho" is a fun way to get started. As you feel the belly move, give the sound some extra length following a forceful "h-h-h"-"h-h-h-a-a-a." Play with this. It will feel easy and natural and make a full deep sound as the diaphragm opens. When done properly, the sound is loud, bouncing out effortlessly and filling the room. It combines power with ease, and should not require straining. For instructors, take a few moments to help the class feel comfortable with making a rich "h-h-h-a-a-a" sound.

18. Up and Down Ha Breath

This is the first and best known of the Ha Breath postures. Dr. Stone called this the "Exercise for Polarizing the Energy Currents,"[28] an indication of its multiple values for all parts of the energy anatomy.

The primary effect of the Ha Breath is on the Fire center, located in the solar plexus. It can be described as the stoking and heating of a furnace, in which the solar plexus represents the fireplace containing hot embers, the brachial plexus and chest represents the air supply, and the thighs represent the fuel. All parts of the system are activated and stimulated by the movements, generating increased circulation and power.

In addition to its effect on the Fire systems, this Ha Breath is also stimulating to the pelvic area (the Water Principle and Element), and the diaphragm (the Air Principle). To continue the furnace analogy, the pelvis is like a water basin. Heated by the increased action of the nearby fire, the basin's contents of old feelings[29] are activated and moved upward across the diaphragm towards expression at the throat. Expression is a significant way of release or elimination, important for health (see pages 86, 94).

In addition, the upper back is activated by the position and action of the arms and hands. Thus the Ha Breath is one of the most stimulating and comprehensive of all Dr. Stone's exercises.

This movement is one of several of Dr. Stone's postures that have proven to be useful in bodywork. The more stimulating exercises accomplish energy activation that can be difficult for a therapist to induce without extremely deep contact. The Ha Breath, Pyramid, Cliffhanger, Woodchopper, and others can be used to quickly increase energy circulation without using deep contact.

Like the Cliffhanger, the Up and Down Ha Breath should be done with caution. It should be avoided or modified to reduce the movement by those with sore knees or sore backs.

Method

To do the Ha Breath, stand with the legs slightly more than shoulder width apart. Lean forward so the hands rest on the knees, fingers conveniently aligning vertically with the energy pathways of the "Long Current" or Water Principle.

From this partially-bent position, slowly lower the body to the position

---

28. Stone, Health Building, p. 162.

29. "In the pelvic basin at the bottom is the sum total force accumulation of all the sensory tension and emotional frustration." Stone, Polarity Therapy Vol. I, Book 2, p. 16.

shown in the illustration, letting out a deep full "ha" sound as you go. Relax your neck (everyone will need to be repeatedly reminded of this), and bend with the legs not the waist. The back stays straight, almost parallel to the floor, and the head stays down in the lowered position. The chest opens and closes as the arms push up and down: this activates the chest and diaphragm, creating a bellows effect to "fan the flames" of the solar plexus.

From the lowered position, push (hands on thighs just above the knees) back up to the upright position as shown in the illustration. The arms, not the legs, should be doing the lifting work: you should be able to feel movement in the shoulder blades. Once up, drop down again with another strong "Ha" sound. (Relax your neck). Repeat this as many times as feels appropriate for your body and the situation. If you are seeking relief from angry feelings or wanting to dramatically increase fiery qualities, the Up and Down Ha Breath can be done many times.

Variations

For an easier variation, sit in a chair with the legs more than shoulder width apart, hands on knees as described above. Proceed the same as above, but adjust your movements to suit the limits of sitting in the chair. Remember to PUSH with the arms as you come up and make a nice full "ha" as you go down. As always, remember to relax your neck. This is a way for seniors and those with weak knees or back to benefit from the exercise.

An advanced variation uses the same up and down movements but with the arms behind the back, hands clasped as shown in the illustration on page 58. This creates a dramatic opening across the front of the chest area.

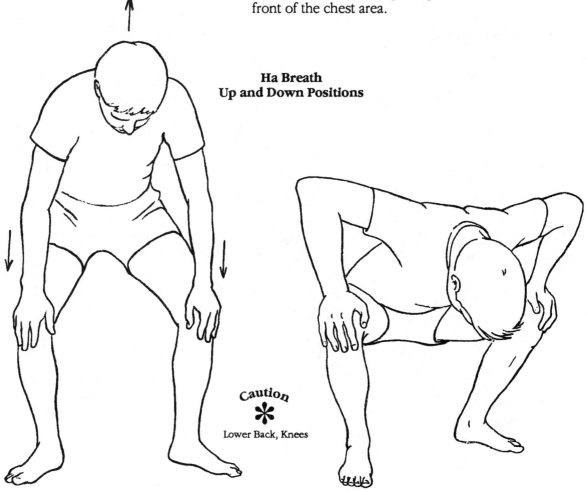

**Ha Breath
Up and Down Positions**

Caution

✳

Lower Back, Knees

Benefits

- Stimulating for physical and emotional energy levels. One of the most comprehensive self-given "Energy Session" exercises, with both top-bottom (Water Principle) and front-back (Fire Principle) balancing effects.
- Relief from gas.
- Relief from nervousness.
- Opens diaphragm.
- Tones back, especially lower back.
- Relaxes muscles around the brachial plexus.
- Fire is activated by sound and by thigh action.
- Brings what is inside to the surface.
- Expansive sound frees expression.

References

Stone, <u>Health Building</u>, p. 162.
Stone, <u>Polarity Therapy Vol II</u>, p. 191.
Sills, <u>The Polarity Process</u>, p. 153.
Seidman, <u>A Guide to Polarity Therapy</u>, p. 137.
Francis, <u>Polarity Self-Help Exercises</u>, p. 19.

Sciatic Ha Breath

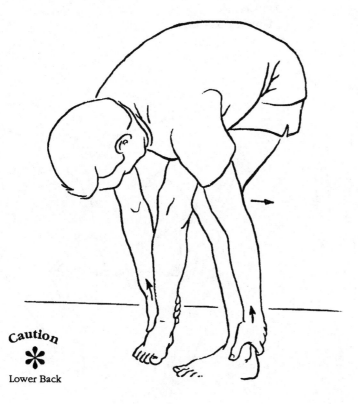

Caution
✱
Lower Back

19. Sciatic Ha Breath

The Sciatic Ha Breath is a demanding but beneficial releasing exercise for the lower back and legs, especially the hamstrings and sciatic nerve path. It retains the up and down movement of the regular Ha Breath, but is much slower, with a groaning slow sound instead of the forceful Ha. For acute Sciatica, the Squat is sometimes preferred over the Sciatic Ha Breath, which can be too strenuous.

Method

Stand with feet about ten inches apart, toes turning inward. Bend over and grasp the heels with the hands, pulling down to lengthen the lower back. For most people, this requires bending the knees; flexible people will need to straighten the knees and bend the elbows, keeping chest to thigh as the legs straighten. Inhale as you bend the knees, making it easier to hold the ankle, then straighten the legs as you exhale with a steady groaning sound. The effect is an activation for the back of the legs, isometrically opposed by the arms gripping the heels.

Benefits

- Lengthens muscles around the sciatic nerve and back of the legs.
- Improves posture, especially problems with tilted pelvis and stressed sacrum area.
- Integrates and balances the top and bottom of the body, the path of the Water Principle (Long line or Bi-Polar current).
- Useful for developing flexibility with Yang challenges such as using authority and making decisions.
- Lengthens the back. Grasping the back of the ankle stimulates the Achilles heel reflex to the lower back. The fingertips press the inside of the ankle, a reflex to the pelvis and emotional history (see hallucis tendon, page 51).

20. Arch Pull Ha Breath

The Arch Pull Ha Breath is another advanced variation, which specifically lengthens and tones the lower back and thighs. Like the Sciatic Ha, it is strenuous to do. The movement is an isometric pull with a slow groaning sound. It should be avoided by those with knee or back pain.

The Arch Pull Ha Breath resembles both the regular Ha Breath and the Squat (page 54). Its unique feature is the placement of the hands under the arches, a reflex connection for the umbilicus and solar plexus.

> This neutral position of the body is completed with the hands under the arches of the feet, so the Polarity Currents can be completed and flow freely.[30]

Method

Bend over and place the hands under the arches of the feet. Breathe in, then pull with the hands to lower the body down to a Squat position with a groaning Ha exhalation. The hands pull on the arches throughout the movement. While pulling

―――――――――――――――

30. Stone, Polarity Therapy Vol. II, p. 193.

down, resist with the legs; while moving up, resist with the arms. The greater the resistance, the greater the heat generated.

After a few up-and-down movements, stay down in the squat position and rock gently from front to back, then side to side, then in circles. Continue breathing fully, with a groaning Ha sound on each exhalation. Again, remember to keep pulling on the arches throughout the exercise.

Benefits

- Stimulates front and back of the torso. The front-back dimension is the path of the Umbilical current or Fire Principle.
- Beneficial for Fire Principle systems, including back muscles, solar plexus, and thighs, which are the negative pole of the Fire Element; generates intense heat.
- Counters nervousness.
- Good for releasing gas.
- Strengthens pelvic muscles.
- Tones thighs and back.

References

Stone, Polarity Therapy Vol. II, p. 193.
Stone, Health Building, pp. 162-163, 171.

21. Pierre Ha Breath

This dynamic Ha Breath was devised by Pierre Pannetier. Most people are able to do it easily, and it is fun for groups or classes. It makes use of a technique called "Crossing Over" which appears in several other Polarity Therapy movements. Passing the arms or legs back and forth across each other stimulates energy flow and balance. An analogy for this is the dynamo, which generates electricity by revolving a magnet within a magnetic field, "crossing over" the magnetic poles.

In terms of energy theory, this movement accentuates the Air Principle, the side-to-side movement of energy throughout the body. This dimension of energy is activated simultaneously by several movements

Arch Pull Ha Breath

Caution

✳

Lower Back
& Knees

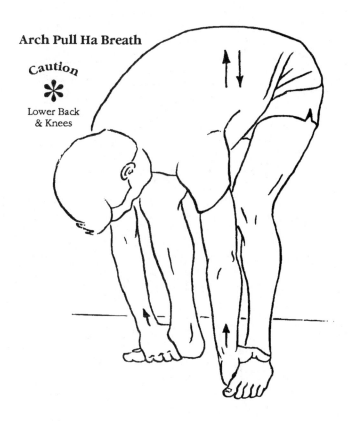

here: the opening and stretching of the "air oval" in the chest for greater breathing, the opening of the diaphragm muscle through the "Ha" sound, and the activation of chest and diaphragm reflexes while lifting up on the balls of the feet for the "Ha." The active movement, strong sound and rhythmic repetition combine to make a stimulating, light hearted exercise.

The Pierre Ha exercise is a dynamic version of the evolutionary Taoist Arch pose, described earlier (p. 30). Moving the arms forcefully back and projecting the chest opens the heart area and stimulates the thymus. Thus this exercise could be grouped with the Chest area exercises, with the functions and benefits described there.

Method

Begin with some warm up movements for the shoulders and neck. Stand with the feet a comfortable, supportive distance apart. Practice lifting up to the balls of the feet to check your balance and stability. Make a practice "Ha" sound or two and then add a crossover arm move-

ment. Put the arms out in front with the palms facing up. Cross them quickly by moving right over left, left over right, right over left three times (see illustrations) and then swing them back briskly with a loud "Ha." The timing of the Ha! is important; it should be at the point of fullest extension. If it is just right, the sound will pop out effortlessly. The exercise takes on a "1-2-3-Ha!" rhythm. Now add rising up on the balls of the feet (a reflex for the chest) as you reach the "ha" in the movement. This can take a little practice, but it is fun and easy to do. Remember to take a quiet moment standing after completion, eyes closed, knees slightly bent, to experience the results of the exercise.

Variations

For those with stiff shoulders, it is not necessary to have the palms facing upwards, and preliminary warm-ups may be necessary. The arm activation techniques described earlier can be good for this.

For the Pierre Ha, here's a quick activation warm-up. With the arms straight

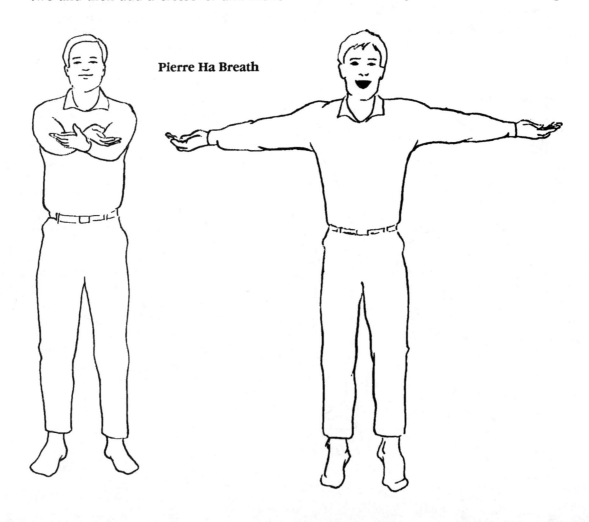

Pierre Ha Breath

out to the side and thumbs pointing up, inhale and "float" the arms back. Exhale and push against an imaginary force that holds the arms from going forward. Inhale and let the arms float back again. Repeat this as long as the arms' range of motion keeps increasing, then allow them to float forward and rest. This isometric technique may also be done pressing against a doorway or wall, and is especially helpful for people whose shoulders curve forward excessively.

Benefits
• Energizing, relaxing, fun for a group.
• Opens the chest, shoulders, breathing, diaphragm.
• Brings alertness and clarity of thought.
• Good for postural slumping shoulder problems.
• Balances side to side Air Principle.

22. Side To Side Ha Breath

The Side To Side Ha Breath is highly popular for many reasons. It is very effective, giving a direct experience of energy flow to many who try it. It is also easy to do and is thus well-suited to seniors or beginners classes.

In energy theory, this version adds a stimulation to the Transverse Current (side-to-side, Air Principle) to go with the Long-line current (Bi-Polar, Water Principle) effect of the Up and Down Ha Breath. As always, the Ha sound stimulates the front/back dimension of the Fire Principle.

Method
Begin in a standing position, feet 24 inches or so apart. Lean forward to place the hands on the knees, keeping the back straight. So far this posture is similar to the Pyramid, and the two can be mistaken in Dr. Stone's illustrations. Here, however, the weight of the torso is never transferred fully to the arms/shoulders. Instead, the weight is evenly distributed between arms and legs.

From this position, begin the Ha Breath sequence by moving smoothly to place the chest down on one thigh as you exhale with a "H-a-a-a" sound. From the low position, chest on one thigh, inhale and use the arms to raise the torso back to center, then exhale and go down to the other side, chest on thigh again with a "H-a-a-a" sound. The upper body makes an arc, from one knee to the other.

We have experimented with a wide range of sounds and tempos here, soft and slow for relaxation, loud and forceful for stimulation; experiment to determine the sound and speed that is right for you. Repeat several cycles to feel the benefits.

Benefits
• Good posture for feeling energy movement.
• General energy balancing for all major systems; especially appropriate for left-right Air Principle imbalances.
• Can be soothing or stimulating, according to tempo and volume of movement and sound and the amount of pressure exerted by the hands on the legs.
• Gentle stretch for the spine, suitable for all ages (can be done in a chair).
• Soothing internal massage for the abdominal cavity.
• Facilitates movement and elimination of gas.

References
Stone, <u>Health Building</u>, pp. 160-161.
Francis, <u>Polarity Self-Help Exercises</u>, p. 20.

Side to Side Ha Breath

Caution

✳

Lower Back

23. Woodchopper

The woodchopper could be located in many sections of this book, since it affects the whole system. It emphasizes connecting top and bottom, and stimulating the back side and fire element energies. It is an advanced, strenuous technique not to be used by those with back problems.

The Woodchopper is a forceful involutionary-to-evolutionary movement, adding action to the positions of the Taoist Arch and the Squat. It also resembles the Rocking Cliff in embodying the involution/evolution positions.

Method

For safety, warm up for the Woodchopper by lengthening and movement. Key areas are the hamstring (see p. 101), back (p. 47) and pelvis (p. 50). Stand with feet a little wider than the shoulders, knees slightly bent. From a standing position, hang down and let the arms swing freely like an elephant's trunk. Then stand with hands on hips and rotate the pelvis, like a hula dancer. Place the hands on the hips and practice the up-and-down movement: pelvis forward, then back, as the chest expands forward then falls to th knees in a smooth motion. The hands-or hip variation is safer because there is les leverage on the back. Other warm ups fc

the Woodchopper are Rowing (p. 64), Hamstring Lengthening (p. 101) and the Pierre Ha Breath (preceding page).

The movement is a natural swinging motion as if holding an axe and chopping wood. Starting with hands clasped and reaching high above the head, rock the pelvis forward to start an undulating swing which goes all the way down and through the legs. Let out a solid "Ha!" at the end of the stroke. The sound should pop out almost on its own as you reach the bottom. This movement can be repeated many times, taking on a rhythmic feeling. The effect is like a wave which ripples up and down the spine as you swing and return, from pelvis through shoulders and arms. Remember that the movement is generated by the pelvis, not the arms. Be careful not to go too fast, and be moderate in using the Woodchopper. Too much force and speed leads to dizziness and strain.

Benefits

- Integrates top-bottom dimension of the Water Principle. Opens the diaphragm, the bridge between upper and lower areas.

- Activates Fire Principle and Element: good for stimulating authority and assertiveness.
- Alternates involutionary Yang (curved in the front) and evolutionary Yin (arched to the back) poses for balancing.
- Grounding: generates a feeling of practicality and a "can-do" attitude.

References

Stone, Health Building, p. 159.
Stone, Polarity Therapy Vol. II, p. 191.
Berkson, The Foot Book, p. 130.
Francis, Polarity Self-Help Exercises, pp. 37-38

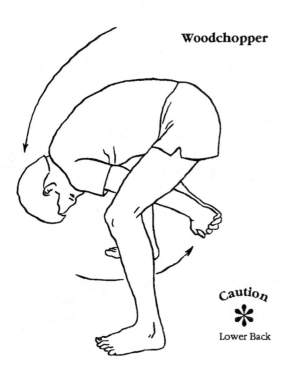

Woodchopper

Caution
✳
Lower Back

Lower Back

The lower back is a common source of tension for many people. Pains in this area can be frequently traced to tension in the front.

Abdominal tension and stress are frequently at the root of lower back pain, for as the muscles in the belly tighten and contract, they begin to tug on the muscles which surround the spine, forcing them to become contracted and rigid.[31]

This link between front and back can be described in terms of emotional experience. The Yin front with its stored emotions is a powerful motivator for the action-oriented Yang back. Actions undertaken for extreme emotional reasons (compulsive behavior, obsessions, addictions, etc.) are invariably stressful and exhausting.

The lower back area is associated with Yang involution, generating new life through sexuality, and "involvement" through creative action, materialism, and power. The sacrum at the base of the spine serves several functions in the Energy Anatomy, including being the center of this involutionary force, the negative pole of the spinal system and the animalistic complement to the higher powers of the brain above. Advanced techniques in Polarity Therapy analyze the alignment of the sacrum in the pelvic basin to indicate the condition of energy currents throughout the system.

The lower back also has a major structural significance. Posture, the presence of a short leg, curvature of the spine, and sinus problems are all related to sacrum/lower back condition by Dr. Stone.

---

31. Dychtwald, <u>Bodymind</u>, p. 27.

24. Back Reflexes

The most commonly used reflexes for the lower part of the torso are found in the heel, achilles tendon and instep. Use light or deep pressure with the fingertips to stimulate and massage these areas. The Achilles tendon is often tight and sore when lower back tension is high. The back of the heel relates specifically to the sacrum.

Along the inside edge of the foot, the spine reflexes range from lower back at the heel to upper back near the toe. The curve of the spine and the shape of the inside edge of the foot are similar, making it easy to locate specific corresponding areas.

Another relaxing reflex area is the ear.

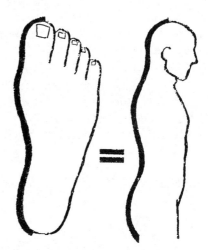

Back-Foot Relationships
Press along the inside of the foot for spinal reflexes, wider for outer areas of the back. Also see the chart on p. 114.

Take each hand and pull lightly along the edge of the ear, especially at the bottom, a reflex to the pelvic area. Lift up firmly on the ridge directly above the ear canal. Similarly, the nose is a reflex to the spine and can be lightly pulled downward or moved in a small circular motion for a relaxing effect: reflexes are arranged from top to bottom corresponding to the area from shoulder to sacrum.

References

Stone, <u>Polarity Therapy Vol I</u>, Book 2, pp. 11, 24, 38, 40, 79; Book 3, pp. 45-49.

Stone, <u>Polarity Therapy Vol</u> II, pp. 105-109, 118, 163, 198, 201.

Berkson, <u>The Foot Book</u>, p. 56.

Stokes & Whiteside, <u>One Brain</u>, chap. 8, p. 9.

25. Gluteal Activation

Most people, especially those with tightness in the lower back, have tension in the gluteal muscles. This posture creates a gentle pressure in a direction opposite to that which we actually want to release, to facilitate the lengthening of the gluteal muscles.

Method

Lie on the floor with the legs straight. Slowly slide one heel toward the chest so that the knee comes up to a bent position. Slowly raise that one knee and bring it

Gluteal Activation

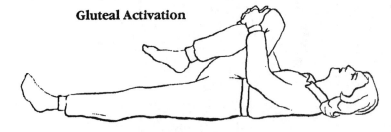

close to the chest, embracing it with the arms to support its resting position. Take a deep breath in and, as you exhale, push the knee (with about 25% of full force) into the arms. The arms exactly meet the force of the push so there is no resulting movement.

As you inhale, relax your leg and allow the knee to drop more closely to the chest. Do not pull or force, "allow." Take up any slack with your arms and repeat the exhale-push-inhale-relax two more times.

Rest the leg in this new position and allow the body to experience and register this new leg position. This may also be done with the arms between the knee and the calf to affect a slightly different area.

Repeat with the other leg, and then with both legs together. This is a great warm up for the "Back Curl," immediately following, which is done in this position. Another activation which replicates more of the traditional squat is to grasp the feet and activate by pushing with the legs and resisting with the hands, similar to the position in Rowing (p. 60), and in the Arch Pull Ha Breath (p. 39).

Benefits

• Relaxes the lower back area
• Lengthens the gluteal muscles.

Reference

Stone, <u>Health Building</u>, p. 134.

26. Back Curl

This is a relaxing variation of the Squat which is specific for the back. It is well known in many therapies for relief of back pain. It can be very relaxing in bed as first aid for insomnia and for "unwinding" from a busy day, before

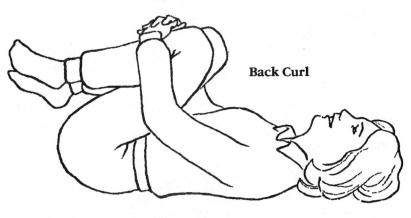

Back Curl

sleep. It re-creates the shape of the squat, without strain on the knees or ankles.

Method

Lie on the floor or bed with the legs out straight. Slowly slide the heels so that the knees come into a bent position (feet still resting on the floor). Slowly raise the knees and bring them close to the chest. Embrace them with the arms. Rock gently from side to side and then stop and relax, feeling the benefits of the posture. As a variation, move the knees from side to side with minimal movement in the back, giving a gentle wringing motion to the back muscles. For a different variation, activation for the back can be done by pressing the legs against the resistance of the arms or hands.

References

Stone, Health Building, pp 132-137
Berkson, The Foot Book, pp. 87-88.
Lowens, The Way to Vibrant Health, p. 102.

27. The Clock

This mindful differentiation sequence comes from Moshe Feldenkrais. It works with the spine, spinal muscles, pelvic muscles, neck and the deeper postural muscles in front and back.

Method

Lie on the back with the knees up, feet comfortably apart, hands resting at the sides. Imagine that you are resting on the face of a clock. Gently rock your pelvis toward your feet (toward "6 o'clock") so that the tail bone comes closer to the floor. Now gently and slowly rock your pelvis up the other way (toward "12 o'clock") so that your lower back curve (lumbar spine) moves closer to the floor. The movements are slow and gentle. Only subtle muscle movement is required and experienced. Do this "6" to "12" and back to "6" slow rocking motion several times, noticing the movement of the head and chin as well as the pelvis.

Next, begin a slow movement toward "9 o'clock." The knees will move slightly and the weight will shift to the right hip. Return with a movement toward "3 o'clock" and the weight shifts onto the left hip. Do this several times, rest, and begin again. When you have completed these basic up-down and side-to-side motions, "rock around the clock" very slowly.

Start at "12 o'clock" and do a clockwise rotation, "12-1-2-3-4," etc. Observe the difference between the right and left sides. After several times, repeat in the other direction. Let the head move too. Whenever movement doesn't feel smooth and circular, stop and imagine a circular movement.

As a variation, move back and forth between opposite points on the clock: from "12 to 6" and back, then "1 to 7," etc. Feel how you move and stay comfortable.

Reference

Feldenkrais, Awareness Through Movement.
Bach-y-Rita, "Feldenkrais at Home: Aligning Your Body" (cassette).

28. Pelvic Lift

A pelvic-strengthening exercise can be done from the same position. Lift up the buttocks by pushing down with the feet. In this raised position, use small differentiation movements to isolate different pelvic and lower back muscles. Then lower the back slowly, one vertebra at a time, until it rests back on the floor.

The Clock

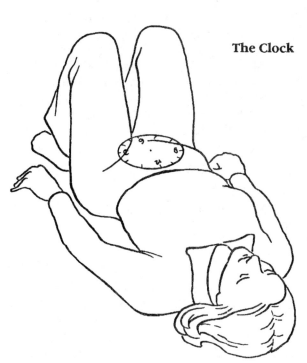

Pelvis

The pelvic basin is a factor in all major energy centers and pathways. It is significant in virtually all aspects of energy therapy, being the "negative pole" of the magnetic field of the torso. Relaxation of the pelvis is an essential part of Polarity Therapy, which began when Dr. Stone experimented with perineal techniques relating to the muscles of the pelvic floor. He found that pelvic therapies made chiropractic adjustments last longer, and gave insight into the emotional origins of tension.

The pelvis is the foundation of structure, the seat of regeneration, the source of courageous confidence, and the storage vault for old unprocessed feelings. Repeating one of the most-frequently quoted lines from Dr. Stone,

> In the pelvic basin at the bottom is the sum total force accumulation of all the sensory tension and emotional frustration.[32]

Therapeutic exercises for the pelvic area can be expected to have a significant impact elsewhere.

> Our experience indicates that the hips are the basic structural element in the body and that balancing the lower back also corrects problems in other areas.[33]

This significance is particularly useful in emotional processing: it is common for old memories and unexpressed feelings to be liberated in the presence of therapeutic touch or movement of the pelvis. Tightness here can indicate unresolved emotional tension from the past, chronic "holding on" to pain, guilt, bad feelings, or excessive concern (or anti-concern/ abandonment) for loved ones.

Indeed, it can be said that attempts to improve posture alone will inevitably require attention to emotional issues.

> To alter faulty habitual erect carriage is, in everybody's opinion, a very difficult enterprise. Especially striking is the case of persons seeking guidance of their own initiative. From the obstinate resistance encountered in such cases, it is obvious that what is attempted is really a major operation on the personality of the subject. All workers in the field agree on this point.[34]

The pelvis is associated with the Water Principle, and the Water and Earth Elements.

29. Pelvic Reflexes

Major pelvic reflex areas are found in the jaw, the fourth toe, the inside and outside of the heel, and the hallucis tendon on the side of the ankle. As with earlier reflex movements, we use small circular motions with the fingertips to probe a reflex area for stimulation, and both hands (one on the reflex and the other on the pelvis) for energy balancing.

For the jaw, touch the muscular areas where the jaw hinges to the skull. Feel for tension in this area. With a gentle circular motion, rub as you open and close your mouth. Make an "a-h-h-h" sound or yawn with this light or firm contact. This is similar to energy yawns in Brain Gym. A second method is a general rubbing motion, pulling down on the facial tissue all around the jaw, from the side, where the downward rubbing can be felt all the way to the ears, to the front. Pull the mouth open with a firm stroking motion from the lower lip to the Adam's apple area.

---

32. Stone, Polarity Therapy Vol. I, Book 2, p. 16.
33. Barhydts, Self-Help for Stress and Pain, p. 38

34. Feldenkrais, Body and Mature Behavior, p. 119.

The fourth toe marks the water element line in the foot, the densest (most distant from the core) part of the water system. Feel for tender or tense areas and use your hands to release tension by circular movement, activation or pressure. Use firm pressure to follow the tendon of the toe along the bottom of the foot.

Hallucis Tendon

The hallucis tendon which passes through the inner heel is an important pelvic reflex. The tendon originates at the big toe, the most distant extension of the Ether energy center at the throat. The Ether center governs emotions; the hallucis is thus located at a junction of Ether (emotions) and Water (attachment) zones; relating specifically to the storage of old feelings. It is an access point for old emotions stored in the pelvis. It is frequently used in bodywork for this reason.

To find the hallucis, probe with the fingers in the area just to the rear of a line between the ankle and heel. The hallucis feels like a thick guitar string, running up the inside of the leg just behind the ankle. It may be deep or shallow, so you may have to push in to find it.

It can be used with foot flexed up or down. Once you find it, push with steady pressure (light to balance, moderate or deep to promote change) to activate energy movement. Making sound helps dissolve the tenderness.

The hallucis has been called the "twanger," sometimes manipulated with a crossing motion which feels like "twanging" a guitar chord. Done this way, the contact is dramatic and usually painful; this is avoided by some for being too forceful, and emphasized by others for the same reason.

References

Stone, Polarity Therapy Vol. I, Book 2, pp. 20, 24, 34, 40, 75; Book 3, p. 45-49.
Stone, Polarity Therapy Vol. II, p. 118.
Dennisons, Brain Gym, p. 29.

30. Butterfly Activation

This activity uses strategic placement of the legs and the activation technique to create release in the pelvic area, including the inner thigh and psoas muscles.

Method

Sit on the floor with the knees bent and the soles of the feet touching. The legs will naturally rest at the comfort level. Place the hands on the insides of the knees. Inhale and, as you exhale with pursed lips, push the legs into the hands with about 25% of your potential force.

The legs do not actually move on the push. On your inhale, as you relax, allow the legs to sink lower if they do so easily. Take up the slack with the hands. Repeat the activation from this new position. Do three times or more and then rest, allowing the body to enjoy this new position.

If desired, this can be done leaning against a wall or other back support.

Benefits
•Lengthening of postural muscles.
•Release of tightness in the psoas and adductor area, restoring flexibility to the inner leg-pelvic relationship.

References
Francis, Polarity Self-Help Exercises, p. 44.
Gach, Acu-Yoga, pp. 90 and 112.

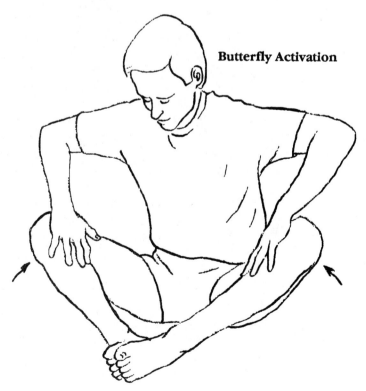

Butterfly Activation

31. The Pyramid

Many teachers consider this the most artful of all Dr. Stone's "easy stretching postures." This exercise releases the hips, pelvis and shoulders, elongates the spine and opens the diaphragm. Virtually all the major pathways of energy are activated, with a simple posture that is quick and easy to do in any situation.

Method

Beginners will benefit from preparation before doing the Pyramid. Good preparations are psoas, hamstring and adductor lengthening exercises, pelvic or lower back reflexes and the butterfly activation. Beginners can also "warm up" by doing portions of the posture or variations before the complete version.

To begin, stand with the feet wider apart than the width of shoulders. Lean forward, placing the palms of the hands (fingers outside, thumbs inside) on the thighs, just above the knees, and transfer the weight of the body from the legs to the shoulders. We are creating a "suspension bridge" with the arms as posts and the shoulders as cables. As you drop into the suspended position, adjust the feet a little wider to create a 90° angle at both ankle-floor and upper leg-lower leg. The knees should be directly above the ankles, and the arms and back should be quite straight. The feet should be aligned parallel to the thighs. The shoulders should be up toward the ears. Lean forward and push the knees out with the hands to emphasize the suspension.

Once you have the posture right, experiment with gentle movement, either pulsing <u>very lightly</u> up and down or rocking from side to side. Then come to standing and take a moment to experience the results of the posture. You may want to do the reflexes (pelvic or shoulder) again, and then go back to the Pyramid to see if it is easier. If you are tight in the inner thighs and pelvis, use the suggested preparations. If you are unable to keep your arms straight, do the alternative Shoulder Release Pyramid on the next page.

After you are familiar with the posture, check these points for fine-tuning. Make sure the gluteal muscles and lower back are relaxed: the full weight of the torso should be on the hands and knees. Feel the spine hanging in full suspension, lengthening from its own weight. Make sure the back and arms are straight.

Pyramid

Pyramid in a Chair

This variation is good for older people and for those quite stiff in the pelvic area. We have used this with seniors groups. The chair seat should be high enough to allow leg extension, so a cushion may be necessary. Sit on the chair in such a way that the legs are "in pyramid position," out to the sides with the ankles and knees making 90° angles. Place the palms of the hands on the knees (with straight arms) and gently transfer some of the weight of the torso to the shoulders. Push outward to open the pelvic area, elongate the spine, and release neck and shoulder tension. Gently rock forward and back or side to side.

Shoulder Release Pyramid

In this variation, the hands turn inward, with the fingers on the inside of the thigh. As you "suspend" the torso, the elbows bend and the shoulder blades are pushed toward each other in the back.

This posture helps free the shoulder blades, which can become buried in tension. Rotate them forward and back, both together and alternately. You can feel the shoulder blades move and squeeze together and apart. Experiment with moving the elbows in wide circles, and pressing them toward the floor. When done, come to standing, bring the feet together, relax, breathe deeply and experience the results.

Spinal Twist Pyramid

This variation adds a twist of the spine to the normal pyramid, taking advantage of relaxation in the lower back-pelvic area and elongation of the spine to further open and energize the spinal area. This position is considered an advanced posture, so it should not be used by those who are unable to do the regular pyramid.

For the spinal twist pyramid, start in the regular pyramid posture. While maintaining straight arms, drop one shoulder forward. This will create a "spinal twist." Turn the head to look at the floor, over the lowered shoulder, then up toward the ceiling over the upper shoulder, for further release. Make sure that the body stays

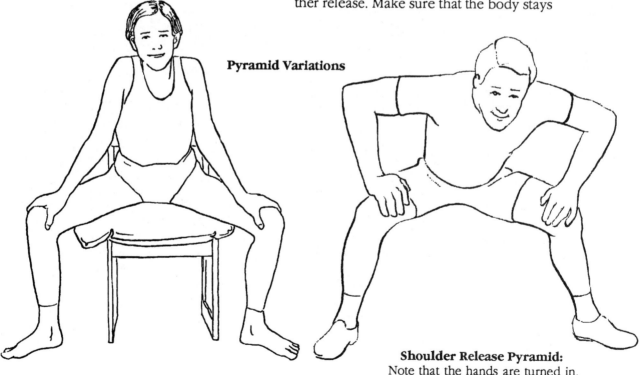

Pyramid Variations

Shoulder Release Pyramid: Note that the hands are turned in. This stimulates movement of the shoulder blades.

in the center. Breathe and relax. Repeat the twist with the other shoulder forward. When done, come to a relaxed standing position and feel the results. Listen to your body and use the degree of stretch and amount of time that is easy, gentle and releasing.

Leg Stretch Pyramid

This variation gives a good stretch to the back and inner portions of the thigh (adductor and hamstring muscles). Start in the regular pyramid position. Keeping the buttocks low, straighten the left leg while shifting the torso right. Make a gentle pulsing movement to lengthen the straight leg, and flex the foot at the ankle to rock back up on to the heel. The pressure of the heel (a reflex to the sacrum) on the floor is beneficial for additional relaxing of the lower back. Repeat with the other leg, and alternate each side a few times. This variation can be used to take a break from having the body weight resting in the center.

Benefits

- General tension release: the Pyramid is one of the best postures for overall energy balancing.
- Because it is so quick and easy to do, even in street clothes, it is recommended for use during the day to ward off fatigue and tension.
- Stimulates circulation of cerebro-spinal fluid.
- Opens pelvic basin, allowing energy to flow up and down the legs. This is rejuvenating, good for circulation, and has a grounding effect.
- Stimulating, especially due to pressure on thighs and pulsing movement.
- Relieves compression on spine.
- Stimulates shoulders (+), diaphragm (0) and pelvis (-), the three poles of the torso, unifying and amplifying energy flow and movement.
- On the level of energy theory, all systems are engaged: it is a good companion for Energy Balancing bodywork, accelerating energy

movement in a way which would otherwise require deep contact. An excellent case history of this type of application is offered in Sills' book, referenced below.
- Excellent for pregnancy, opening the pelvic floor and toning its support muscles.

References

There are many variations for the Pyramid, and yet relatively little mention of the posture in Dr. Stone's writings. A "Pyramid-like" illustration in Health Building (p. 160) actually describes the Side-to-Side Ha Breath, and the reference in Volume II (p. 192) is a brief one sentence and again accompanies the Side to Side Ha Breath. There is a photograph of Dr. Stone in the posture in Health Building (p. 170), but again, there is relatively little description. An explanation is offered in the editors' footnote on page 164 of Health Building. The posture's popularization and development is a function of Dr. Stone's verbal classroom instruction (rather than written work), and the creativity of subsequent Polarity instructors. As its benefits were experienced, it received more attention and use, an examples of the organic, evolving nature of the art of energy-based therapies, and a validation of Dr. Stone's often-quoted motto, "What works, works!"

Stone, Health Building, pp. 160, 170, 182-183.
Stone, Polarity Therapy Vol. II, p. 192.
Francis, Polarity Self-Help Exercises, pp. 33-34.
Seidman, A Guide to Polarity Therapy, p. 138.
Sills, The Polarity Process, pp. 149-152.

32. The Squat

The squat is the foundation of all Dr. Stone's Easy Stretching Postures.

After years of study of every health posture and exercise including the eighty-four Yoga postures, I have found none equal to this one which combines squatting and stretching for relaxation and well-being...

What simple thing can one do to preserve bodily functions at par and stay well, or even to regain health with the expenditure of the least amount of effort and time? The answer is an Easy Stretching Posture which is so natural that it takes only three to five minutes, once or several times a day if necessary, to increase the release of gases and the consequent intake and absorption of oxygen in the body, and to quickly release mental and emotional tension.[35]

The squatting posture is a natural position assumed by much of the world's population for all kinds of daily activities. In western cultures where so much time is spent sitting in chairs and where most lives have high tension levels, many have lost the flexibility needed to do this posture. People with back problems, varicose veins and knee problems will find it difficult and possibly contraindicated. As a general rule, if there is pain anywhere, stop.

The reasons for the squat's effectiveness are explained in great detail by Dr. Stone in <u>Health Building</u>.

> ...man can take body postures which place the polarity energy fields-- one immediately above the other-- into action under a mild stress (or stretch) which forces them to work in two ways; first by the electromagnetic polarity; second by physical effort and gravity function, blended with the proper mental attitude. The body, the mind and the subtle energies are therefore all engaged simultaneously.[36]

Thus the primary reason for the squat's effectiveness is the close proximity of calves, thighs, solar plexus and chest, which enhances current flow in the main energy fields of the body. The squat is similar to the fetal position, creating the "path of least resistance" for energy circuits in the original weaving of the body. This position reflects the fulfillment of the involutionary energy impulse (the Fire Principle), represented by Dr. Stone's "Interlaced Triangles" geometric star, discussed on page 76.

Secondly, leveraged opening and lengthening of the pelvis and spine activates the body's natural tendency for self-correction. Just getting in this position is rejuvenating, soothing and energizing.

For many people, squatting is difficult. But it is well worth the continued effort. Dr. Stone himself could not achieve the squat position at first, but found an answer:

> The author passed his 64th birthday on February 26, 1954. He had not been able to correctly take these postures until the discovery of the gentle rocking motion to shift the polarity constantly from one group of muscles to another, which made the accomplishment of the posture possible.[37]

The Squat

---

35. Stone, Health Building, p. 122.

36. *Ibid.*, p. 111.

37. *Ibid.*, p. 98.

If this posture is difficult, use movement to facilitate progress. Dr. Stone lived another 28 years after the comment above, and was pictured in the squat on many occasions, including the photos on pages 170-171 of Health Building, taken in the 1970's when he was in his mid-eighties.

How to overcome initial difficulty? Stand with weight shifting from side to side and gradually begin the process of lowering the body down, with up and down movements. One way to help is to use a board or book under the heels (or wear shoes with heels) at first, to reduce the stretch of the calves; another is to use both sides of a door handle (see illustration, page 93) to keep balanced and support the lowering movements. We emphasize perseverance, for the benefits are well worth the effort. Specific aids for the squat found elsewhere in this book are the calf lengthening, foot flex, hamstring lengthening, scissors kick and pyramid.

Exercise instructors may consider having the class do the squat first, because of its central place in these exercises. Students will get an idea of their flexibility. All the other exercises will build toward the squat, so they can refer back to it periodically to check their progress.

> It is not the accomplishment of a position that we are after, but the stimulating actions of the currents set into motion by these posture stretches. Those who need them the most will at first feel that they accomplished the least, but they will slowly feel the benefits just the same. It is like turning on a switch and allowing the currents to do the work, instead of wasting a lot of energy in performing acrobatic stunts. All this is based on Nature's finer forces in motion.[38]

---

38. *Ibid.*, p.139.
39. Stone, Polarity Therapy Vol. I, Book 2, p. 84.

Method

Dr. Stone described two squatting positions, "wide" and "narrow." He used the term "Youth Posture" for the wide position, and "Health Posture" for the narrow. They are similar in that they both require lowering the torso and resting on the haunches. In the wide position, the feet are about 12 inches or more apart, and the elbows are inside the knees, pressing out. In the narrow position, the feet are as close as possible, and the arms wrap around the legs, pressing in.

Once in the squatting position, gentle rocking will facilitate movement of energy currents and release of tension. Rocking movements can be front to back, side to side, or circular. Deep breathing, emphasizing the exhalation with a loud sigh, will also enhance the effects. After completion, which can mean a short or long period depending on the individual's needs and capabilities, take a resting pose, either seated on the floor, resting fully extended on the back, or standing with knees slightly bent.

To come back to standing, allow the hands to drop forward to touch the floor. Lift the back and straighten the legs, slowly uncurling to a vertical position. This "uncurling" movement is preferred over the more common vertical lift from the knees.

For therapeutic applications, Dr. Stone recommended squatting for "Three minutes several times a day."[39]

The squat is also used in bodywork. The practitioner may assist the client in assuming the position for a short time, as a preparation or complement for other bodywork. The gravity, energy, and leverage at work in the position applies more force than the practitioner usually can, in a more gentle way, for deeper results.

In exercise classes, the squat can be done with partners for fun and benefit. One person can stand behind the squatting student and hold the shoulders while guiding movement. Another way to work in partners is to face each other and grasp each other's wrists. Then lower each other down into the squat, each supporting the other and assisting movement.

Narrow Squat

The Health Posture has the feet about 6 inches apart at the heels, or closer. Rock into the position gently, beginning with a bend at the knees and sinking down and rising back up again. When ready to go all the way down, the hips drop toward the heels and the armpits rest on the knees. The close position of the feet gives support to the abdomen which rests on the thighs. Now begin a back and forth rocking motion.

In this position, the chest, colon and calves, the Air Principle's +, 0, and - poles, are pressed tightly together. Thus it is specifically recommended for colon function and elimination of gases.

Narrow Squat with arms wrapped

For this version of the Health Posture, take the narrow squat position and wrap the arms around the knees, hands locking together. This posture should not be used by people with varicose veins. The knees are pushed together, lengthening muscles and opening the hip joints to bring spring to the step. Rock back and forth, side to side, and in a rotating motion. With locked hands, exert a gentle stretch on the arms and take a deep breath in. Exhale with a grunt or sigh-- increasing relaxation. Dr. Stone's famous comment on making sound for tension relief fits well here:

> The gallant Frenchman will groan himself well while the stolid Englishman succumbs to the malady.[40]

This squat frees the brachial plexus, moving gases and opening the heart and

lung areas. It is also good for constipation, toning the abdomen and thighs, and for improving all eliminative functions. For a specific discussion, see Health Building, pages 134-136.

Many arm movements may be added to complement the squat. The arms may be clasped behind the back and lifted up, with the weight rocking forward to the front of the foot. The hands can be clasped behind the head, elbows lifting to open the chest. For greater lengthening lower in the back, each hand can grasp the opposite elbow behind the head, with continued rocking from the feet. Experiment and develop your own preferences to take advantage of the squat's many benefits.

Wide Squat

The "Youth Posture" has the feet wider apart, at least 12 inches wide at the heels. The arms are placed inside the knees and the elbows exert an outward

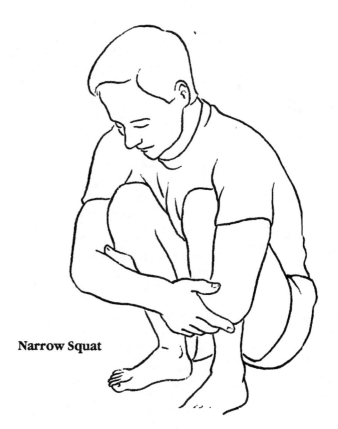

Narrow Squat

---

40. Stone, Health Building, p. 135.

push. The hands are held firmly with interlaced fingers, a reflex shoulder release.

A balancing position can be created by placing one hand over the other in a double fist, and pressing the extended thumbs to the eyebrows. This is the "Ridge Meets Bridge" contact shown earlier (page 17). Contact here is a reflex for the shoulders and a balancing for the Yang Fire Principle's Interlaced Triangles pattern (see page 76). Remember to rock back and forth, side to side, in a circle, and in a twisting motion.

Many variations are possible with the Squat. The arms may be extended in back, as shown in the illustration, for releasing the shoulders. The feet and toes may be massaged in the position, and the Neck Lift or Neck Activation may be added. Be creative and explore the many possibilities of the Squat position.

Benefits
• General enhancement of energy flow throughout the body, involving all Three Principles and Five Elements. Dr. Stone called this the "Youth Posture for Balance and Elasticity."
• Good for muscular elasticity and relaxation.
• Opens the pelvis where unexpressed emotions are stored, helping these to be released and come to consciousness.
• Relaxes the hips and perineum (especially useful in pregnancy). The latent energetic forces of the pelvis are released for rejuvenation and self-healing.
• Releases gases and stimulates the downward current of elimination.
• Eases pressure on sacrum.
• Preventative for back problems; provides a self-correcting influence for spinal tensions.
• Assists concentration and focus, centering and grounding.
• Self-nurturing; restores inner calm.
• Lengthens Achilles tendon, "unwinding" the natural stress response of the "tendon guard reflex."
• Improves colon function.

References
Stone, <u>Health Building</u>, pp. 98-157.
Stone, <u>Polarity Therapy Vol. 1</u>, Book 1, p. 49; Book 2, pp. 84-85.
Berkson, <u>The Foot Book</u>, pp. 78-79.
Francis, <u>Polarity Self-Help Exercises</u>, p. 11.
Sills, <u>The Polarity Process</u>, p. 150.
Siegel, <u>Polarity Therapy</u>, pp. 94-96.

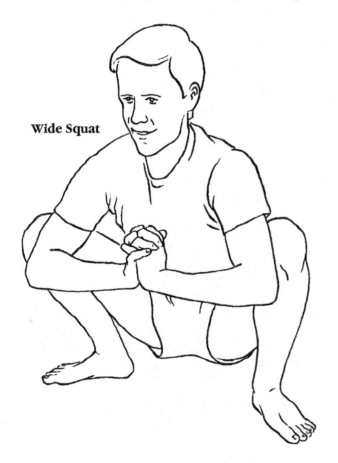

Wide Squat

Arm Stretch Squat

33. Scissors Kick

This is a gentle yet powerful exercise for opening the hip and pelvic areas. It has two effective actions for energy movement. First, the rocking of the hip joints creates expansion and contraction of the hips, which alternately puts pressure on and then releases the sacrum. This creates a pumping action which facilitates cerebro-spinal fluid circulation. Second, swinging the legs enhances the "transverse" energy currents using the "crossing over" dynamo effect described earlier in the Side to Side Ha Breath.

Because of the reflex relationship between sacrum and cranium, this type of movement of the hips leads to cranial adjustment and pressure relief; Dr. Stone recommended the Scissors Kick for relief of sinus congestion. If the nose is blocked or the head is stuffy, ten to twenty minutes of Scissors Kicks will give relief.

Method

Lie face down with the head resting comfortably on crossed arms. Lift the feet so that the lower legs are perpendicular to the floor. Swing the feet rhythmically outward and inward, alternating which foot crosses in front. Some people find this easier if they emphasize the out swing, then just let the legs move on their own back to the inward position.

Repeat this easygoing motion for 5 or 10 minutes. Experiment with varying paces. Stop, lower the legs, and roll over for a period of rest. The rest period is taken on the back for a reason, because we have greater sensitivity when the sensory (front) side of the body is exposed.

As an additional energy balancing during the rest period, assume the Interlaced Triangles Balance pose (page 77), which is also based on the sacrum/cranium relationship. Touch the center of the forehead with the left thumb (turning the head to the left side makes it possible to do this with the left elbow still on the floor, thus keeping the body more relaxed). At the same time, touch the pubic bone with the right thumb. These contacts balance the circuitry of the "Interlaced Triangles," a geometric pathway closely associated with the sacrum/cranium reflex relationship. This pattern is also shown on page 77.

The Scissors Kick can be done on the floor or on a bed. Some like to do it before rising in the morning, or to fall asleep more easily in the evening. It can be done while reading or watching TV, and is a good supplement to weight management, hip toning (if done for twenty minutes or more daily), or back therapy programs. Both this and the following exercise are sometimes fondly called "windshield wipers." In an exercise class, this is often done at the beginning as a warm up or at the end as a cooling down exercise.

Caution should be used for those with lower back pain or knee problems. For back protection, press the pubic bone into the floor. To protect the knees, flex the feet. If there is pain in any joint, restrict the out kick.

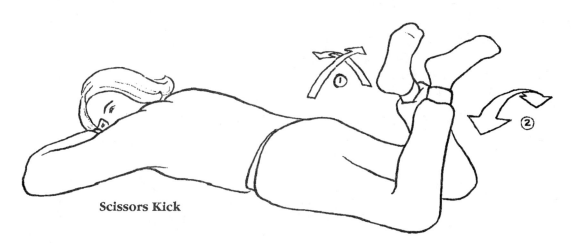

Scissors Kick

Variations

This can be done in pairs, with one person holding the left hand on the occiput and the right hand on the sacrum of the person who is doing the Scissors Kick. This is an energy balancing contact for the Fire Principle's Interlaced Triangles.

Benefits

• Good general energizer and balancer, increasing alertness. Often used as a warm-up in exercise classes. The side to side motion benefits left/right brain integration.
• Releases lower back, especially sacrum and sacro-iliac junction.
• Easy to do; good for elderly and infirm.
• Tones thighs and buttocks.
• Benefits circulation of cerebro-spinal fluid from sacrum to head, promoting mental clarity.
• Specific for sinus congestion relief.
• Releases nervousness.
• Releases tensions stored in the legs; good for "grounding" and feeling more solidly rooted in the legs and feet.

References

Stone, Polarity Therapy, Vol. I, Book 2, p. 61; Book 3, pp. 45-49.
Francis, Polarity Self-Help Exercises, p. 13.
Seidman, Guide to Polarity Therapy, p. 139.
Berkson, The Foot Book, pp. 178-179.

34. Seated Scissors Kick

This exercise has mechanics and benefits similar to the Scissors Kick, but it can be done by those unable to do the regular posture. The rocking motion alone restores flexibility and circulation for people with limited movement capabilities.

Method

Sit on the floor (or in a chair) with the legs extended in front at a comfortably wide angle. The hands are placed flat on the floor slightly behind the body, supporting the body weight. This hand position activates wrist/pelvis reflex relationships, with additional reflex benefit coming from the pressure of the leg weight on the heel (another pelvic reflex specifically for the sacrum).

Rock the feet rhythmically, in and out. You should be able to feel the whole leg rotating up to the hip joint. Do this for five or ten minutes. Then stop and rest, seated or lying down, experiencing the results of the exercise. The "Interlaced Triangles" contact points may be touched (left thumb to forehead, right thumb to pubic bone) as an extra balancing position.

During the rest period, close your eyes and feel the tingling sensation moving through the legs. Notice where it stops or feels blocked. You can then find an exercise to work with the blocked area. Check again later as a comparison: this exercise can be used as a gauge of energy movement in the body.

Variations

This may be done leaning against a wall if the wrists are not strong or flexible

Seated Scissors Kick

enough to hold the body weight. It also may be done seated on the edge of a chair. A natural variation of this exercise can be seen when we rhythmically swing one leg as we sit in a chair with one leg crossed over the other.

Benefits

- Generates energy flow throughout the body.
- Opens pelvis and activates cranium/sacrum energy pathway of the Yang Fire Principle.
- Stimulates circulation.
- Side-to-side movement stimulates Air Principle balance, giving a sense of calm and rest.
- Good for elderly and infirm.

35. Light Rocking Perineal

It has been said that all of Polarity Therapy evolved from Dr. Stone's search for explanations for the demonstrated effectiveness of techniques involving the perineum, or pelvic floor.

> The perineum is the lowest major point of gravity...[and]...the major negative pole of the body...[It] holds the key to all negative and irrational impulses and perversions of the currents in the energy field.[41]

> Perineal treatment correctly done will unlock energy blocks quicker than most other methods because it deals with the vital force of emotional locks and frustration.[42]

The Rocking Perineal gives an easy way to experience some of this therapeutic power. It is a natural aid to young children preparing for sleep, and first aid for emotional upset or anxiety. "The perineal contact is the best treatment for nervousness and hysteria..."[43]

This posture uses the hands to connect the energy field of the pelvic floor to the upper fields of the head and shoulders. The gentle rocking motion stimulates energy movement and relaxation. Bodywork techniques taught by Milton Trager emphasize rocking and have been much appreciated.

Method

Lie on the left side and place the left hand comfortably on the neck and the right hand on the hip, fingers reaching over the gluteal muscle and toward the pelvic floor. The little finger of the right hand should be near the coccyx. A small pillow may be used for the neck and head. Have the knees slightly bent in a position that allows stability and flexibility for rocking. When you are correctly positioned, the body will rock easily back and forth with a slight, almost-effortless movement of the upper leg. Rocking can continue for a few minutes or more.

Variations

The Light Rocking Perineal may be either done individually as illustrated on page 8, or by another. The "giver" of the exercise sits or kneels at the "receiver's" back, with right hand on the hip, fingers

---

41. Stone, Polarity Therapy Vol. II, p. 87.
42. Stone, Polarity Therapy Vol. I, Book 2, p. 37.
43. Stone, Polarity Therapy Vol. II, p.185.

Light Rocking Perineal

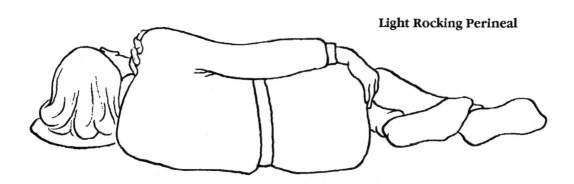

toward the perineum, and the left hand on the neck/shoulder junction. The giver rocks lightly, carefully being sensitive to the receiver's preferred tempo and movement. Giving and receiving a Rocking Perineal is a very nurturing experience.

Benefits

- Soothing and balancing for the nervous system. Perineal technique is specifically recommended for the Air Principle's parasympathetic ("vegetative") nervous system governing functions of regeneration and assimilation.
- Gives relief from nervousness or hysteria.
- Stimulates flow of energy from pelvis to shoulders and neck.
- Helpful for calming or insomnia.
- A nice way to rock babies and children.

References

Stone, <u>Polarity Therapy Vol I</u>, Book 2, pp. 36, 37.
Stone, <u>Polarity Therapy Vol II</u>, pp. 198.

36. Foot Flex

This exercise works with the reflexes related to the sacrum and their influence in pumping cerebro-spinal fluid. When walking, the rocking motion of the heel is a constant energizer. The heel itself is a reflex to the sacrum and lower back. A firm grasp of the Achilles tendon and behind the knee assist the calf muscles in lengthening; contacts on the calf itself affect colon, chest and digestive system.

Shoes play a role in energy movement: rigid soles or high heels inhibit or negate the natural therapeutic lengthening of the Achilles tendon with each step, with serious consequences for the whole body.

Method

Sit comfortably with one foot crossed over the other thigh so you can easily reach anywhere on the lower leg. Find and press tender spots, pushing the thumbs away from each other to encourage lengthening; the touch may be gentle or firm. Grasp the Achilles tendon with one hand and the calf behind the knee with the other hand. Flex the foot and hold for a count of eight. Now alternately flex and point the foot while maintaining the grasp. Do one leg and then the other. Others areas may also be touched to further assist release.

Benefits

- Increases flexibility in the heel-calf area.
- Enhances the flow of cerebro-spinal fluid, thereby increasing mental alertness and clarity.
- Enhances ability for self expression.
- Excellent for those who feel tightness in the

Light Rocking Perineal
Position for Giving and Receiving

shins from exercise.
- Especially good for women who wear high heels, as a correction for the shortening of the Achilles tendon and lack of rocking motion. The wearing of high heel shoes is very stressful for the feet, pelvis and spine and therefore for all of the body.

References
Dennisons, <u>Brain Gym</u>, p. 19.

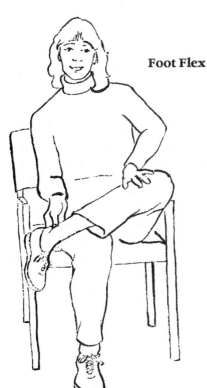

Foot Flex

37. Sacral Rocking

This simple rocking motion massages the sacrum area. Through a flexing movement, the sacrum/hip area self-corrects and re-aligns itself. As the sacral area is relaxed, the spine and cranial bones may also self-adjust.

Method
Sit on the floor with the knees raised. Support your weight partially with your hands, which rest behind you. Rock slowly and gently on the gluteal muscles in all different directions. Circles and figure eights are two good methods. The posture may also be done with partners. Standing behind the receiver, the giver gently creates and guides the movements.

Benefits
- Relief from some lower back problems, by lengthening the lower back. Reflex pressure on wrists stimulates pelvic area.
- Relaxes hip and gluteal tension.
- Improvement of cranio-sacral fluid rhythm and function.
- Promotes mental clarity.

References
Mahoney, <u>Hyperton-x</u>, p. 66.
Dennisons, <u>Brain Gym</u>, p. 11.
Siegel, <u>Polarity Therapy</u>, p. 99.

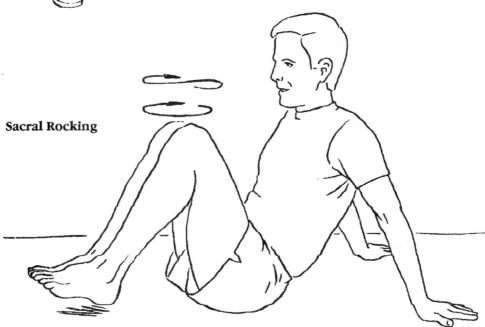

Sacral Rocking

38. Rowing

This exercise engages several muscle systems and energy pathways simultaneously. It is grouped with pelvic exercises because its movement opens the pelvic basin and energizes the belly and lower back. The brachial plexus and shoulders, legs, lower back and pelvis, and pelvic reflexes in the heels are also vigorously affected.

Rowing is stimulating and balancing for the Yang, or motor and muscular, systems. The full body rocking motion eases and strengthens the back, and facilitates top to bottom balancing. Like the squat, rowing makes use of the involutionary fetal position, reflecting the compressed shape of the Fire Principle's "Interlaced Triangles" pattern (see p. 78).

The exercise has an isometric resistance between the muscles of the arms and upper back, and the legs. The degree of resistance and tempo of movement can be varied, from fast and easy to slow and hard. The upper back will be more affected with the knees bent high, and the lower back with the legs more straight.

Method

Sit with legs extended in front, knees bent. Experiment with how much to bend the knees. Reach the hands over the toes so that the palm of the hand holds the ball of the foot and the toes are pulled up and back. The fingers are thus aligned vertically with the corresponding energy lines in the feet.

Begin a motion of gentle rocking forward and back, using back muscles to pull and leg muscles to push forward. Then push forward with the feet and resist with the arms, letting the feet "win." Then pull back with the arms and resist with the feet, letting the arms "win." Feel the back and shoulders open and lengthen, and the pelvis flex. Keep the head low so that the neck stays relaxed.

Breathe evenly in time with the movement, exhaling forward and inhaling back. Experiment with varying tempos according to preferences and situation. The amount of time in the exercise can depend on your goals: it can be aerobic and toning if done extensively. When you are ready, stop to rest (the motor balance position, page 67, would be especially appropriate for this) and feel the results.

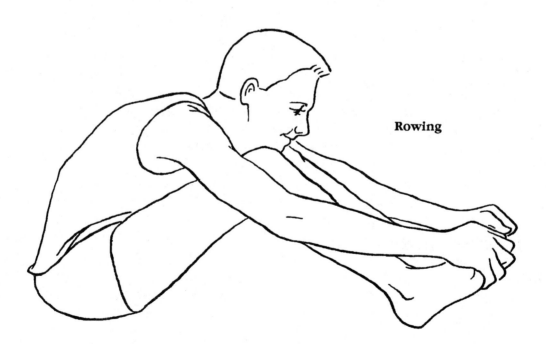

Rowing

Variations

Increased resistance changes the dynamics of the exercise, making it a more strenuous workout for the back. By increasing the activation of the thighs, the negative pole of fire element, additional stimulation of Yang energy is created. Because it is strenuous, high-resistance rowing should be done carefully, avoiding back strain.

Another variation of Rowing is done with partners. Sit opposite a partner, feet touching, both with knees bent to a comfortable degree. Join hands and take turns pulling/resisting. This can be strenuously or lightly, rapidly or slowly. Partners should be matched in general size, fitness and strength, and resistance should be sensitively applied. A class may enjoy singing "Row, row, row your boat" for fun while rowing in partners.

Another variation is combining Rowing with Toe Activation (page 16). The hands are the neutral pole and the feet the negative pole of the whole body, so the fingers and toes have a direct energy link. The fingers and toes are placed in resistance while the Rowing movement continues.

Benefits

- Opens and relaxes pelvis.
- Exercises upper back, shoulder and chest areas.
- Good as a toning exercise for the back and legs.
- Multiple reflexology actions are used: heels (reflex to sacrum area) are pressed to the floor, fingers and toes are linked, balls of the foot (reflex to upper chest and back) are stimulated and connected with the corresponding zone of the hand.

Balancing Postures

The following postures are for quiet relaxation and rejuvenation.

The idea presented here is that the body can be put in a [neutral] position of rest, the same as any machine. The act of standing still is anything but rest for the body. The same can be said about sitting on a chair. Even lying down has its phases of better positioning for complete motor relaxation and repair of tissues. These ideas are more or less startling until they are put to use, when we feel the difference and no further explanations are necessary.[44]

We often assume postures that give natural self-correction. Simple observation reveals many examples: the resting of the forehead on the thumb and forefinger in deep thought, the placing of the hands behind the skull when lying on the back, and the clasping hands over the abdomen and crossing ankles while sitting. All of these commonly-assumed postures make sense from an energy anatomy perspective, unconsciously placing the energy fields in appropriate relationships for balancing. Dr. Stone's analysis of energy fields and reflexes gives meaning to what can seem to be arbitrary everyday events.

Much emphasis is placed on doing and achieving, and little value is placed on stillness. These postures facilitate spending some inward time to balance all the outward activity, to refresh our mental, emotional and physical resources, and to allow contemplation of inner values.

Stillness is a quality of the neutral Air Principle (*Satva*, which means Truth in Ayurveda), the subtle blueprint for the whole system. These postures are all Satvic expressions of the Air Principle.

---

44. Stone, Polarity Therapy Vol. II, p. 127.

The secret to learn here is for man's consciousness to remain still in the CENTER OF BEING, in its eternal essence. Then things will right themselves. The Holy Bible states this in simple terms: "Be still, and know that I am God."

The whole body recuperates when life's Central Energy is permitted to flow naturally, without interference by our own mind's desires, etc...

Paracelsus, the great alchemist, observed this also when he stated <u>man is ill because he is never still</u>. He said there was great healing in the quiet depths of space, but man never tuned into it by being quiet himself! [45]

39. Sensory Balance Posture

In this posture the body is comfortably arranged to resemble the shape of the Yin evolutionary energy. The evolutionary attitude looks beyond material concerns in its quest for re-union with its heavenly source. Thus this posture is associated with cultivating receptivity, and is sometimes used as a meditation position.

> It is also...a philosophic posture for bearing the ills of the day with a confident faith in God's Providence. [70]

A secondary benefit is created energetically because the arms and ankles are "crossed over," affecting the Air Principle. It connects transverse (side-to-side) currents and inhibits further incoming stimulation from the outside. Thus a quality of stillness is usually experienced.

The word "Sensory" has broad implications here. Sensory and Motor are words

---

45. Stone, <u>Polarity Therapy Vol. II</u>, p. 57.

used to summarize the functions of Yin and Yang, respectively. For more on this, see p. 124.

Method

Sit cross-legged and rest the hands on the front of the opposite side calf area. Close the eyes and relax. At first, breathe consciously, with a deep inhale and exhale; then forget the breathing and rest quietly. Allow the internal energy currents to come to balance.

This can be done when sitting in a chair, either by bringing the legs up, or by extending them out and crossing at the ankles, with hands lightly clasped in front. The Sensory Balance Posture is similar to Cook's Hook-ups, p. 69.

Benefits

•Soothing, relaxing.
•Rejuvenating for the senses, especially when "overloaded." The posture integrates sensory input with mental absorption.
•Useful for meditative practices, or "getting away from it all." Helps bring the attention inward.

Sensory Balance Posture

- Beneficial for excess or deficient Yin condition, cultivating discrimination and acceptance.
- Helps relieve the stress of exhaustion, the feeling that "we've had it up to here."

References

Stone, <u>Polarity Therapy,</u> Vol. II, pp. 56-57.
Francis, <u>Polarity Self-Help Exercises,</u> p. 45

40. Motor Balance Posture

This position is the Yang complement to the Sensory Balance position. The pose takes the shape of the involutionary aspect of energy, the fetal position of action and involvement. The back of the head (positive pole of the motor current) is balanced with the neuter palms of the hands. The spine and back is gently lengthened. The non-crossed, straight posture affects the Water (north-south) and Fire (back-front) Principles' energy pathways.

It is not necessarily a position of true relaxation, but rather a dynamic feeling of building and potential power. "Motor Balance" makes sense in the context of the Yang functions of action and creativity. The posture is especially used following

---

47. Stone, <u>Polarity Therapy Vol. II</u>, p. 57

very active exercises like Rowing, the Ha Breath, or the Woodchopper.

Method

Sit on the floor with knees comfortably bent. Lean the elbows forward to rest on the knees and clasp the hands behind the back of the head. Breathe deeply at first, then normally. Relax and allow the energy currents to balance. Do not be concerned if the posture does not feel truly "relaxing" as it is a somewhat different state, of readiness or potential action. A restful variation of this is when we lie beneath a shade tree, hands clasped behind our head, gazing at the sky above, "...the life of relaxation."[47]

Benefits

- Relaxes, energizes before and after muscular activity
- A good complement to vigorous motor exercises like the Woodchopper and Rowing.
- Gives a gentle lengthening of spinal muscles.
- The elbow-to-knee contact is a connection of neutral (acute) and negative (chronic) diaphragm reflex points.
- Prepares the body for creativity and action.
- Balancing for front/back dimension, the Fire Principle.

References

Stone, <u>Polarity Therapy Vol. II</u>, p. 57.
Francis, <u>Polarity Self-Help Exercises</u>, p. 46.

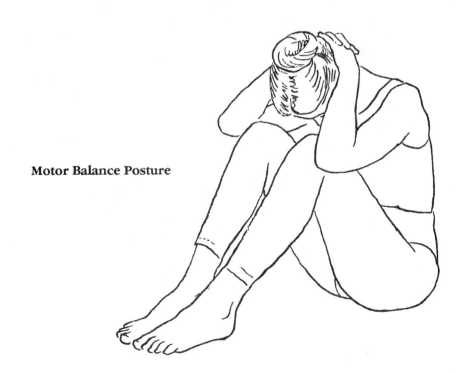

Motor Balance Posture

41. Wise Man Of Old

This energy balancing pose was "...used by sages and wise men for their deeper penetration into the Inner Mysteries of life."[48] With a typical splurge on adjectives, Dr. Stone also calls this "the Ideal Neutral Position Squatting Posture, plus local special sense balancing through finger locations."[49] It has the benefits of the squatting posture, with the addition of finger/face contacts for sensory relaxation and energy balancing for the Five Elements.

The finger contacts balance the five senses, reducing pressure at the positive pole with a neutral hand contact. The thumbs in the ears provide a connection with the etheric functions of expression, sound and hearing. The first fingers (lightly over the eyes) soothe the heat and fire of the body and the sense of sight. The middle finger position over the nose relates to the gases or air of the body and the sense of touch. The ring finger over the mouth relates to the fluids and water of the body and the sense of taste. The little finger on the chin relates to the earthy solids of the body and the sense of smell.[50]

Method

Take the squatting posture (or one of its substitutes, if squatting is not comfortable), with the elbows or armpits resting on the knees, and place the fingers as noted above: thumbs in ears, first fingers

---

48. Stone, <u>Polarity Therapy Vol. II</u>, p. 57.

49. *Ibid.*, p. 56.

50. For a complete description of these element/senses relationships, see Stone, <u>Polarity Therapy Vol. I</u> , Book 1, p. 4.

lightly over the eyes, middle fingers on the sides of the nose, ring fingers on the top lip and little finger above the chin.

Variations

This may be done seated in a chair and leaning forward with elbows on the knees, or with the elbows resting on the arms of the chair.

The Wise Man of Old also combines well with Humming (page 87).

Benefits

- Quiets the senses. Gives a sense of introspection and inner contemplation, disengaging the mind and senses from outer stimulation. "The Wise Men" knew that it was necessary to close off the outer senses in order to be open to the inner world.
- Balances the "vital pattern of the mind," the subtle core function of the Air Principle.

References

Stone, <u>Polarity Therapy, Vol. II</u>, pp. 56-57.
Francis, <u>Polarity Self-Help Exercises</u>, p. 42.

Wise Man of Old

42. Cook's Hook-ups

This posture comes from Educational Kinesiology, or Edu-K. It has two parts, which are similar to the Sensory Balance Posture (part one) and the Motor Balance Posture (part two). With both parts, a complete balance of energy currents is accomplished, involving Air, Water and Fire Principles.

We do Cook's Hook-Ups whenever we feel sad, confused or angry. This cheers us up in no time.[51]

This posture was developed by Wayne Cook as a way to process stimula-

tion. It restores balance to disturbed energy circuits. Paul Dennison describes using it to counter emotional or mental stress, creating calm and release of old and new trauma.

This posture is naturally taken and commonly seen. It is often interpreted as suggesting a closed off or resisting state of mind. However, from this perspective, the person may be seen as temporarily loaded with stimuli and taking a necessary self-processing stance. For example, it may be used when flying on an airplane, to keep or restore balance in a very stimulating environment

Method

For part one, sit comfortably with the legs crossed at the ankles. Cross the arms over the chest with hands under the

---

51. Dennisons, <u>Brain Gym</u>, p. 31.

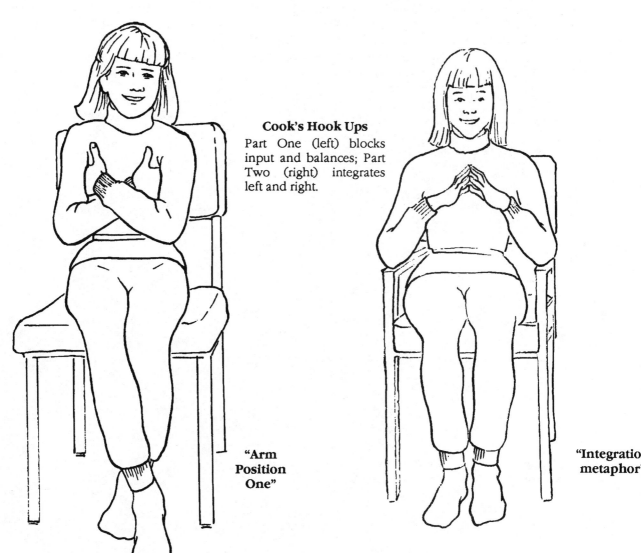

Cook's Hook Ups
Part One (left) blocks input and balances; Part Two (right) integrates left and right.

"Arm Position One"

"Integration metaphor"

armpits, thumbs out and up. Hold this position until you "feel complete."[52] Some people can feel the actual balancing taking place as tingles, shudders, throbs or other sensations or movements. Stay in part one until you feel this energy release: if you are very stressed, this could take some time, so be patient.

For part two, uncross the legs and arms and place the finger tips together in a "rainbow arch." Many people feel the tingling of energy crossing the fingers and balancing. This is similar to the integration metaphor part of Dennison Laterality Repatterning (page 89). Again, do this until you "feel complete."

Variations

Part one may be done in several different ways. The above posture is called a "crossover." You may also (2) "double cross" the arms and turn them under (see upper drawing) or (3) "leg cross" while seated, with one leg over the other side's knee. Hold the ankle with one hand and the ball of the foot with the other hand, so that the forearms are crossed. This is a blend of the Foot Flex (page 62) and the Sensory Balance Posture (page 66). It has the added benefit of connecting the upper and lower body.

The double cross (2), shown below, is a favorite for many. Children will challenge you to move a particular finger when the hands are clasped and turned in this way. To take the position, cross the wrists and turn the palms facing each other, then clasp the fingers. Next, turn the hands under until they rest on the chest. If this is comfortable, rest and continue. If not, use one of the other options.

Versions (1) and (2) may be done while seated, standing or lying. Version (3) is only for a seated position.

Benefits
- General relaxation and concentration. This position has proved itself in a wide variety of applications and is highly recommended.
- Release of tension. Removes distractions and allows integration of mind and emotions.
- Combines benefits of Sensory Balance and Motor Balance positions.

References
Cook, Universal Truths, p. 132.
Dennisons, Brain Gym, p. 31.
Stokes and Whiteside, One Brain, Ch. 8, p. 12.

---

52. CranioSacral Therapy describes a self-correcting mode called the "stillpoint." The stillpoint is a moment in which the body relaxes, adjusting energy surpluses and deficiencies on its own. Subtle energy balancing postures make use of this natural self-correction. When the adjustment is complete, we get a new feeling of being ready to move on to a new activity. CranioSacral therapists call this subjective feeling "being done" or "being complete." Most people can identify this time readily. For a description of this phenomenon, see Upledger's CranioSacral Therapy, pp. 238

"Arm Position Two"

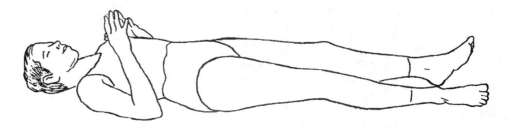

Cook's Hook-ups:
Variations in prone position

Integration metaphor

Balancing Touches

The use of touch is an extension of bodywork. It can be used for stimulation, creating change, balancing, or soothing. These touches can be first aid for a wide variety of stressful, painful, or difficult situations. While they are described as being self-given, all the contacts given here may also be done with two people, a "giver" and a "receiver."

A digression on the use of hands for health is useful here. We will take a moment here to give some background on the why, how and where of therapeutic touch.

First, the point is well-made by Dr. John Thie[53] that our modern life includes far too little touching. When people touch, it is usually for very limited purposes, in extreme cases just punishment or sex. The well-documented health benefits of touch are not appreciated or employed in many conventional health care treatments. Thus Thie called his system "Touch for Health," being a distinctively "new," different and good reason to touch one another.

Generally, the hands are considered to resemble the jumper cables of a car battery system, with the right hand charged positively and the left hand charged negatively.[54] This may be visualized as an outpouring fountain on the right and an incoming suction on the left.

Dr. Stone differentiated treatment into two categories, with placement of the hands determined by the purpose of the treatment.[55] He called these two types of treatment "centripetal" (from the outside in and the feet upwards) and "centrifugal" (from the head down and the inside out). Generally, centripetal treatment is recommended for stimulation, and for "chronic or subnormal" conditions; centrifugal is for soothing, for "acute and painful" conditions.

In practice, the right hand is placed lower on the body (closer to the feet) than the left hand for the centripetal treatment, and the left hand is placed lower than the right for the centrifugal. We can visualize the effect by placing two magnets close to each other. One way has an repelling, inhibiting effect (touching the lower or negative pole of the body with left or negative hand), the other an attracting, enhancing effect (touching the negative pole of the body with the right or positive hand).

Dr. Stone emphasized the use of positive/neutral/negative poles in bodywork, and many contacts call for placement of hands according to a top-to-bottom arrangement of polarity zones (see page 15). Polarity fields are also used with a front/back (negative/positive, respectively) or left/right (negative/positive, respectively) orientation, but top/bottom orientations are more frequent in the literature, reflecting the vertical arrangement of the spine and chakras.

Centripetal Treatment Predominates

The positive (right) hand to negative (lower) pole centripetal treatment is most frequently used.

---

53. Thie, <u>Touch for Health</u>, p. 7.
54. Stone, <u>Polarity Therapy Vol II</u>, pp. 208-209.

---

55. For a complete explanation of these two treatment modes, see Stone, <u>Polarity Therapy Vol</u> I, Book 3, pp. 40-41. These concepts should not be considered rigid rules, but rather guidelines to supplement the practitioner's observation and experience.

The operator's right hand should be on the most negative pole-- the toes, the left hand on the neuter pole, in the middle, or on the neck or head if the aroused current is strong enough to carry that far. If it is not, merely go a little above the lower contact, establish a current between the two hands by kneading and pressure, then proceed in this matter up to the neuter center pole, thence to the positive pole above that.[56]

Understanding why this is the common placement of hands requires a larger analysis. "Energy blocks" occur when the impulse of cosmic force flowing through the body is disrupted or impeded by distorted pathways caused by trauma. This can be imagined as malfunction caused by tangled, twisted, or broken wires. The result is usually a reduced capacity for current flow, experienced physically as reduced vitality or health problems, emotionally as reduced capacity for love, and mentally as reduced ability to learn and change.

Energy pathways have a dual function: conducting current down into the tissues (involution, the Yang function), and conducting a return flow back up and out (evolution, the Yin function). Dr. Stone emphasized the return current, the evolutionary function, as the critical focus of therapy.

> The real picture of energy block due to depolarization is given here: Wherever the negative pole of matter is in excess and rules, the positive energy field and function are crowded out. Then a shutting-in and deadlock of energies occur.[57]

Sills' pages on this in The Polarity Process are excellent.[58] This is "The Journey of the Soul," a topic expanded later (p. 123). Energy comes down into matter, but is unable to go back. We inev-

itably become attached to the forms of our minds, feelings and bodies. We gain knowledge of matter through involution (the eating of the apple in the Garden of Eden), but the ensuing attachment blocks us from moving on to knowledge of spirit through evolution.

We hold on, through the emotions of the five elements (vanity, greed, anger, lust, attachment), and the circuit is unable to be fully completed. Thus the Yin, evolutionary aspect of human experience is essential, becoming an ultimate therapy for all dis-eases. This explains the predominance of centripetal, right-hand-below hand placement in Polarity energy balancing, as well as Dr. Stone's emphasis on perineal technique to reduce inhibitions in the five-pointed star Yin function. It also is compatible with attitude-based therapies espoused by such authors as Bernie Siegel, Louise Hay, Norman Cousins and others.

Another way to explain the emphasis on Yin in therapy is in terms of the development of emotions. Traumas incurred in the first few years have a primary importance. In this formative period, from conception to age seven, we are very impressionable. From this period we gain most of our attitudes and expectations, and during these years emotional situations have their greatest impact. Insults, abuses and insecurities experienced during these years set a tone for later issues and feelings.

In these formative years we are invariably occupying the Yin, receptive position in our relationships: the child is powerless

---

56. Stone, Polarity Therapy Vol I, Book 3, p. 40.

57. Stone, Polarity Therapy Vol II, p. 138.

58. Sills, The Polarity Process, p. 80-82. Juhan, in Job's Body (p. 181) has a similar opinion in the context of nerve message function: "We must admit it is the descending... sensory [Yin] current that is most important [conducting the brain's response to stimuli]...it is the process of selection and interpretation that makes us respond differently, makes each of us the unique individuals that we are."

to resist the offenses of the adults, to stop the divorce of the parents, or to remove painful irritants from the environment. Such traumas set the stage for the fateful holding on described above. With early Yin experience being the source of so much later energy blockage, later Yin therapy makes sense as a primary treatment strategy.

Another aspect of Yin-oriented therapy relates to the nature of modern life. We live in a very Yang world, with constant pressure to expand and create. Meanwhile Yin qualities of receptivity and contentment are discouraged and unappreciated. The Yin, centripetal treatment counters this tendency.

Thus the right hand below/left hand above placement is commonplace in Polarity Therapy.[59] For many people, amplifying and facilitating the return current is a priority. The exceptions are in the instance of pain, inflammation, or spasm (when the hands are reversed), and in contacts in massage or some forms of acupressure, in which hand placement is de-emphasized or considered insignificant.

---

59. In Gordon's Your Healing Hands, p. 25, this is carried to an extreme: the right hand below positioning is erroneously expressed as mandatory .

60. Stone, Polarity Therapy Vol I, Book 2, p. 78. Stokes and Whiteside give a slightly different arrangement in One Brain (chapter 6, p. 2), with the polarity reversing in each finger from right to left hand. Thus the index finger is positively charged on the right, negatively charged on the left. They agree with the thumb being considered neutral, and the overall polarity relationship of the two hands; compromising their viewpoint with Polarity, the index finger on the right and the ring finger on the left would make a strongly-polarized pair.

Stokes and Whiteside's characterization of the four lower fingers as governing categories of needs in four groups-- electrical (earth or little finger), emotional (water or ring finger), nutritional (fire or middle finger) and structural (air or index finger)-- fits well with and adds significantly to Polarity theory concepts.

Finger Polarity

On each hand, each finger has a charge; they alternate from little finger to thumb: fifth finger positive, fourth finger negative, third (middle) finger positive, forefinger negative, thumb neutral. Of the positive fingers, the middle (fire) finger on the right hand has the strongest outgoing charge, and the fourth (water) finger on the left the greatest pull. Thus these two fingers are often used for specific applications of directional Polarity contact.[60]

The Three Touches

Three touches are described by Dr. Stone: light (for balancing, called Satvic, from the Sanskrit for the Air Principle), moving (for stimulation, called Rajasic, from the Sanskrit for the Fire Principle), and deep (for changing, called Tamasic, from the Sanskrit for the Water Principle). These balancing, stimulating, and changing touches reflect the qualities of the three Godheads of Hindu mythology, the Creator, Sustainer, and Destroyer.

Generally, the balancing Satvic touch is light and soft. The Rajasic stimulating touch involves movement and light or medium pressure. The movement can be by kneading, rocking, or other methods. The Tamasic changing touch is firm and deep, usually without movement.

All three touches are available to the sensitive practitioner, although the deep touch, which is often painful, has been de-emphasized or deleted by some. However, our experience agrees with Dr. Stone's words:

> A good manipulation of Polarity Centers is sometimes painful and far removed from the languid relaxation associated with magnetic treatments.[61]

---

61. Stone, Polarity Therapy Vol I, Book 3, p. 41.

43. Jelly Roll

The Jelly Roll is one of the best known balancing touches. It works with the Fire Principle, governing digestion, circulation, action and confidence. The Fire Principle radiates in a spiralling oval out from the umbilicus. It is the power called the *hara* in Martial Arts, the center of gravity and outgoing force. Many people can feel the radiant movement of energy from the umbilicus after the Jelly Roll, and it is often used in Polarity bodywork.

This posture, has grown in popularity with use; it is minimal in Dr. Stone's written work, given as a variation of a treatment for "umbilical congestion and eye trouble."[62]

Method

Comfortably lie, sit, or stand. Place the left hand on the forehead and the right hand on the navel; the belly button can be

---

62. Stone, <u>Polarity Therapy Vol I</u>, Book 3, p. 78.

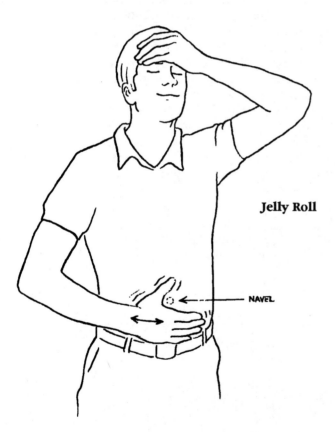

Jelly Roll

NAVEL

between the thumb and forefinger. Stimulate the umbilical area by rocking the lower hand from side to side, at a tempo which feels comfortable: fast and firm will be stimulating, slow and soft will be soothing. When ready to stop, maintain the hand contact and feel energy movement as a surge, tingling or other sensation. If resting on the floor, turn the head to the left so that the left elbow can rest on the floor. We can feel energy movement best when completely relaxed.

Variations

This is frequently done in pairs, and often used as an introduction to the experience of energy.

A more specific use of contacts on the same points is offered by the Barhydts. The forehead is touched in the hollow above the eyebrows by thumbs and fingers, while the navel area is massaged deeply with fingertips, thumb directly in navel.

Benefits
• Balances Fire Principle and Yang functions.
• Stimulates and balances digestion functions; soothes an upset stomach.
• Good for building confidence.
• Frequently used to comfort young children before nap or bedtime.
• Can be used in preparation for active movement.

References
Stone, <u>Polarity Therapy, Vol. II</u>, p. 180.
Stone, <u>Polarity Therapy</u>, Vol. I, Book 3, pp. 78-79; Book 2, pp. 8-11, 18.
Barhydts, <u>Self-Help for Stress and Pain</u>, p. 28.

Buttons

The Buttons series come from the Dennisons' <u>Brain Gym</u>. Each set of "buttons" stimulates and balances a set of acupuncture meridians based on the Chinese energy anatomy model. When the systems related to these meridians are out of balance, we feel fatigue, confusion, or poor performance. When proper energy flow is restored, feelings of clarity, balance and effectiveness are regained. Each set of points is stimulated only briefly; the most time is used for holding, with a light touch. Energy moves on the basis of the contacts and does not require pressure.

The light, balancing Satvic touch used here is deceptively powerful. The movement of Rajasic touch and the penetrating, changing force of Tamasic touch are often more dramatic, but many practitioners feel the Satvic to be most powerful because it reflects the subtlest level of energy function, the "blueprint," or Air Principle. The "Buttons" series uses the Satvic touch to balance the three dualities or dimensions of brain function and energy movement: top/bottom (earth buttons), front/back (space buttons), and left/right (brain buttons).

44. Earth Buttons

Method

Place two fingers of one hand directly above the pubic bone and two fingers of the other hand just below the lower lip. Stimulate with the two upper fingers and then gently hold both contacts. Breathe deeply, visualizing the movement of energy up the center of the body. Add looking up and down with your eyes (without moving the head) to assist the top-bottom connection. When "complete," remove the hands from their contacts. Repeat with the opposite hand holding the points. Finish by looking all around in a downward direction: downward eye

placement activates the brain's top/bottom dimension. This emphasizes the feeling of stability and anchors in a feeling of being grounded.

Benefits

- Helps to restore energy flow in the Central (or "Conception") Meridian which comes up the center of the body on the front starting directly above the pubic bone and ending below the lip. This corresponds to the Water Principle and the Earth Element in Polarity.
- Integrates top/bottom dimensions, for "grounding" or feeling more stable and practical.
- Good for precise activities like mathematical calculations or balancing a checkbook.

Reference

Dennisons, <u>Brain Gym</u>, p. 26.

45. Space Buttons

Method

Place two fingers of one hand at the junction between the coccyx and the sacrum, the hard boney area at the base of the lower back. Place two fingers of the other hand on the "moustache area," between the upper lip and nose. Stimulate with the two upper fingers and then hold. Breathe deeply, and imagine a movement of energy up the back and over the top of the head to the "moustache area." You may experience energy movement and balance. Stop when you feel complete.

Earth Buttons

Space Buttons

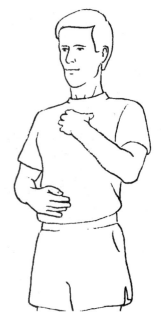

Brain Buttons

Repeat with the opposite hand holding the points. Finish by looking all around in an upward direction. This emphasizes the upward direction and anchors a feeling of the expansiveness of space.

Benefits
- Helps restore proper energy flow to the Governing Meridian which comes up the center of the body from the tail bone over the head to directly above the upper lip. This corresponds to the Fire Principle in Polarity.
- Helps with back-front brain integration, controlling such activities as quick decision making.

Reference
Dennisons, Brain Gym, p. 28.

46. Brain Buttons
Method
Place one hand so that it covers the navel. This is a linking point for all the acupuncture meridians. With the other hand, touch on either side of the sternum (breast bone) just under the clavicle (collar bone). In acupuncture, these points are called K27 and are the top of the kidney meridian. Use two fingers to contact one side and the thumb to contact the other. Rub with the upper hand to stimulate and then stop and hold. Move the eyes left and right, crossing the midline, as an optional extra stimulation. Stop when you feel complete.

Benefits
- Integrates left and right brains.
- Restores energy flow in the kidney meridian. This corresponds to the Air Principle in Polarity.
- Facilitates activities that require total brain function such as reading or using eyes in concentrated study.
- Opens the mental perspective when you feel overly focused on details or "one-sided" on an issue. Helps make both sides visible.

Reference
Dennisons, Brain Gym, p. 25.

47. Brain Energy Balance
This three-part posture is a quick and simple meridian balance taught by the Barhydts, combining the three preceding poses.

Method
In all three parts, hold one hand so that the fingertips surround the navel. For right/left balance, stimulate and hold the same acupuncture points as brain buttons, on each side of the sternum, called K27. For top/bottom balance, stimulate and hold with the thumb below the lower lip and two fingers above the upper lip. For back/front balance, stimulate and hold directly behind the navel on the back. Stop each section when it feels complete.

Benefits
- Balance of the top-bottom, left-right, back-front dimensions of energy flow and brain function.

Reference
Barhydts, Self-Help for Stress and Pain, p. 19.

48. Balance Buttons
Method
Place one hand with the fingertips covering the navel. With two fingers of the other hand, contact the indentation at the base of the skull about one inch behind the ear. Combine deep breathing with visualizing the movement of energy up from the navel to the head, holding for a minute or so. Do one side, then switch hands and do the other. Sense the effect on the body and stop when you feel complete.

Benefits
- Links the navel with points affecting balance, creating a state of relaxed body, alert mind.
- A good stress release break for computer workers.

Reference
Dennisons, Brain Gym, p. 27.

49. Positive Points

These contacts are called "Positive Points" in <u>Brain Gym</u> and "Stress Release Points" in <u>Touch for Health</u>. The position and effect is similar to Dr. Stone's Wise Man of Old.

Holding this area of the forehead helps to process emotional stress from past and present. These are reflex points for emotional centers of the brain.

Positive Points are useful to calm a stressful emotional response, or to help process an emotional memory. The contact is also used for soothing another person, such as a child who is upset or during an emotional release accompanying bodywork.

Method

Contact the forehead lightly on both sides, just above the eyebrow and midway between the hairline and brow. Use either both hands, two fingers on each side, or one hand, thumb on one side and two fingers on the other. A slight bulge, the frontal eminence, is the exact location. Hold this gentle contact until you feel complete.

Benefits

• Ability to approach goals with less worry and emotion. Makes it easier to face situations that have been upsetting.
• Defuses emotional tension

References

Thie, <u>Touch for Health</u>, p. 36.
Dennisons, <u>Brain Gym</u>, p. 32.
Stone, <u>Polarity Therapy Vol. I</u>, Book 2, p. 52.
Barhydts, <u>Self-Help for Stress and Pain</u>, p. 16.

50. & 51. Interlaced Triangles & Five Pointed Star Balances

The next poses create balance in two basic circuits of the energy anatomy. The Five Pointed Star and the Interlaced Triangles (or Six Pointed Star) are two of the most frequently used maps in Polarity Therapy. These geometric shapes track wireless circuits which have a major significance in all three principles and all five elements. The Interlaced Triangles pattern describes the Yang Fire Principle. The Five Pointed Star pattern describes the Yin Water Principle.

This has many implications in exercise and bodywork. If tension is from Yang action (doing, creating, directing), the Interlaced Triangles gives a map for therapy. If tension is from Yin reaction (being, receiving, reflecting), the Five Pointed Star is indicated.

Exercises for the Interlaced Triangles exercises have an inward shape like the Squat. This mirrors the fetal position, in which the body materialized as it became "involved" (involution) in the world. It exposes the back Yang side and protects the front Yin side. The top and bottom points of the triangles are emphasized. Five pointed Star exercises have an outward shape, like the Taoist Arch. These mirror the evolving search for meaning (evolution) beyond materialism. All five points are significant. They show the actual shape of the body. Many exercises deliberately go from one pattern to the other: the Woodchopper and Rocking Cliff are examples. These are embodying a smooth transition and balance from Yang to Yin and back.

50. Interlaced Triangles Balance

The "Interlaced Triangles" reflect the involution of primal energy into physical form. On the spectrum of spirit and form, it is the spirit end, the launch pad for movement to form. Generally, its points and contacts are more subtle than the Five

Interlaced Triangles & Five Pointed Star Patterns
Each pattern is present in both men and women

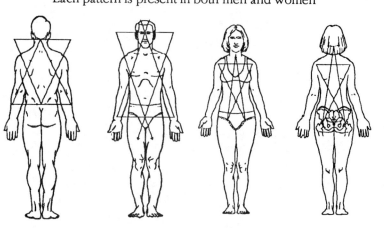

Pointed Star, since only two points are actually in the physical body. It is associated with the powerful relationship between cranium and sacrum, and with the sympathetic nervous system.

This star shape is an ancient symbol for polarity. It symbolizes mankind's essential choice between materialism and spirituality. In front, the two points in the body are the "Third Eye" at the top, and the genitals at the bottom. The Third Eye at the pineal gland is considered the gateway at which the primal energy and mind/body meet. The genitals at the bottom are the location of sexual pleasure and the creation of children, mankind's ultimate experiences of materialization.

In back, the two points are at the occiput and sacrum. Polarity and CranioSacral Therapy both emphasize the major therapeutic opportunities at both locations. In advanced methods, subtle factors relating to these areas' positioning and pulsation receive primary attention.

Subdividing the overall pattern,[64] the downward pointing triangle represents involutionary movement of energy into the body. It is associated with the (Yang) air and fire elements and the Fire Principle. The upward-pointing triangle represents the evolutionary movement of energy back out of the body, from the sacrum to the eye center, and is associated with the (Yin) water and earth elements and the Water Principle.

In Oriental medicine the shape of the Interlaced Triangles is considered significant in body characteristics of men and women.[65] The downward pointing energy of the Yang triangle is reflected in broader shoulders, downward pointing beard, and protruding sexual organs of the man. The upward moving energy of the Yin triangle is reflected in a woman's broader hips, higher voice, indented sexual organs, and other characteristics. Both man and woman have both triangles (and both stars), with the impact of one slightly predominating according to gender.

Method

The balance involves systematically touching the six points of the star, right hand below and left hand above. The thumbs may be used for the front, but any relaxed and comfortable contact is acceptable. The points of the star are forehead to pubic bone in front, occiput to sacrum in back, and a same-side connection of shoulders to hips. While lying down is most relaxed, these contacts may be made

---

64. "Any Yin or Yang aspect can be further divided into Yin and Yang."
--Kaptchuk, The Web That Has No Weaver
pp. 7-12

This is always true in energy theory. Any section of the body will have all three principles, just as cutting a bar magnet into pieces will create new magnets, each with new positive and negative poles. Similarly, the foot, which is negative relative to the head, has positive (toes), neutral (middle) and negative (heel) zones when considered alone.

65. Michio Kushi, The Book of Macrobiotics, pp. 86-87, 9. Also see Muramoto's Healing Ourselves, pp. 8-9, 21-37. Sources from the Orient are strong in describing Yin and Yang characteristics in all aspects of life. Integrating Oriental and Polarity energy models is the subject of an essay in Part Four (p. 126).

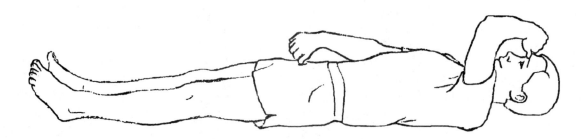

Interlaced Triangles Balance

with the body in any position. It is easy to do seated in a chair.

Benefits
• Balances the Yang Fire Principle, enhancing responsibility and creativity.
• Balances the back motor current side of the body.
• Soothes the nervous system.
• Relaxing for feelings relating to authority, forcefulness, confidence and action.
• Assists movement of cerebro-spinal fluid.
• Complements bodywork or exercise for the back.

Reference
Stone, Polarity Therapy Vol. I, Book 2, p. 18.

51. Five Pointed Star Balance

Considering "spirit" and "form" to be opposite ends of the cycle of involution and evolution, the Five Pointed Star represents the "form" end of the spectrum and the launch pad for movement toward spirit.

The pelvis and throat are highlighted by this pattern. The pelvis is the storage vault for feelings, the "reactions" to earlier stimulation. It is linked directly to the arms, which are used to reach out for what is wanted, and especially to the throat, where feelings are verbalized. Feelings must be able to be expressed, or they become emotionally toxic to the energy systems.

Five Pointed Star contacts are especially significant in emotional processing. They are also used for improving abdominal and thoracic organ functions, like digestion and breathing, and for facilitating expression of feelings. They are commonly used when working with eliminative functions including colon.

Method
For the Satvic Five Pointed Star contact, lie comfortably on the floor or bed. Touch the left pelvic area with the right palm, and the right upper chest area (fingertips touching the shoulder) with the left hand. Hold this position until you feel complete, which may be experienced as tingles, softening, heat or pulsation, followed by a quietness or settled feeling. Some people are able to actually experience the energy pathway itself.

Next, move the upper hand to rest gently in the throat area, making a contact at the top of the five pointed star. Now the link is between the pelvic area and the throat. Again wait for the energy to release and balance.

Next, do the same contacts to the right pelvic area with the left hand and the left shoulder with the right hand and then moving the upper hand to the throat.

Be conscious of the energy movement and when you feel complete, take a moment to relax and experience the new balance.

A "butterfly" variation is shown in the illustration. Lie on the back with the knees bent and the soles of the feet touching, knees widely open. Let the weight of the legs gently open the pelvis as the five pointed star contacts are made.

Benefits
• Balances the Yin Water Principle, enhancing receptivity and contentment.
• Opens and lengthens pelvic muscles.
• Helpful in emotional release and balance.
• Provides a complementary postural balance following exercises for the back, as it opens and balances the front of the body.

Reference
Stone, Polarity Therapy Vol. I, Book 2, p. 16.

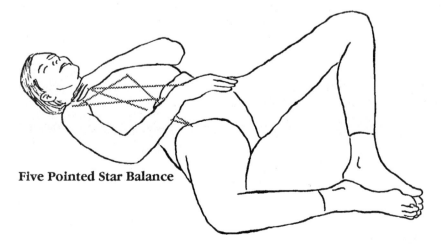

Five Pointed Star Balance

52. Bridge Reflex

These points relate to the junction of neck and shoulders. When this area of the body is blocked, the brachial nerve plexus is inhibited and breathing and relaxation suffer. These points are also used to release eye tension.

Method

Take a position in which the head can rest on the hands: squatting is best, or seated at a table. Place the curled fist of one hand inside the other, leaving the thumbs extending out and next to each other. Use these two thumbs to contact the area just to the side of where the bridge of the nose and the ridge above the eye meet (these spots may be tender). Maintain the thumb contact. Pressure or a circular motion here may assist in release.

Benefits

• Helps to restore balance in breathing and movement of gas.
• Balances side-to-side Air Principle.
• Good to counteract dizziness after exercise.
• Releases shoulder-neck tension and allows the circulation to balance between the head and the rest of the body.

References

Stone, Polarity Therapy Vol. I, Book 2, P. 85.

53. Sympathetic Balance

This combination of contacts comes from an advanced Polarity Therapy technique. It is primarily for use in a Polarity session, with a giver and a receiver. However some of the benefits are also available for the individual using just the part of the technique which can be done alone.

The sympathetic nervous system is the Yang component of the three-part nervous system (Parasympathetic being the neutral Air Principle and Cerebro-Spinal the Yin Water Principle). It is the "fight or flight" response, by which we react to stress.

The point has been well made by Pelletier (see page 107) and others that modern life often affords neither fight nor flight as an option. Thus the sympathetic system can be "on" all the time, leading to exhaustion. Often chemical treatments (sedatives, sleeping pills, blood pressure regulators, intoxicants) are used to artificially give relief from chronic sympathetic nervous system overload.

This balance has been proven to have a powerful effect on relieving this pressure. It is based on the reflex relationships between spinal vertebrae and their reflexes in the feet and legs.

Method

Lie down on the floor or bed, or recline in such a way that the weight of the head is entirely supported and the neck is relaxed. With the fingers touch the sides of the neck firmly to determine

(+)	(0)	(-)
C1	T3	L5
C2	T4	L4
C3	T5	L3
C4	T6	L2
C5	T7	L1
C6	T8	T12
C7	T9	T11
T1	T2	T10

Chart of Spinal Relationships

The vertebrae are linked according to these relationships. Find the sorest cervical vertebra from the column at left, and press contacts from the column at right, then the column at center, to release the sympathetic nervous system. Start with reflexes in the foot, then the leg next, then the back itself. This technique gives dramatic relief from stress. Also see Pelletier note, p. 107, and Stress essay, p. 134.

which side and which vertebral spinous process (the bone projecting from the sides of the spine) is more painful.

Start at the head behind the ears, and touch firmly on each side of the neck, in steps going down. Estimate which vertebra is most sore and find it in the left column in the chart. Then look next to that vertebra, in the center and right columns, for the lower related vertebrae. Then use the drawing to figure where the reflexes to these vertebrae are, on the feet and in the leg. The full treatment in an advanced Polarity session makes progressive contacts starting at the foot, touching each reflex firmly, and ending at the top in the neck where we started.

For the self-given version, we touch only the foot and leg. Using the chart to approximate the right location, press deeply on the inside edge (the Ether line) of the foot. The right hand starts near the toe, the other in the arch. The "right" spot will be painful to the touch.

Feel for a release of these points, then move on. Now the hand that was at the toe moves up to replace the hand near the arch, which in turn finds the next spot, inside the heel. Again, press firmly until you feel energy release as a pulse, tingling or relaxation.

Next, move up again. The lower hand assumes the position at the heel, while the upper hand finds the next spot near the Achilles tendon on the outside of the leg behind the heel. After a time, the upper hand moves up again to the next place in the calf, on the rear outside below the knee, then finally to the top leg position in the thigh.

After the sequence is complete, go back to the spot on the neck that was sore. Very often the pain will now have melted away!

Step by Step:

1. Find sorest cervical.
2. Look up corresponding vertebra on table at left. Follow that pattern for balance procedure.
3. Start at foot and work up: press & hold approximate reflex points

Benefits

- Good for stress, sleeplessness, agitation, exhaustion, anger, or fearful conditions.
- Combines well with the Light Rocking Perineal (page 61).
- Gives a sense of centered balance and calm power.

Reference

Stone, Polarity Therapy Vol. II, pp. 85-91, 163-165, 197.

Sympathetic Balance Touch Sequence

Use this chart to locate reflexes according to the table on the left.

54. Ear Reflexes & Thinking Cap

The ears are microcosmic representations of the whole body; ear acupuncture is a sophisticated specialty in the Orient. The ear shape reflects the shape of the fetus in the womb: shoulders at the top, pelvis below, with the ear canal relating to the umbilicus. The customs of puncturing the earlobe (a pelvic reflex) at puberty, and wearing gold (a stimulant) can be interpreted as subconscious energy adjustment for sexual stimulation.

Dr. Stone considered the ear lobe to be an indicator of vitality, the positive point (wrist bracelet being neutral and buttocks being negative poles) indicator of vital force or reserve energy. The amount of this vitality is inherited, a reflection of the diet, lifestyle, and emotions of parents and previous generations.

Method

Sit, squat, or lie down comfortably. The fingertips are placed in the ear canals with light pressure, light movement, or soft touch. In addition, pulling and twisting the ear in all directions activates reflex relationships to the whole body.

Variation

The Dennisons' "Thinking Cap" exercise, used for improving concentration in Edu-K, consists of "unrolling" the ears, repeated three or more times. In educational therapy, this improves listening concentration and comprehension.

Benefits

- Affects sense of sound, relating to the central core of the body. Combines well with making sound for refreshed concentration and calm.
- Gives a general reflexology treatment for the whole body.
- Firm contact on the ear canal in four main directions (up/down, back/front) is a release for Yang motor tension.
- Enhances balance functions, and digestive functions of the umbilical area.

References

Stone, <u>Polarity Therapy Vol. I</u>, Book 2, P. 79.
Stone, <u>Health Building</u>, pp. 150-153.
Francis, <u>Polarity Self-Help Exercises</u>, p. 16.
Thie, <u>Touch for Health</u>, p. 120.

55. Tennis Ball Head Cradle

This simple procedure from Upledger's CranioSacral Therapy is a powerful way of inducing self-correction. By lying with the head resting on two tennis balls, we induce what is called a stillpoint, which Dr. Upledger defines as:

> ...a therapeutic interruption of craniosacral rhythm which allows the craniosacral system to reorganize its activity for more optimal effect on the body.[66]

The cranio-sacral system is the central core of the body including the spine, cranium and sacral area. Polarity Therapy has several maneuvers for cradling the head,[67] and Dr. Stone was quite familiar with cranial technique:

> POLARITY CURRENT RESEARCH IN CEREBROSPINAL FLUID AND IN CRANIOPATHY: The life-breath or Prana current moves in the cerebrospinal fluid conductor to all tissue cells and communicates with other internal secretions and body fluids, like a living cosmic breath. This may be called the primary respiratory

---

66. Upledger, <u>Craniosacral Therapy</u>, p. 238
67. This has similarities to the "North Pole Stretch". (Stone, <u>Polarity Therapy Vol. II</u>, p. 139) and other head cradle positions.

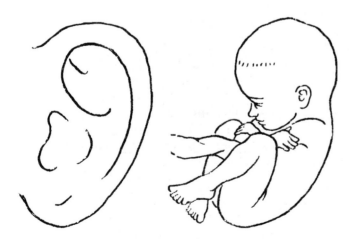

The ear is a reflection of the whole body.
Contact on the ear will stimulate energy movement in the corresponding body area.

cycle of energy flow, with its own cranial rhythmic impulses as a physiological wireless energy response, like atomic current circuits. It is prior to and distinct from the regular respiration of the lungs' cycle of oxidation and pulse beat.[68]

Method

This exercise requires a prop, two tennis balls bound closely together. This is done either by tying them snugly in a sock or by putting a string through holes in them and tying them together. They must be bound so that the balls stay together. The Energy Exercise classroom can have these available for use.

Take the "tandem tennis balls" and place them under the head so its full weight rests on them, one ball on each side of center, about midway up the back of the skull. The specific location can be located by finding the boney occipital prominence at the base of the skull and feeling above it for a slight depression.

Rest the head on the tennis balls for about 15 minutes or a length of time that feels good for you. If needed, adjust the head slightly, with gradual, gentle movement, to maintain comfort.

Variations

Curl the hands into fists and let the head rest on the knuckles as you rest on the floor or bed. This will not work if shoulder tension is created by having the arms raised during the posture.

Benefits

• Adjustment of the cranio-sacral system.
• Reduces stress, enhances body function, relaxes connective tissue, enhances fluid motion, reduces fever.
• Can be effective for headache relief.
• Has been used with persons with auto-immune disease, autism in children, degenerative arthritis and anxiety.

---

68. Stone, Polarity Therapy Vol. II, p. 223.

References

Upledger, CranioSacral Therapy, p. 310-311.
Stone, Polarity Therapy Vol. I, Book 2, p. 49, Book 3, pp. 48, 79, 101.
Stone, Polarity Therapy Vol. II, pp. 45, 162.
Gach, Acu-Yoga, p. 117, also pp. 173-174.

56. Fountain Of Love

This exercise was practiced by Montessori educator Elizabeth Caspari.

Method

There are eight "sets" in the routine, for hands, arms, chest, shoulders, head, torso, legs, and finishing. Dr. Caspari suggested doing them while singing, humming or whistling; she sang the following words from her Mazdaznan song book.

> Fountain of Love, Our source is in thee.
> Living thy will the spirit is free
> O Beautiful day, When all of us see
> The hope of the world is Love

Hands: Shake the hands up and down, loosely held in front of the chest, palms facing the chest. Shake the hands up and down with palms facing downward, elbows bent, arms relaxed, fingertips straight ahead. "Make a parcel:" roll the arms hand over hand away from the body, then do the same toward the body.

Arms: Reach the arms up and out one at a time, shaking the hands as you reach the limit. Repeat doing both hands together. With a loose hand tap one arm, rotating it to reach all surfaces. Do the same with the other arm.

Chest: Hold arms extended in front, palms up. Put the hand into a fist with thumb extended, and press gently into the armpit area. Move the elbows out to the side and back, pressing in with the thumbs.

Shoulders: Roll the shoulders forward and backward in circles as if touching the ears.

Head: Sing with a "La-la-la-la" to the roof of the mouth (it is difficult to sing words while moving the head, and this also stimulates reflexes in the roof of the mouth). Nod the head forward, then rotate left and right. Keep the shoulders down and the head up.

Circle forward circles, then backward circles, with the chin. Then make figure eights with the chin, first one way, then the other. Lean the head over so the ear "listens to the sky," in both directions.

Lightly tap the head all over with the

fingertips, going down to the shoulders.

Torso: Tap the chest all over strongly with the fists. Embrace yourself with both arms and lean forward, lengthening the back. Do this leaning forward to the left and then the right.

Legs: Lying on the back or seated in a chair, lift one knee, then the other as if marching; then lift both knees. Move the toes with legs straight, one foot at a time, then both at once. Circle feet one way, then the other. Shake feet one at a time, then both together.

Finish: Standing up, tap the legs with the side of the hands. Begin at the feet and go up to the side of the hips. Tap the front, sides and back of the legs and buttocks.

Reach the hands up to the left and then the right, fully extending the arms and shaking the hands and "sending love to the world."

Stand quietly and feel your body and how it has both come alive and relaxed.

Benefits

• Dr. Caspari attributes her vitality (traveling worldwide teaching the Montessori Method in her eighties) to this exercise set.
• Gives a feeling of well-being and vitality.

57. Thymus Thump

The controller of energy flow in the body is the thymus gland.... The thymus gland is the first organ to be affected at an energy level by an emotional state.[69]

Method

Use the fingertips to lightly tap the center of the upper chest area. For a more vigorous stimulation, make fists and rap more firmly with the knuckles, like Tarzan. If the setting is right, add a Tarzan yell for extra invigoration.

Benefits

• Increases overall vitality.
• Gives a sense of openness to love.
• Beneficial for the heart and immune system.

Reference

Diamond, Your Body Doesn't Lie, pp. 53, 67.

Balancing Sounds

Audible sounds are a reflection of the essential form of all energy.

...the fundamental level of the whole world, according to the Vedic rishis, is made of sounds.[70]

The Biblical phrase has an esoteric meaning: "In the beginning was the Word, and the Word was with God and the Word was God." Mystic Eastern philosophies describe a cosmic emanation of sound and light which precedes all phenomena. The ability to perceive this celestial emanation with inner senses is a theme of mystic spirituality in many traditions.

Music

Music can be a powerful tool in healing strategies. Music has the power to transform feelings, evoke expression, and inspire change. John Beaulieu cites several events in which patients exposed to music healed more quickly than others.[71]

Different kinds of music have different effects, and the effects may be highly individual according to each person's subjective perspective. Beaulieu gives general guidelines for analyzing sounds according to the elements, using rhythm, speed, volume, pitch and key. The slower and lower the sound, the lower the related energy center.[72] Keys are analyzed as follows:

C (256 cps)	Earth
D	Water
E	Descending Fire
F	Descending Air
G	Ascending Air
A	Ascending Fire
B	Ascending Water
C (512 cps)	Ether.[73]

---

69. Diamond, Your Body Doesn't Lie, pp. 61, 83. The passage continues, "Besides being affected by stress and emotional states, the thymus is strongly influenced by an individual's physical environment, social relationships, food, and posture." (p. 63).

70. Chopra, Quantum Healing, p. 250. Chopra reports good results with a technique called "primordial sound technique" inspired by Ayurveda and Transcendental Meditation.

71. John Beaulieu, Music and Sound in the Healing Arts, p. 131.

72. *Ibid.*, pp. 81-82.

73. *Ibid.*, pp. 95-96.

Yehudi Menuhin summarizes the value of music in his foreword to Patricia Joudry's <u>Sound Therapy for the Walkman</u>:

> Music is the voice of the universe, it is the voice of humanity and is part of our existence. Good music is the harmonization of all the vibrations of which matter consists, and it restores us to ourselves and to our universe. It is the bond that we have between our frequencies and those frequencies which vibrate millions of light years away.
>
> When we hear music we are actually vibrating with the whole audience, and with the performer, and we are thereby put in touch with the composer's mind and heart.
>
> I have always felt that music is basically therapeutic, restoring proportions which are squeezed out of shape by the pressures of the day. In a state of physical disequilibrium of the nerves or the mind, music can reach our subconscious and put things in place.[74]

There are two sides of the sound therapy equation, as Beaulieu points out: changing the music, and changing the listener. For the first, we can actively cause certain types of music to occur, by playing selected sounds, or experimenting with tuning forks[75] or other instruments. The possibilities for doing this, such as playing selected music for specific purposes, singing various kinds of songs, etc., are innumerable.

On the other hand, we can experiment with the receptive approach and develop a consciousness which perceives all sound as music, attuning ourselves to harmonize with the natural sounds of our local environment.

During listening you have the power to resonate with your sonic environment. Suspend your mental attitudes, relax, and open yourself to the energy of sounds. The deeper the relaxed listening, the more there is to be discovered.[76]

This novel concept mirrors Dr. Stone's emphasis on the Yin or evolutionary aspect of energy as a primary focus of therapy. In this receptive listening, we seek greater flexibility, receiving openly and responding spontaneously, instead of following rigid preconceptions. These are the attributes of a healing process for the evolutionary aspect of energy.

58. Humming

Humming in high and low pitch can be used selectively to vibrate any area of the head or body where the hands are placed for polarization.[77]

Humming uses the skull and abdomen to act like the hollow sounding board of a guitar or similar musical instrument. The relationship between types of sound and energy centers can be explained in scientific terms:

> In the case of sound, for example, the air in a cavity will respond only weakly to a sound wave coming from outside, but will begin to 'resonate,' or vibrate very strongly, when the sound wave reaches a

---

74. Joudry, <u>Sound Therapy for the Walkman</u>, p. vii

75. Beaulieu, <u>Music and Sound in the Healing Arts</u>, pp. 95-99.

76. *Ibid.,* pp.123.

77. Stone, <u>Health Building</u>, p. 111..

Position for Humming
Also in this position, see if you can feel the cranial rhythm. Have the fingers touching the head so lightly that only the hair is (barely) felt. The skull "breathes" in a subtle expansion and contraction movement.

certain frequency called the resonance frequency.[78]

Each sound has a vibration of its own and can be used to create vibration in a selected body area. Low pitched sounds resonate with the lower centers of the body and the denser tissues. High pitched sounds resonate with the higher, less dense centers. Similarly, a guitar string will begin to vibrate when a companion string of the same pitch is plucked.

Another dimension to the sound of "Hum" is found in esoteric Tibetan Buddhism, the spiritual tradition was summarized in the sound "Om Mani Padme Hum"[79] which reverberates in chanting and prayer throughout the region.

Each part has a meaning: "Om" refers to gathering the outward tendencies and directing them up the chakras toward the eye center. "Mani" is the jewel or philosopher's stone of transmutation, by which the ordinary has the potential of transcendence. "Padme" is the evolutionary process symbolized in the opening of the lotus flower. "Hum" is transcending material illusion, above and beyond the eye center. As we hum, we momentarily partake in a profound and ancient system of spirituality whose cosmology is similar to Polarity.

Method

Find a comfortable posture in which to hum. The squat is excellent, especially the "wise man of old" posture, or another position in which you can comfortably place the thumbs or little fingers in the ears with the arms supported. Humming is done with the throat, mouth and jaw areas relaxed. The lips are barely closed and the teeth slightly parted.

Experiment with different pitches to intuitively choose the "right" one for the moment. Do that one pitch for one full breath or more, to completely experience that pitch. Then repeat, or do another, different pitch, higher or lower.

It is generally easier at first to feel the effects of different pitches in the face and skull. With time and practice, cultivating increased sensitivity, the effect can be felt in the torso as well.

Variations

In Health Building (p. 150), Dr. Stone describes humming to release the ear canal itself for people with ear problems and head noises. The little finger of each hand is placed in each ear and used to lift and dilate the canal. Pressing in different sides of the canal (front, back, up, down) gives different effects.

Hum different pitches until you "feel" the vibration in the selected area. Hum that pitch for a minute or so. When the problem is in the middle ear, press with both fingers equally. When the problem is more to one side, using one hand only may be preferred.

Humming is popular in an exercise classroom setting, as a great sound of varying pitches wells up in the group. It takes on increased impact with this increased volume and diversity.

Benefits
- Release and relaxation: the humming sound is both energizing and soothing, relaxing the nervous system and energizing the areas of the body which resonate with the sound's particular pitch.
- Humming pulls the attention inward; the effect is almost immediate. It is a great way to induce a centered feeling and to help the transition from mental activity to a state of inner calm.

References
Stone, Health Building, pp. 150-151.
Stone, Polarity Therapy, Vol. I, Book 2. p.79.

59. Ha!

A "Ha" sound contrasts greatly with the hum. Rather than soothing, it has a stimulating and warming effect. Its force-

---

78. Capra, The Tao of Physics, p. 269.

79. Lama Anagarika Govinda, Foundations of Tibetan Mysticism. Sills' The Polarity Process has a knowledgeable summary of the linkage between the Polarity model and Buddhism. Once again, the Polarity model successfully incorporates the central themes of an ancient world-view.

fulness expels old gases from the lungs and creates the space for new fresh air to come in. The diaphragm muscle moves powerfully and opens and balances itself. The expansive sound brings us into expression and movement with openness. Whereas "Om" and "Hum" are evolutionary, inward and stilling, "Ha" is involutionary, outward and creative. A loud, expressive sound like Ha can be quite liberating emotionally. The making of loud sounds, such as the cheering experienced at sporting events, can be very beneficial. Some teachers have suggested making loud Ha (or other) sounds when driving on the freeway, to release tension.

Method

See "Ha Breath" (page 40).

Variations

This sound can be quite loud and may not be appropriate in all situations. It is possible to do it with minimal sound, with only the "h-h-h" is audible.

Benefits

- Increases warmth and heat in the body.
- Stimulates self expression.
- Releases anger, facilitating expression of warmth and love.

60. Roar

The roar is a sustained sound that has many of the same benefits as the "Ha." It is warming, activating and releasing for the diaphragm, and encourages expression. The difference between this and the "Ha" is the steady sustained release of the sound: where the explosive "Ha" creates expression, the steady roar gives the power to sustain it.

Method

See Lion Roar, page 38.

61. Ah

A relaxed, sighing "ah" is used to release breath and tension, assisting the eliminative, letting go process.

Method

Allow a deep full "a-a-h-h-" to come out on your exhalation until the lungs are totally empty. As you get to the end of the breath, "blow out the candle" to completely expel the old air. Use the vibration of the sound to release tension and relax.

Benefits

- Assists complete exhalation. This is important in several exercises, such as the Cliffhanger and some breathing exercises.
- Turns on the gestalt or reflex brain hemisphere so we can relax and not "try" so hard.
- Uses sound vibration to aid tension release in many exercises.

Laughter

Several authors, most notably Norman Cousins, have described the health benefits of laughter.

> Salivary immunoglobin A, which is believed to have a protective capacity against some viruses, increased significantly in the saliva of students who viewed a humorous videotape.[80]

In addition to dispelling tension, laughter has also been identified with thymus gland stimulation, reflexology benefits (with specific reflex points in the upper cheek area), relaxation of the brachial plexus and diaphragm, and other positive effects.

One simple game to make everyone in a group laugh is "Ha Ha." Lie on the floor, each person's head on the next person's stomach in a long chain. The first person loudly says "Ha," the next, "Ha Ha," and so on, each adding one more "Ha." It usually does not take long until it dissolves into laughter for all.

---

80. Cousins, Head First, p. 139. In Anatomy of an Illness, Cousins reported that 10 minutes of solid belly laughter gave him two hours of pain-free sleep (p. 126).

Brain Integration

Just as the body has polarized currents and functions, so does the brain. The enormous subtlety and power of energy balancing for the brain is a relatively new area, and not found to great extent in Dr. Stone's writing. His system anticipates and complements the remarkable recent advances in the field.

Research into the brain's polarized functional relationships is entirely consistent with Dr. Stone's basic premises, and unveils large new areas for therapeutic application. The three principles seem to be perfectly reflected in the three dimensions: left/right being the Air Principle, top/bottom being the Water Principle, and front/back being the Fire Principle. Applications of these correlations are discussed in a separate essay in Part Four.

People have a dominant side of brain function and sense function. For the eyes, a simple test to show which eye is habitually "on" is to make a small circle with both hands at arm's length, and sight through the circle to a distant object. Then close one eye at a time. With one eye closed, the image will be the same; with the other eye closed, it will "move." Of course, nothing is moving; rather, one eye is "dominant." The dominant eye is the one for which the image remains the same.

One side of the brain is more logical, sequential and language oriented. Edu-K calls this the "try" brain. This is usually but not always the left hemisphere. The other hemisphere is intuitive and gestalt oriented. In Edu-K this is called the "reflex" brain; this is usually but not always the right hemisphere. A person who is not integrated in brain function, can have difficulty making full use of both sides.

Dr. Stone used the phrase "effortless effort" or "Wu Wei" to describe an integrated state, combining the effort of the try brain and the effortlessness of the reflex brain for optimum function.

Use of the term "switched on," suggesting an electrical switch, is appropriate, for when the brain is integrated, performance is dramatically improved: the image of a light bulb going on is based on proven theory here. This has been demonstrated in the use of brain integration techniques to teach drawing: students routinely "break through" to sudden major improvements when using these techniques.

The light bulb in the brain image, popularized in cartoons, is also supported by modern brain research. The front brain Conscious Associational Thinking (CAT) area is the site of new experience and insight, and has the seldom-used capacity to override all habitual patterns.

> ...when artificially stimulated in test situations, CAT registers a single specific response, LIGHT.[82]

Not surprisingly, it has been found that trauma and past experience play a key role in whether we are "switched on" or "switched off" in certain situations.

> In almost every instance, "learning disabilities," popularly termed "dyslexia"-- result from emotional stress at the time of learning, a stress so intense that the individual programs in a blind spot to a given learning skill due to fear, fear of pain, or pain itself.[83]

Energy balancing for the body is inevitably balancing for the brain as well, and vice versa. These exercises are subtle, powerful ways to work directly with activating smooth use of the whole brain, and enhance the natural ability to switch back and forth into different functions as needed.

---

82. Stokes and Whiteside, <u>One Brain</u>, chapter 1, p. 22.

83. *Ibid.*, chapter 1, p. 3.

62. Lazy 8's For Eyes

In Lazy Eights for Eyes we activate both sides of the brain, both eyes, and the natural link between brain, eye and hand coordination. This exercise makes use of the concept of "crossing the midline." For the eyes, crossing the midline refers to the process by which we switch primary use from one brain hemisphere to the other as we move the eyes across any visual field. For many people, "crossing the midline" is difficult, and activities such as reading and coordination suffer.

Method

This fun activity can be done several different ways. The simplest way requires no extra materials and can be done anywhere. Stand or sit comfortably. Hold one hand extended in front of the nose, thumb up on the midline in the center of the body. Fix your sight on the thumbnail. Now move the thumb in a "lazy eight" (∞) shape, by moving it up the midline and circling to the left. Make a full circle back to center and then another circle over to the right.

Continue this lazy eight motion and follow each part of the movement with your eyes. The head remains centered and relaxed and the eyes follow slowly so they do not miss any section of the eight and move easily.

After eight times or more, use the other hand to draw the lazy eight, again following continuously with the eyes, head remaining centered. After eight times or more, draw the lazy eight with both hands together.

This can also be done with colored pencils, markers, or crayons on a big sheet of paper or chalkboard. Make sure to keep the nose as the midline and follow with your eyes. Another possibility is using a child's toy car or train that has a figure eight track.

The Elephant

Crossing the midline can be a problem in hearing as well. For this the Dennisons developed the Elephant in which the head rests on the shoulder and moves as the arm traces lazy eights.

Benefits
- Eases reading. This exercise has given dramatic benefit to people with reading problems.
- Improved hand/eye coordination.
- Connects and balances left and right brain functions.
- Gives a sense of stability and calm.

References
Dennisons, <u>Brain Gym</u>, p. 5.
Stokes and Whiteside, <u>One Brain</u>, chapter 8, pp. 16 ff.

63. Dennison Laterality Repatterning

"Repatterning" is a term for brain integration therapies created by Paul and Gail Dennison. In Repatterning, simple movements are employed to activate both sides of the brain and improve communication between them.

Repatterning is often used in relation to a particular task. Often we want to be good at something, but find it just gets more difficult the more we "try" to do it. Similarly, we may know our attitude is defeating us in a particular task, yet we are unable to change to an attitude that would be successful.

**Use a large version of this figure
to trace the Lazy Eights**

Use a figure at least two feet wide traced at full arms-length away. Either follow your thumb or use crayons or markers to draw the Lazy Eight. Go up in the middle and down on the sides

In this situation it is sometimes said, "You don't really want to change or you would do it." To the observer, this seems the only plausible reason for failure. But the problem is not so simple. The unfortunate person can be locked in a "homolateral" state in which the intercommunication of the two brain hemispheres is shut down or short circuited. The more this person tries, the more difficult it actually does get. The "try" hemisphere (usually but not always the left) is working hard detailing and organizing, but the "reflex" hemisphere (usually but not always the right) is shut off from the action.

A person may be "homolateral" for certain situations or actions and not others, often in response to childhood trauma and experience. One might be well integrated as a skier and homolateral as a cook, or good at writing but poor at sports. Lost skills are re-integrated with this process.

Usually this method is taught using a biofeedback system called "muscle checking." For more information on this, see the Bibliography in the back of the book. References here to Kinesiology are the beginning of a very large subject, and further study of details is highly recommended to the Polarity student.

In this exercise the "reflex" brain hemisphere is connected with a movement that uses both sides of the body at once, and we activate the "try" brain hemisphere is connected with a movement using one side only. Then the two parts are integrated for whole brain functioning.

The movement consists of "marching in place" in two particular ways, and bringing the hands together. Bringing the hands together prompts the two brain hemispheres to begin communication. The actual link is a central brain area called the corpus callosum; the hand movement represents the movement of messages back and forth across this bridge. In Polarity terms, the connection of right and left in the neutral pole (the hands) completes a circuit, inducing a similar connection in the positive pole (the brain).

In addition to movement, sound and sight are employed. For sound, the reflex (usually right) brain is activated by humming, while the try (usually left) brain is activated by counting. Many people can actually feel the difference, and can readily identify which side is active in which activity. When humming, hum on only one note. When counting, count crisply and clearly without singsong or rhythm.

The reflex brain is activated by looking up and the try brain is activated by looking down.

Method

If you are repatterning for a specific action, think of it or do it and notice how your body feels. Now "cross crawl" (opposite arm and leg moving simultaneously) and notice how that feels. Then do the "homolateral crawl" (same arm and leg) and notice how that feels. Often the cross crawl will feel more awkward when we are switched off. It requires using both brain hemispheres at once and becomes difficult when there is a lack of integration.

Now begin the actual re-patterning movements by humming, looking up and "cross crawling" in place. The "Cross Crawl" replicates a stage of crawling for young children which is critical to brain development. As you look up, look to the left, the center and the right, moving only the eyes. Find the direction that makes marching easiest. Continue looking in that direction, humming, and marching until you feel easy and natural with the movement. This is becoming your easy or "high gear."

Next, look down while counting and doing a "puppet" march, in which the same side arm and leg rise together. This is called the "Homolateral Crawl." Look down in the direction opposite that which was easy during cross crawling. Homolateral crawl until it becomes awkward or tiring. This is becoming your "low gear."

Now reach your arms out to the sides with hands open. Imagine one brain hemisphere in each hand, getting ready to come together. Slowly move the hands together until clasping, fingers interlocked, holding until you feel complete. Take your time and move however feels right for you.

A therapist can monitor the craniosacral rhythm as the hands are being held. The person will often be in a cranio-sacral stillpoint, processing for some time. Many people can feel the energy releases happening as tingles, pulses, or brain activity, and it is clear to them when they are "complete."

Finally, cross crawl and look in all directions, then homolateral crawl while looking in all directions. Then briefly cross crawl again. Always finish with the cross crawl.

Last, do some version of the original activity, and repeat the two methods of marching. Notice the difference from the beginning to "anchor" the change.

Variations

For a quick integration you can first hum, then count, and then count to a

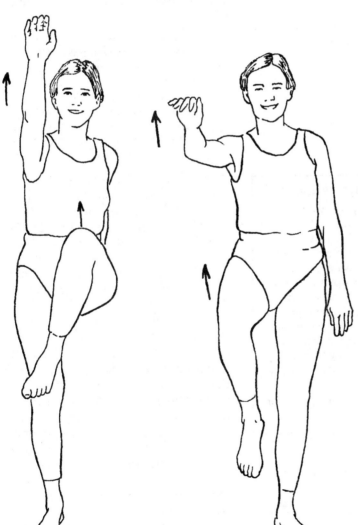

First Marching in Place
The Cross Crawl
Hum and look up

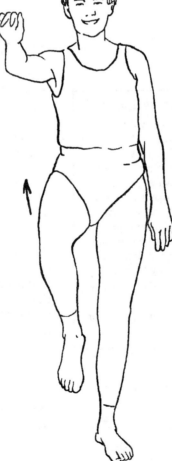

Second Marching in Place
The Homolateral Crawl
Count and look down

The Integration Metaphor

After both marching in place movements, including appropriate eye placement and sound, do the Integration Metaphor. Stretch the arms out wide in front and slowly bring the hands together until they are clasping. Hold this position until you feel "complete." Clasping the hands symbolizes renewed and integrated communication between left and right sides of the body/mind.

familiar tune (such as "Row your Boat" or "Happy Birthday"). Make sure to look different directions: up, down, right, left, center. Experiment with eyes open and eyes closed. This is fun and can be effective for easing a difficult activity. Also, in a classroom situation, it helps people feel the hidden machinery at work in consciousness.

Benefits
- Improves ability to function with "effortless-effort," ease of action especially for attitudes or activities which are chronically difficult.
- Release from feelings of blockage and obstruction.

References
Dennisons, Edu-K for Kids, p. 20.
Dennisons, Brain Gym, p. 4.

Water: Essential to Brain Balance

Being composed primarily of water, the body naturally needs water to maintain balance. While this is true on all levels, it is especially important in brain function. The electrochemical process depends on correct water levels for proper function. Often the correction to feelings of sluggishness or confusion can be as simple as drinking some water. Avoiding dehydration is especially significant under stress, and in lifestyles in which frequent drinking is difficult. For example, a closed-air office building with a fast pace of activity will be especially conducive to dehydration.

Take time to drink plenty of pure water for health benefits on all levels!

Breathing that Balances

We have never seen a disturbed person who did not have some abnormality of breathing.

--Kurtz & Prestera, The Body Reveals, p. 83.

Breathing is an essential part of energy exercise. Awareness and development of breath is an age-old component of all energy-based healing systems. Well known in yogic and martial arts practices, it is present in every tradition. We believe full and balanced breathing is a benefit for all health conditions and often the first and greatest self-help step any person can take.

While working with the S.A.G.E. project, I and others experimented with a variety of growth techniques and practices in an attempt to revitalize the minds and bodies of older men and women. Among the practices that we experimented with were relaxation training, electromyograph biofeedback, deep breathing, hatha yoga, bodymind awareness exercises, massage, Feldenkrais exercises, individual counseling, meditation, T'ai Chi, music therapy, and Gestalt Therapy. After the first year of practice and research we interviewed the participants about which of the techniques seemed to be most effective for them in the restoration of emotional energy, physical well-being, and feelings of interpersonal connectedness. The answer was almost unanimous: deep breathing.[84]

The concept of "Prana" is an important part of breathing for energy benefit. Prana (the Oriental equivalent is Ch'i or Ki) is a word for the subtle cosmic life force which rides on air, sunlight and moving water. Just as the cells need oxygen, the energy systems need prana. It is thought to be absorbed through a membrane at the top of the nasal passage,

---

84. Dychtwald, Bodymind, p. 147

hence the emphasis on inhalation through the nose. Some yogis are reputed to live on breath alone, obtaining life energy from prana only.

Therapeutic breathing can be differentiated into its three parts: inhalation, exhalation, and rest. This cycle mirrors the three stages of energy movement, or three principles. Many people breathe unevenly, over- or under- emphasizing one or another part. Thus they are habitually over-expanded or under-filled or without stillness. These characteristics of breathing can be "read" as an accurate way of self-discovery, indicating imbalance in the system. Breath indicates inner conditions on mental, emotional, and physical levels.

On the popular health issue front, many disruptive flora (such as the fungus Candida Albicans) are anaerobic, thriving without oxygen. As we oxygenate the body through deep inhalation, these make way for healthier flora. Oxygen is also needed for the chemical reaction required to burn fat or use energy properly. For weight loss, this is accomplished by aerobic exercise: deep and full breathing supports such a program.

Exhalation is equally important, if more subtle. It is the essential elimination of cellular waste. Exhalation is associated with the critical emotional function of letting go, an eventual goal (after first facing the pain) in the recovery from emotional trauma. More people seem to have trouble with exhalation than inhalation, perhaps due to the materialistic nature of modern times: we live in a time in which Yang qualities are glorified, and Yin is poorly understood and underappreciated.

After the exhale is a moment of rest. In our accelerated lives, this rest point is sometimes forgotten. This indicates a loss of neutrality and stillness emotionally, characteristic in a person "caught up" in busy activities with "no time" to contemplate new or deeper meanings. This is also found in people with childhood trauma of such severity as to create "disassociation" of the mind, emotions, and body from each other. Locked in to habitual patterns of reaction to the trauma, it is difficult to rest or be neutral.

Energy exercises offer a general opportunity to become more aware of breathing, and to practice full, balanced breathing using the whole body. In addition, several specific breathing exercises are offered here.

64. Inhale 2, Hold 8, Exhale 4

This is a stimulating, oxygenating breath. Take the time for a "breathing break." Sit, lie or stand in a comfortable posture in a place where the air is the freshest available. Inhale strongly and deeply to a slow count of 2. Hold for a count of 8. Exhale fully for a count of 4. Repeat five to ten times. Slow exhalation is relaxing, strong exhalation is stimulating.

Reference

Robbins, Unlimited Power, p. 171.

65. Belly Breathing

This is a relaxing and soothing breath. Rest the hands on the abdomen. Inhale slowly and deeply, feeling the belly fill up like a balloon. As you exhale, purse your lips slightly and breathe out in short little puffs like you're keeping a feather in the air. Feel the rhythm of the belly softly rising and falling. To take the air deeper, arch your back after inhaling.

References:

Dennisons, Brain Gym, p. 12.
Barhydt, Self-Help for Stress and Pain, p. 43.
Lowens, The Way to Vibrant Health, p. 99.

66. Watch Your Breath

This technique brings relaxation through contemplation. Find a comfortable position and close the eyes. Concentrate on the breath, without any intention of changing it in any way. "Watch" what it does. It will adjust without conscious effort.

67. Alternate Nostril Breathing

This is a yogic breathing exercise which facilitates balance of the right and the left nostrils, brain hemispheres, and sympathetic and parasympathetic nervous systems. During the day we normally switch breathing for time periods (when healthy, every 50 minutes to 2 hours), so that one nostril and then the other predominates. The right (Yang side) nostril is activating in its effect and the left (Yin side) nostril is relaxing.

Breathe and "watch" the breath. Determine which nostril you are currently using. Next, purposefully alternate nostrils by using the thumb and forefinger to close off one nostril and then the other by pressing just above the flared portion of the nostril. Close off the right nostril with the thumb. Inhale and then exhale through the left nostril. Switch so the forefinger is closing off the left nostril. Inhale and exhale through the right nostril. Continue this process and notice the effects.

This exercise can take some time to perfect. While it sounds simple, it is subtle and profound. Do it daily for a week, to develop sensitivity and skill.

Benefits
• Re-establishes balanced breathing.
• Concentrates attention.

Reference
Stone, The Mystic Bible, p. 114.

Elimination functions of Each Element	
Earth	Bowels
Water	Urine
Fire	Sweat
Air	CO2
Ether	Expression

Exercises for Elimination

Inevitably, exercise programs and elimination programs overlap. In our progress toward better energy and vitality, increased function of the elimination systems is very significant. There are five systems of elimination, one for each of the five elements or chakras: earth/bowels, water/urine and lymph, fire/sweat, air/carbon dioxide exhalation, and ether/expression of feelings. Lack of function of any of these will eventually be fatal, and declining health is accompanied by difficulty in the appropriate zone. Exercise can play a part in all of these areas, with fire and air the most obvious: any physical activity will increase perspiration and breathing rate.

Diet

A brief statement on diet is appropriate here. There are two approaches to take when improving elimination functions: enhancing removal, and reducing the toxicity of material taken in. Both are important. For the second approach, we advocate a lacto-vegetarian or vegan diet, in keeping with Dr. Stone's teaching:

> The proteins of flesh meats and eggs have many by-products in them, such as... wastes of the animal system. These must be eliminated in order to maintain health.[85]

There are many good reasons to be a vegetarian: our favorite books on the subject are Robbins' Diet for a New America and McDougall's The McDougall Plan.

Dr. Stone taught extensively on using the vegetarian diet for specific purposes. He described two sub-categories of vegetarian eating, the "Health Building" and

---

85. Stone, Polarity Therapy Vol. I, Appendix, p.115.

"Purifying" Diets. For elimination and cleansing, the Purifying diet, consisting of raw and cooked vegetables or fruit (minimizing protein, starch, and oil and avoiding salt and sugar altogether) has been proven to be effective. Dr. Stone also recommended an orange juice/olive oil "Liverflush" followed by an herb tea formula, which has since been called PolariTea, to complete the cleansing program. Details for these dietary strategies are given in Health Building and in the Murrieta Vegetarian Cookbook.

Deep Bodywork

There is a direct link between deep pressure on the body and elimination. This was discussed earlier in the context of "Touches that Balance." Each Principle has a corresponding touch: light and balancing for Air, vigorous and stimulating for Fire, deep and changing for Water. Elimination is a primary function of the Water Principle, and deep "Tamasic" touch amplifies and stimulates this, the Yin part of the energy system promoting elimination on all levels.

The Box
This shows a simple way to create a Box at home, with a 4x4 post and a doorway.

68. The Box

Dr. Stone used "the Box" as a way to put deep pressure on the feet. As we discussed in "Touches that Balance" in noting the predominance of Yin therapy, energy tends to get "stuck" in this distant area. Energy is able to go out, but unable to get back. The pelvis and the feet, as the "negative poles" of the torso and the whole body, respectively, are the locations of this tendency to become fixed. In using the box, we forcibly "soften" this dense energy field, simultaneously engaging shoulders (via the muscular activity of the hand support) and torso (by moving in various positions). Since all parts of the body have reflexes in the feet, the Box can be used to facilitate elimination and change in any of the five elemental zones.

To create a box, an edge and a hand support are needed. The edge should have a slightly rounded corner, without danger of splinters, about 4 to 8 inches above the floor. This can be a framed box of wood, the edge of a stair, or a large timber. The hand support can be a bar fastened to the wall, a staircase bannister, a door handle or the edges of a door frame, a stout broom handle wider than the doorway, etc.

Method

To use the box, step on the edge and experiment with different postures: leaning back, squatting, shifting from side to side, etc. Breathe deeply and make sound. This can be painful, and each individual has to set his or her own pace. If the feet are found to be very rigid and sore, do the Box or something like it daily.

Benefits

- Deep pressure is applied on the feet, while colon reflexes in wrists, calves and neck are simultaneously activated.
- Use the Box when you want changes to occur on any level.

References

Stone, Health Building, p. 167.
Lowens, The Way to Vibrant Health, p. 76.

Earth Elimination Exercises

Exercise is only part of the methods available for improving elimination for the Earth Element. Herbal programs, the use of psyllium as a bulking agent, the drinking of adequate amounts of water, avoiding animal foods, and cultivating an attitude of relaxation and "letting go" are all worthy of mention. Gray's Colon Health Handbook is highly recommended.

Squatting

The Squat is a key defense against colon problems, not only for its already-described value as an exercise. The topic of posture during defecation has been discussed by many authors, who invariably struggle against the indelicacy of the subject and people's reluctance to discuss, much less change, such intimate personal habits. The modern toilet has been identified with a host of modern health problems, such as a malfunctioning ileocecal valve (one study estimated this at 80% of the population)[86] constricted colon (constipation), autointoxication, prolapsis of organs, swelling of the abdomen, and several degenerative diseases including cancer.

This is not a new debate: a line of brave doctors has preached the same message throughout the century, to no avail. In recent years, Dr. Welles of San Diego has taken up the campaign, including designing and selling devices to facilitate squatting during defecation and in exercise.

An agile person can squat on an existing conventional toilet, while others can design or acquire appropriate fixtures (platform, hand rails, etc.) for most frequently used facilities. If squatting is impossible, one can lift up one or both feet to the seat while still seated. If one foot is used, the left (descending colon side) is recommended, to support the abdominal wall. An easier alternative is to have a low bench next to the toilet to hold the foot somewhat raised.

69. Skin Brushing

Five minutes per day of skin brushing is easily worth 30 minutes of vigorous physical exercise in this respect [colon therapy].

--Gray, The Colon Health Handbook, p. 23.

The interrelationship of skin, colon and lymphatic system is a complex subject, whether considered in terms of orthodox anatomy or energy theory.[87]

Let it suffice to say that skin brushing, if done regularly, is a profoundly beneficial exercise. It activates the colon, assists in the discharge of old fecal matter, accelerates the flow and elimination of lymphatic fluid, and imparts a lustrous tone to the entire body.

At home, use a long-handled (so the back can be reached) natural hair brush to stroke the bare skin evenly for about 3 to 5 minutes each day. The skin and brush should be dry, and a systematic, one-directional movement should be used. Go from the extremities toward the abdomen. Brush up the legs, then up the arms, then down the torso, etc. "Sweep" all surfaces except the face.

---

86. Welles, "The Hidden Crime of the Porcelain Throne," p. 1.

87. Gray, The Colon Health Handbook, p. 20. "It is the author's belief that the colon is the principal organ through which mucoid matter from the lymph is eliminated, even though this idea would be quite new in orthodox medical circles." (p. 20).

In Energy theory, the relationship is strongly expressed. The colon and skin are linked as functions of Air and Earth: the colon is the neutral pole of the Air Principle and the Earth Element, and skin is a combination of Air and Earth Elements. The lymphatic system and colon have similar energy links: lymph is the negative pole of the Water Principle which is based in the pelvis with the colon, all within the negative pole of the torso.

Another recommended reference for colon health is Jensen's Tissue Cleansing through Bowel Management.

70. Colon Reflexes

There are several reflexology opportunities to stimulate the colon. The colon has overlapping relationships, primarily the Air Principle (Chest-Colon-Calves) and Earth Element (Neck-Bowels-Knees). The most frequently cited colon reflexes in Polarity Therapy are the muscles of the calves, and the feet (in the center area on the bottom, and between the fourth and fifth toes on the top and bottom).

Using the fists to exercise the calf muscle is described on page 34. In addition, calf lengthening (page 100) has a toning colon effect. Squatting is especially beneficial for the colon, bringing chest-colon-calves (the three poles of the Air Principle) into closest possible proximity for efficient energy movement and amplification.

For the feet, gentle or deep rubbing has a stimulating effect. Press along the "web" of the foot between the toes, holding on sore spots. For the bottom of the foot, more pressure can be created by standing on the edge of a board (see The Box, preceding page), book, bottle, can, or other object (a wooden "footsie roller" is made commercially for the purpose).

Another way to press the feet is to sit in a kneeling position, with buttocks back on the heels. Use the knuckles to press in on the calves, then continue down into the foot. The colon reflex area follows the main arch, just below the ball of the foot. Start on the right foot and press up to the outside arch area, then across the foot to the arch instep. Continue on the left foot from instep to outside of foot and down. This path mirrors the ascending, transverse and descending path of the colon.

Dr. Stone also mentions stimulation of the tongue as a colon reflex. Like the ear, the tongue is a complex combination of reflexes for the whole torso. This stimulation can be done by pressing the tongue firmly in all directions, by creating suction, by "scraping" with the teeth (especially the sides of the tongue) or a device made for the purpose, by contact with a tongue depressor, and other means.

Benefits
• Stimulates colon.
• General revitalization for the whole body: colon function has a central significance in all systems. Some authors (Gray, Jensen) have said colon distress is a factor in all degenerative disease.

References
Stone, Polarity Therapy Vol. I, Book 1, pp. 48-49, Book 2, pp. 17, 81-82.
Stone, Polarity Therapy Vol. II, pp 150-151, 183-184, 199, 201.

71. Valve Tapping

A rhythmic tapping with the fingertips at the "corners" of the colon is effective for general relaxation and for stimulating peristalsis and colon valve function. This technique was shown to one of our editors by an Ayurvedic doctor in India.

Method

Tap with light or medium pressure over the ileocecal valve on the right and over the sigmoid valve on the left. These are located on either side of the front abdomen, two inches below and to either side of the navel. Take your time and breathe deeply during the tapping. Afterwards, relax and hold the spot lightly with one hand, while touching the other side with the other hand as a balance.

Related Exercises
Self Organ Drain, p. 38.

Massage the colon with small circular contacts, from right to left following the colon. This direct contact should not be used if there is pain or degenerative disease in the abdomen.

Water Elimination Exercises

The water system responds to healthful liquids, and to movement. Many people are dehydrated, especially in the dry environments of forced air office buildings. Water, herb tea, and juices should always be kept nearby for refreshment, using up to two quarts of water each day for a cleansing program. Sugared, caffeinated or alcoholic beverages supply "polluted" water: the water is used, but unhealthy side effects are experienced.

Movement is the primary mechanical way that the lymphatic system takes waste materials away from the cells. The lymph also receives some pumping action from its duct system. Dr. Stone makes the larger point that circulation of fluids in the body originates in the deep energy currents, the pulsation of expansion and contraction. Mechanical pumps, including the heart, lymphatic ducts, peristalsis and one-way valves, etc. are secondary reflections of pulsating energy, the subtle basis of all pumping action.

72. Rebounding

Of all possible ways of movement, rebounding stands out as the most beneficial for the lymphatic system. Rebounding is light or vigorous jumping on a small trampoline. Its efficiency is due to the up and down motion, in which a miniature weightlessness/gravity-force cycle is created. At the top of the jump, upward momentum balances downward gravity, and a split second of artificial weightlessness is achieved. At this moment, a minuscule de-pressurized expansion occurs throughout the body.

At the bottom of the cycle, momentum and gravity are combined against the resistance of the bouncing surface to create a slight "G-force" situation, causing minute pressurized contraction throughout the body. Thus rebounding facilitates the expansion and contraction of all systems, creating cellular "breathing" to assist drainage of waste from cells, and movement of liquids through lymphatic channels.

The energy exercise classroom will benefit by having a few rebounders, with one or two located by a secure rail for older people to hold while they bounce.

Even the slightest movement is beneficial, improving vitality and circulation without excessive shock to the joints.

Fire Elimination

Sweat is the goal here, so active movement is the primary method. Other alternatives are steam rooms and saunas, and swimming or exercising in medium- or warmer temperature water. We are partial to natural hot springs for this purpose. Saunas are more effective because more sweat is eliminated in the dry environment.

It has been found, incidentally, that exercising in water does not burn fat effectively and is a lower priority method of exercise if weight loss is a primary goal.

Air Elimination

This function is covered in the section on breathing, beginning on page 92. Emphasis is on the exhale, and on an attitude of "letting go."

Ether Elimination

The Ether Center at the throat is the location of self-expression, discrimination, longing and grief. These are all goals of many therapy systems. "Emotional constipation" of not being able to speak one's feelings, whether for internal or external reasons, is a serious prelude to health problems.

Etheric elimination means expression and making sound. The Lion Roar (page 38) and Ha Breath (page 40) are ideal for this.

Music

Music has its own section, on page 84. For purposes of elimination, music can assist in the evocation of feelings, provide a forum for expression (choral singing is especially enjoyable, and a part of holidays and religious events for good reasons from an energy perspective), and encourage liberating movement.

Movement

Certain kinds of movement can also be effective:

Rhythmic expressions of song and dance, which use all the bodily forces and muscles for expression, free the emotions by naturally liberating the energy blocks, suppressions, frustrations and stagnations.[87]

---

87. Stone, Health Building, p. 108

<table>
<tr><td>

Lengthening

</td></tr>
</table>

These simple lengthening exercises are for specific muscle release. They make a good preparation for some of the more complex postures, and can be used with bodywork to accomplish with leverage that which would be hard to do with pressure. Re-read the introduction to lengthening at the beginning of the book (page 17). Remember never to strain or bounce into these postures. Hold, at the "edge of release," and wait for the muscle to let go on its own and reset at a new length. It is very useful to know the location (including origin, insertion point, and tendons) of each specific muscle, and the desired direction of lengthening.

Most people have one or two particular muscles that are tighter than the others. You can figure out which muscles among the following are most important for you, and help create a habit of working on those one or two lengthening postures. If the worst case is improved, all the others (and the whole body) will benefit.

73. Inner Thigh Lengthening

The origin of the inner thigh muscle is in front of the pubic bone. The insertion is along the thigh, beginning just below the hip and going down to just below the knee on the inside of the lower leg.

Method

Start with the feet spread wider than shoulder width. Decide which leg will be straightened for lengthening. Keep the foot of this leg turned out to avoid straining the inner knee ligament. Place the hands on the thigh above the knee of the opposite leg. Shift the hips toward the bent leg and as you bend into that knee you will feel the inner thigh lengthening on the opposite straight leg. Go to a point of tension that feels like it will release gently. Wait in this position until the muscles let go and reset. Then, bend further for another level of release or come out of the posture. Take a moment to quietly experience the new lengthening.

74. Calf Lengthening I

The soleus is a part of the calf muscle, deeper and inside the gastrocnemius. The origin is just below the inner knee on the back of the leg and the insertion is behind the ankle at the heel.

Method

Stand with the feet in a medium-length stride, one foot forward and the other foot back, feet facing straight forward. Bend slowly into both knees and focus on the area of the origin and insertion of the soleus in the back leg. Feel the tension of the lengthening in the Achilles tendon. Stop at the "edge of release" and hold, waiting for the muscle to let go and reset. Repeat with a deeper bend for further lengthening or come to standing and experience the new length in the calf.

75. Calf Lengthening II

The origin of the gastrocnemius muscle is on the back of the leg just above the knee, and the insertion is in the middle of the back of the heel. This is the large double bellied muscle of the calves which lifts the heel in walking. It is also the bottom of the "tendon guard reflex," the body's instinctive response to stress. Wise runners lengthen here before starting.

Method

Place the feet in a long stride with one foot forward and one foot back. Place the hands on the thigh of the forward leg and lean over the front knee, keeping the back flat and maintaining balance as you go. Spread the feet as far as needed to keep a

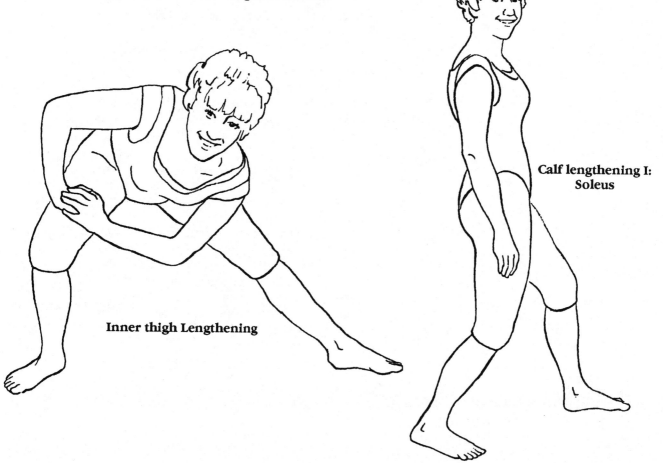

Inner thigh Lengthening

**Calf lengthening I:
Soleus**

tension in the back calf that is on the "edge of release." Wait for the muscles to "let go" to a new length. Then, lean even more or push the back heel further down for more release, or come to standing and do the opposite leg. When complete, come to standing and take a moment to experience the new feeling of length.

76. Hamstring Lengthening

These muscles are located in the thigh. The origin is at the lowest part of the hip bone and the insertion is at the top of the lower leg just below the back of the knee.

This muscle is commonly tight due to the customs of sitting in chairs and rarely walking barefoot. It is also part of the "tendon guard reflex," in which the back side of the body tightens in response to stress. In a high-stress lifestyle, this area can become permanently over-tightened. This position, which has similarities to and can be done with the Pyramid, is a beneficial daily routine first thing in the morning.

Method

Stand with the legs more than shoulder width apart. Place the hands on the thighs just above the knees. KEEP THE BACK FLAT as you lean forward. Push with the hands and keep lifting the buttocks toward the ceiling-- this separates the origin and insertion points. Notice the tension being created in the back of the upper thighs. Go to the edge of release and wait for the muscles to let go and reset. Push more for further release. When done, come to standing and feel this new hamstring length. Notice how overall posture has been affected.

77. Psoas Lengthening

The psoas is a major structural muscle; its origin runs along the spine from the vertebra at the lowest ribs (12th thoracic) through all the vertebrae of the

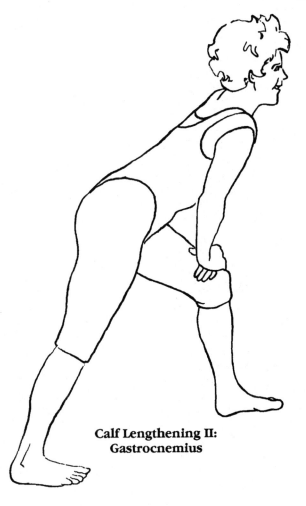

Calf Lengthening II: Gastrocnemius

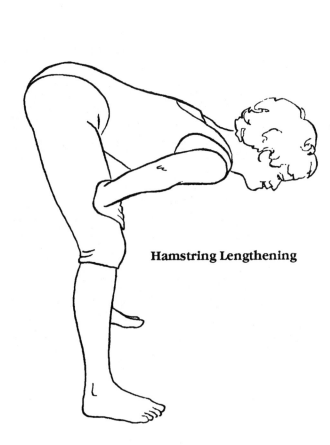

Hamstring Lengthening

curve of the lower back (lumbar vertebrae). The insertion is in the front, on the inside of the upper thigh bone on a level with the pubic bone. This is the muscle used to lift the leg in walking. This lengthening can be used to accompany five pointed star Polarity Therapy techniques.

Because this muscles goes from the front (of the thigh) to the back, tightness here forces a curve (lordosis) in the lower back. This tips the pelvis to make the shortest possible distance from front to back. Lengthening the psoas can thus release the lower back and allow the pelvis to return to proper alignment.

Method

Stand with the feet in a stride position, one foot in front, one foot in back, both feet facing forward. Allow both knees to bend and the back heel to lift, thrusting the pelvis forward and keeping the back straight. Focus on the front inner thigh area. Feel the tension reaching into the psoas.

If you do not feel the tension in the front of the pelvis, spread the feet further apart. Make sure the pelvis is thrust forward by pulling the navel in toward the back and if necessary squeezing the buttocks. Contraction in back creates extension in front.

Hold at the edge of release until the muscle releases and resets. When done, stand up and feel this new openness.

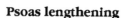

Psoas lengthening

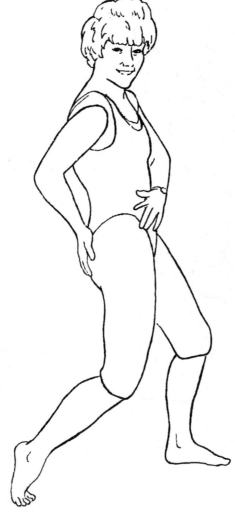

Part Three
Body Reading

"A person's past is his body."

--Lowen, Bioenergetics, p. 34.

"To every emotional state corresponds a personal conditioned pattern of muscular contraction, without which it [the emotional state] has no existence."

--Feldenkrais, Body and Mature Behavior, p. 93.

"Now we know that the mind and body are like parallel universes. Anything that happens in the mental universe must leave tracks in the physical one. As you see it right now, your body is the physical picture, in 3-D, of what you are thinking."

--Chopra, Quantum Healing, p. 69.

Appreciating the link between physical, emotional, and mental levels of our being is absolutely essential to understanding the energy approach to health. This section presents Polarity Therapy's approach to making the link direct and tangible.

For most people, pain is felt physically. Some are sensitive to emotional pain, but it is more subtle, as we do not have the sensory equipment to perceive it so directly. Mental pain is most subtle of all: while many may feel vague distress, only a few can recognize specifically when an unrealistic expectation or unworkable attitude is causing problems. We feel a splinter in the finger quite directly; an emotional "splinter" or hurt feelings, or a flaw in the mental blueprint, is much more difficult to perceive.

Body reading is a primary tool for the energy practitioner. It provides information to serve many purposes, from identifying current and future health event probabilities, to linking the obvious symptom (in the physical body) with the subtle cause (in the emotions and mental patterns). The whole notion of body reading is a revolutionary idea in the health field,

and often difficult for the conventional practitioner to accept.

Giving a physical foundation for psychiatry... was also a new concept.[88]

The first premise... is to assume that all movements of the body have meaning... I find this... most difficult to accept.[89]

In our experience, bodyreading is best used as a gentle indicator, rather than hard fact, and its goal primarily the prompting of self-understanding, not the diagnosis of disease. In the Orient, body reading has a far more elevated place. Virtually all health systems from the East use some form of body reading: pulse diagnosis, physiognomy (reading the face), analysis of the eye, the ear, breath, voice quality, the torso, the hands and feet. In some cases these are very difficult for the Westerner to penetrate: Chinese pulse diagnosis in particular requires an intuitive sensitivity that eludes most western practitioners. Dr. Stone mentions that ancient

---

88. Stone, Polarity Therapy Vol. I, Book 1, p. 8.

89. Fast, Body Language, p. 151. This was one of the first popular works on the subject.

Chinese pulse diagnosis distinguished over 600 different pulse qualities, far too complex for the newcomer to find useful.

> The Chinese physician can detect imbalances in meridians by feeling the pulses, but this is a sensitive touch, and it may take 10 to 20 years to develop proficiency with it.[90]

Dr. Stone's Polarity Therapy made extensive use of bodyreading, and in a way that is relatively easy to understand.[91] His system is based on the Ayurvedic system of India, although it is generally confirmed and supported by other systems which have made it to the West, such as Macrobiotics and Shiatsu.

There is a problem in the fact that bodyreading systems and techniques from the Orient do not necessarily agree entirely with each other. This makes the study of body reading less tidy, and less valid for some: theoretically, if the information was accurate, all systems would say exactly the same thing, which they do not. Our recommendation is to proceed with caution and sincere curiosity, using experience as the primary validating procedure and emphasizing open-minded sensitivity in applying abstract ideas to individual cases.

> Information does not become knowledge unless it has relevance to experience...Knowledge becomes understanding when it is coupled with feeling."[92]

90. Thie, Touch for Health, p. 17. He continues: "Touch for Health uses muscle testing to detect these same imbalances, taking advantage of the body's own wisdom to let us know what's going on." Muscle testing is a significant new addition to the art of body reading.

91. The Polarity model offers an umbrella to unify many different systems, and an answer for the problems faced by earlier Western commentators on body reading. "What must be found is one common system that will work for all cultures and all ethnic groups." (Fast, Body Language, p. 151).

92. Lowen, Bioenergetics, p. 62.

The Energy practitioner is like a detective, searching for clues which could explain events. There are many sources for clues, and body reading is one of the best.

Replicated Patterns

The basis for Polarity body reading is thinking of the different areas (face, torso, hands, feet) as replicated patterns of a single design. The key to the design is the arrangement of energy zones, centers and fields along the spine, with their increasingly dense vibrations, located in a vertical order. This is the Caduceus (see page 11). We have discussed this idea of repeating patterns earlier with Babbit's Atom (p.12) and Reflexology.

What do we look for when beginning body reading from a Polarity perspective? There are two groups of questions for the beginner to ask: comparison of symmetries, to assess Three Principles (left/right, top/bottom, and back/front), and analysis of horizontal-zones (of marks, swellings, lines or deviations from the norm), to assess the Five Elements. More advanced practitioners will look for more subtle cues, including more sophisticated views of top/bottom symmetry, front/back balance, posture (especially hips and shoulders) and others.

The two beginning questions (comparison of symmetries, location of marks) can be applied to any part of the body, but the face, torso and feet seem to be most immediately useful. In this section, we will discuss the face and torso; body reading for the feet has its own section, immediately following.

Symmetry

Very few people have symmetrical bodies. One side will be smaller, as measured from the bottom of the eye to the corner of the mouth, or from shoulder to hip. The short side shows where tension originates, and more subtly, the aspect of experience that causes more stress. The right side suggests the condition of the Yang energy, the ease of Yang (creative, responsible, outgoing, logical, giving direction)

25 Combinations: Weaving the Body with the Five Elements
Source: Stone, Polarity Therapy Vol. II, p. 226-227.

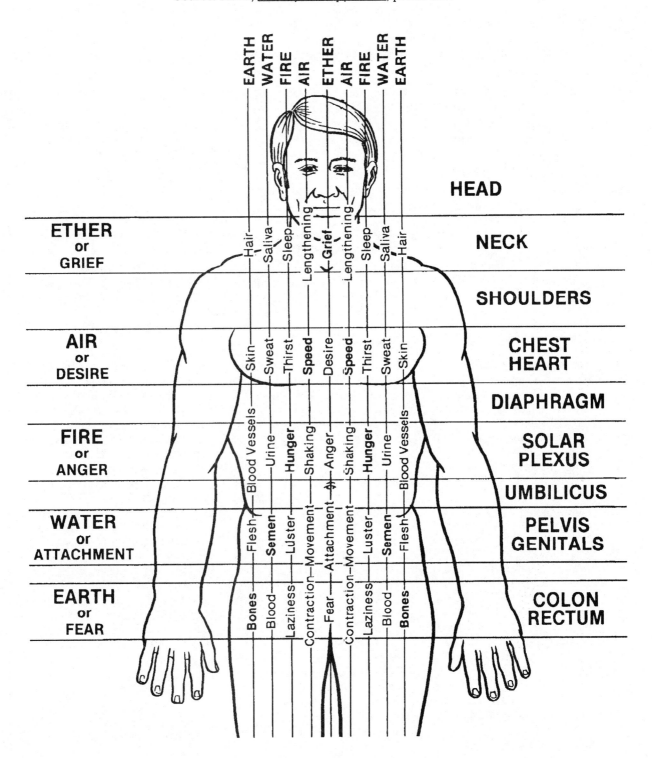

This chart is a summary of Dr. Stone's "Enquiry into the Gross Body" charts, which in turn came from ancient India. The center line shows the emotions for each elemental zone. This is the basis for Polarity Therapy's linking of body and emotions, which is a major part of body reading.

for the individual, and the contribution of the father. The left side indicates the ease of Yin experience (receptive, yielding, intuitive, listening) for the person, and the contribution of the mother.[93] Which side is contracted? That will be the aspect of life and parental mind-pattern of greatest stress.

Horizontal Energy Zones

Second, survey the area for marks and distortions. Which zone is disproportionately expanded or contracted? Where are the lines and bumps, how is makeup used, where are scars or injuries? Into

which of the five horizontal zones do these fall? According to our theory, these are not accidental, but in keeping with the overall subtle energy field of the individual.

This last statement is controversial for some, and requires a digression. Is there

---

[93] "...the left is the side with which we take things in. It is receptive. The right side is outgoing, expressive, the side with which we act." (Kurtz and Prestera, The Body Reveals, p. 47). Dr. Stone (Polarity Therapy, Vol. 1, Book 3, p. 29) and Dychtwald (Bodymind, p. 27) both agree with this.

Medical Politics

"The two medicines do not have to be antagonists, but for the moment they clearly face in opposite directions."
--Chopra, Quantum Healing, p. 141.

"It is unfortunate that mainstream medicine still acts as if it believes the Newtonian concepts, that have been proven to be an inaccurate model for fifty years, are real."
--Norman Cousins, quoted in Gerber's Vibrational Medicine, p. 27.

Energy-based health systems are often considered antithetical to conventional western medicine. In body reading, where we attempt to directly link physical qualities with emotional/mental factors, this potential conflict is brought to center stage, because the idea is so alien to the mechanical model.

The conventional separation of body from emotions and mind is understandable because of the difficulty and complexity of working with such subtle factors. There is a long history of the development of treatments for the physical level in the west, but only a short history for emotional or mental treatment, usually confined to emergency care based on chemical medication. Before Freud, there were few pioneers in the field, and the succeeding generation struggled against a variety of restraints.

Only in the last thirty years has the field expanded rapidly, to eventually begin to reach the common man. There is a grass roots movement bringing these

ideas into common knowledge, often entirely bypassing the conventional system. A sign of this is the popularity of the many "12 Step" programs. Alcoholics Anonymous and its offspring deserve great credit for this.

Physical events requiring medical attention receive treatment aimed primarily at saving the patient from life-threatening symptoms, and relieving pain. These are vital and worthy goals, essential to the quality of life. We are the beneficiaries of the removal of major diseases from our cultural landscape, achieved by this system.

The practitioner of the energy approach can supplement conventional care by helping a person look at the subtle issues involved in disease. No amount of reflexology, exercise or self-understanding will save a person from acute appendicitis; but once saved by drugs and surgery, a follow-up wholistic program of health enhancement will invariably be beneficial. The energy practitioner can support emer-

gency health providers by helping people understand themselves better, helping them see how health problems often originate in more subtle sources relating to diet, lifestyle, emotional experience or mental attitude.

Sadly, these preventative dimensions of public health have been neglected by modern medicine for a variety of reasons. At a time of spiralling health care costs, the very inexpensive, self-regulated techniques of the energy approach could be a great asset to national well-being.

We advocate a cooperative attitude between these two branches of the health care system. Juhan makes an eloquent plea for such cooperation (Job's Body, p. 56).

Western medicine, which has largely to do with the diagnosis of disease and severe malfunction, knows precious little about exercise and other preventative systems. It is neither useless nor unintelligent, only incomplete.
-Horwitz, T'ai Chi Ch'uan, p. 18.

such a thing as a true "accident" or random event? Commonly used language suggests that there is, but deeper consideration suggests not.

> Life is from within out. External trauma and effects are in the fields of the external nature, of mechanical skill and principles. But the within rules the without. All external happenings are precipitated by unperceived, internal (mental-emotional) causes.[94]

It is a central premise of this system that all events have a place in the cosmic plan. From our limited perspective we cannot ever see or comprehend the whole picture. Our quest is to discover those parts and patterns which can be known, and second, to make use of information gathered to increase knowledge and harmony. So with body reading, we assume that all shapes, lines, and events have a significance, even though we are always limited in the degree to which this significance may be understood.

---

94. Stone, <u>Polarity Therapy Vol. I</u>, Book 3, p. 35.

How the Body tells the Truth

A neurophysiological explanation of the truthfulness of body language is given by Stokes and Whiteside in <u>One Brain</u>. Two subdivisions of the brain are noted: between "dominant" and "alternate" halves (a left/right distinction) and between "conscious associational thinking" (CAT) and "common integrative areas" (CIA) (a front/back distinction). Generally, language skills reside in the dominant half, and physical expression resides in the alternate half. The frontal CAT area holds newly-acquired knowledge, while the rear CIA holds survival skills gained earlier in the development of the species. The CIA is located in the dominant brain; the CAT is found in both left and right halves.

The CAT has the ability to control all neurological activity. However, under stress we characteristically "retreat" from the more advanced front CAT area to the survival-oriented, risk-avoiding back CIA zone. With its strong link to the dominant verbal side, the CIA generates the words we use under stress. These words will tend to reflect an association of current sensation with unconscious remembered experience, which has been strongly modulated by expectations and social customs. So for people who are under stress, words tend to express what they think they should say (their habitual pain-avoidance strategies) rather than how they actually feel.

Meanwhile the physical expression function in the alternate brain freely responds to the current sensation directly and independently. Thus the body language message will be simpler, clearer, and more present-oriented than the verbal message, and much more likely to reflect true feelings as opposed to censored verbal interpretations generated by the CIA.

A convincing case has been made by Pelletier showing how modern man is <u>always</u> under stress. The first response of the human system to stress is in the sympathetic nervous system, the "fight or flight" options. However, neither of these is a viable alternative for most modern stressors; we cannot attack <u>or</u> flee from the irritating boss, traffic jam, or stack of bills. This lack of discharge of its programmed response sets up "a prolonged and unabated stress response"[95] by the sympathetic nervous system, leading eventually to exhaustion or to an explosive, hysterical response such as violence and addiction to stress and intensity. Pelletier adds a provocative thought on this a few pages later:

> It is possible that twentieth century man has designed a social and economic structure which is antipathetic to his health and psychological well-being. If this is so, can an evolutionary change help us adapt in a new version of survival of the fittest? Will the social system regulate itself when it becomes evident that its psychological complexity is affecting its members negatively? Or will man take it upon himself to scale down the proliferation of technological progress and concentrate upon a more inner-directed quest to preserve his mental and physical equilibrium?

The idea of a chronically stressful life has many implications in medicine, psychology, sociology, economics, and politics. It accounts for the dramatic effect of the sympathetic balance contacts in Polarity Therapy bodywork, and the popularity of mood-altering intoxicants and medications, which allow the system temporary (the problem is not being addressed) rest from chronic stress.

---

95. Pelletier, <u>Mind as Healer, Mind as Slayer</u>, pp. 69 and 82

Bodymind in Disease

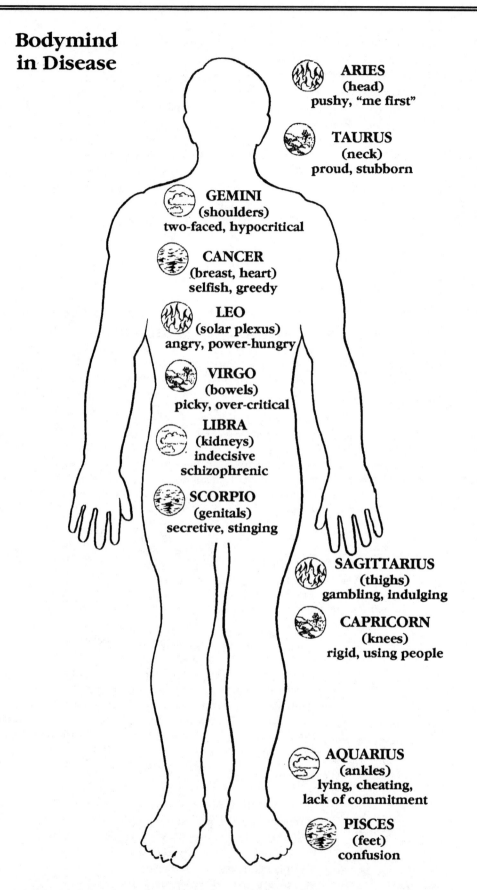

ARIES
(head)
pushy, "me first"

TAURUS
(neck)
proud, stubborn

GEMINI
(shoulders)
two-faced, hypocritical

CANCER
(breast, heart)
selfish, greedy

LEO
(solar plexus)
angry, power-hungry

VIRGO
(bowels)
picky, over-critical

LIBRA
(kidneys)
indecisive
schizophrenic

SCORPIO
(genitals)
secretive, stinging

SAGITTARIUS
(thighs)
gambling, indulging

CAPRICORN
(knees)
rigid, using people

AQUARIUS
(ankles)
lying, cheating,
lack of commitment

PISCES
(feet)
confusion

These charts use the language of Astrology to give a model for Body Reading. Each body area has characteristic qualities: distress in an area suggests distress with the linked experiences.

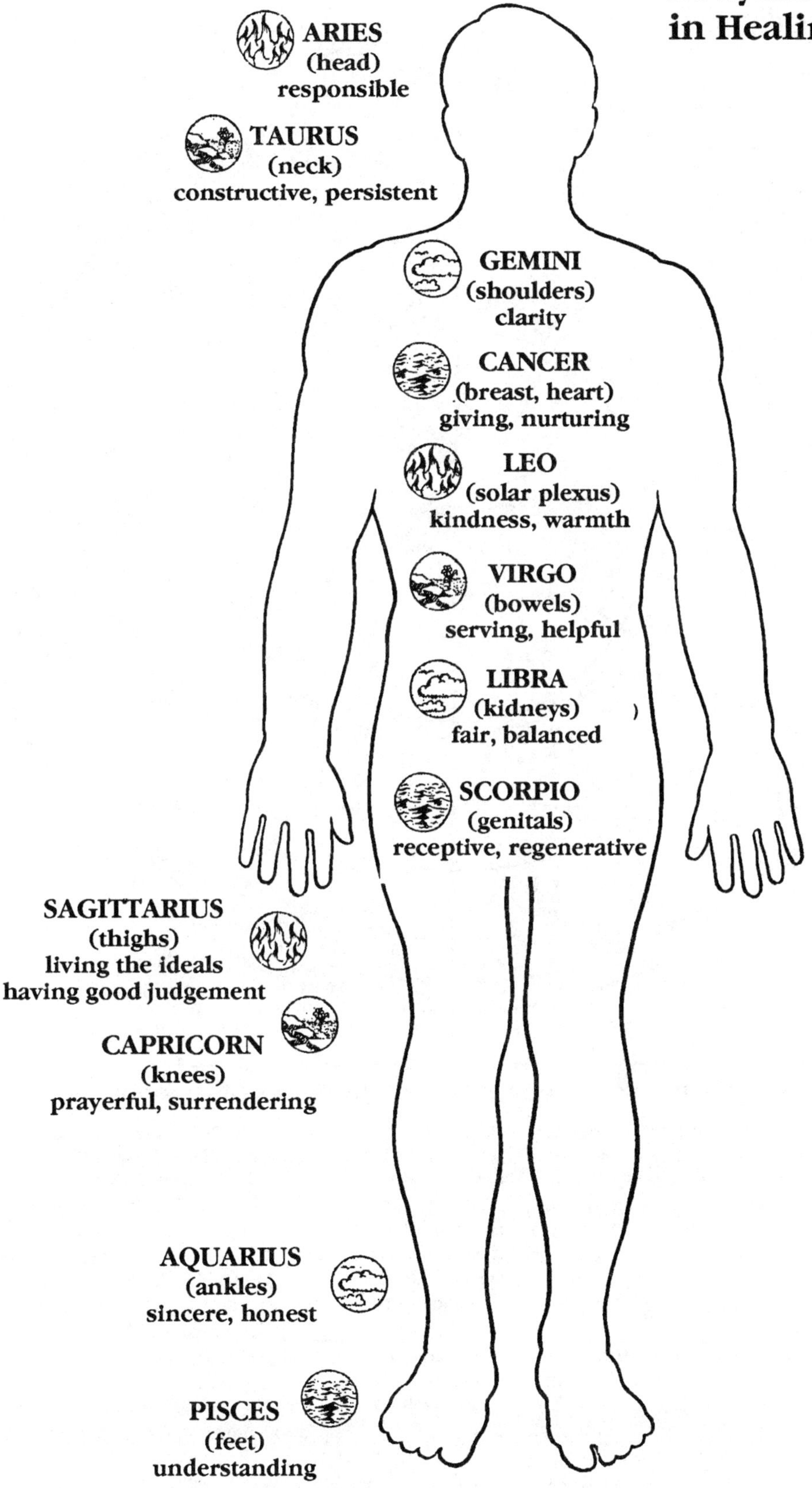

Bodymind in Healing

ARIES
(head)
responsible

TAURUS
(neck)
constructive, persistent

GEMINI
(shoulders)
clarity

CANCER
(breast, heart)
giving, nurturing

LEO
(solar plexus)
kindness, warmth

VIRGO
(bowels)
serving, helpful

LIBRA
(kidneys)
fair, balanced

SCORPIO
(genitals)
receptive, regenerative

SAGITTARIUS
(thighs)
**living the ideals
having good judgement**

CAPRICORN
(knees)
prayerful, surrendering

AQUARIUS
(ankles)
sincere, honest

PISCES
(feet)
understanding

These qualities are emotional antidotes for problems in various areas. Exercises or bodywork relating to body areas can be accompanied by mental/emotional work with the appropriate qualities.

Weaving the Body

Source: Stone, <u>Polarity Therapy Vol. I</u>,
Book 1, pp. 48-53

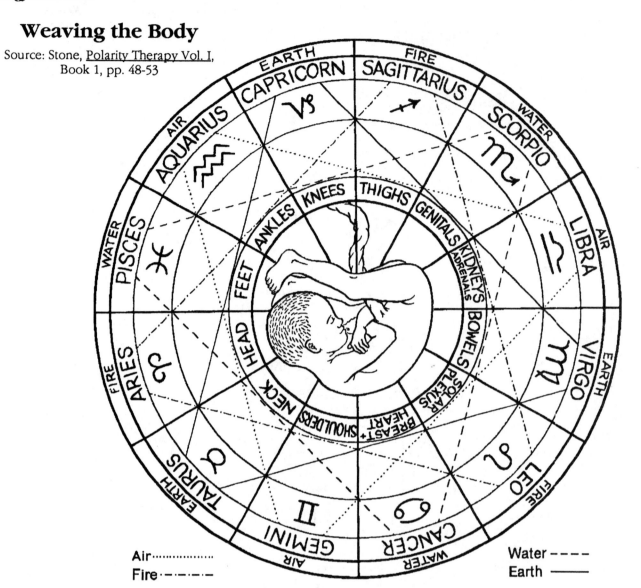

Air ....
Fire ·—·—·—·

Water — — — —
Earth ———————

The Language of Astrology: Categorizing the Subtleties of Body/Mind

On this chart and the two preceding, the language of astrology provides a convenient way to convey subtle physical, emotional and mental nuances.

Languages are filters by which the mind makes sense of input, through categorizing experience into recognizable, meaningful systems. Language has great power, the medium becoming the message. People and objects create expectations according to the language used to name and describe them.

The simplest language is yes/no, or that/not that. This divides experience by two, the smallest possible divisor. Yang/Yin is just such a language. Such a distinction has a great universality due to its simplicity. The naming of objects and events occurs on this simple yes/no level: giving something a name makes it distinct from its surroundings, "that" and "not that."

More sophisticated languages divide by larger factors: to categorize by three leads to the Three

Principles, by four leads to the four seasons, directions, and classic Elements. Twelve (Zodiac, clock, calendar) is a particularly universal divisor, since it neatly incorporates two, three and four. Astrology unifies the ideas of Yin/Yang, the Three Principles and the Four lower Elements into a single system: each sign is a unique mix of these three factors.

As examples of larger systems, ten (numbers), 26 (alphabet), 64 (<u>I Ching</u> hexagrams) show how even more complex filters have been devised to describe human experience.

There is also a quest for no division at all, or oneness. This is a state of mind associated with deep spiritual experience. At this level no language can function. Mystic traditions speak of a level of awareness beyond language in which man realizes and merges with Godness, the "Peace which passeth all understanding."

Body Reading for the Face

"Of all the parts of the body, none is so directly expressive of a person as that complex unity of structure we call a face."
--Kurtz and Prestera, The Body Reveals, p. 89

To analyze the face at an introductory level, we apply the same left/right and horizontal zones approaches. The left/right comparison may be facilitated by covering one side, then the other. Which side is contracted, as measured from corner of the mouth to the eye? Does one side convey a specific feeling more than the other? An interesting study is to use a popular magazine, one with many pictures, and apply this idea to many faces chosen randomly. Very few faces will be symmetrical, and the emotions expressed can be dramatic when one side is covered.

The horizontal zones may be viewed generally or individually. Generally, what is the overall image? Which zone seems most stressed? Stress means marks, scars, discoloration, loss of tone, creases, or other unusual signs.

For specific zones, we begin at the top. The area from the cheeks up indicates the air element, in the chest. The eyebrows reflect the shoulders and the upper cheek the breast/lung area. Dark circles under the eyes mean kidney stress, the kidneys being the neutral pole of the air element. Air is manifested emotionally as desire, including hope and ambition. Thus indicators in these areas of the face suggest desire (including hope or hopelessness) as an active source of stress.

Lower, across the nose and including the lower cheeks and the area above the mouth, is the zone for fire, in the solar plexus. The lines from the nostrils around the mouth reflect the line of the diaphragm in the center of the fire area. The nostrils and tip of the nose are heart indicators. Emotionally unbalanced or stressed fire manifests as anger or "coldness," so deep lines or a swollen nose suggest these as active emotional issues. Conversely, contraction here is a sign of constriction of power and capacity for love.

The mouth area and upper jaw area reflect the status of the water element, in the pelvis. The lips show the condition of the lower abdominal and genital area, with the upper lip related to Yang (outgoing, paternal) and lower lip related to Yin (receiving, maternal). The tip of the tongue also indicates sexuality and genital condition. These may be observed closely when bodywork or emotional process

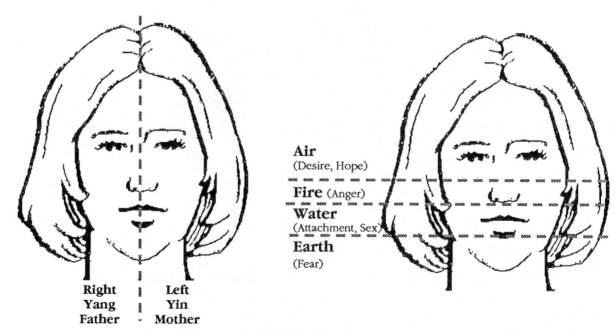

Right Yang Father   **Left Yin Mother**

Air (Desire, Hope)

Fire (Anger)

Water (Attachment, Sex)

Earth (Fear)

The Two First Questions for Face Reading:

Left/right comparison: Which side is contracted?
Horizontal zone analysis: Which zone has distortion or marks?

work is underway, to indicate activation of old emotions relating to attachment or sexuality. The lower cheeks or jowls indicate tone of the pelvic floor area. The emotion related to water is attachment or clinging, so these indicators show the degree to which attachment is a source of tension.

Identification of the lips and tip of the tongue as genital reflexes is a topic which has been described in several sources. Michio Kushi goes on to describe kissing as an unconscious electromagnetic substitute for intercourse through reflex action. Similarly, painting the lips bright colors makes sense as a use of subliminal reflexology to stimulate sexual interest. This leads into other topics, such as the interpretation of other make-up practices (blue and green on the eyes being the colors for ether and air, or loneliness and desire, red on the cheeks as a reflex to the breast, etc.), and the many behaviors based on unconscious reflex perceptions.

The earth area at the base of the spine is seen in the lower chin and jaw line. Lines and marks here suggest tension relating to fear, the emotion manifesting from the earth element. Look for marks, loss of tone, different skin color, and other cues for distress in this zone.

Putting these observations of the face together with our earlier left/right comparison, we can offer a few guesses about the individual. Which element (and therefore emotion) is indicated, and in which style or from what parent? Which areas in the torso are likely to be involved?

In bodywork and other therapy, the practitioner watches the client's face closely. Movements and gestures can be subtle and easily missed. The face reflects current-time activity and is invaluable as a window on inner experience.

As a final comment on body reading for the face, the eyes need special atten-

tion. This is outside the left/right and horizontal zone analyses, and not derived primarily from Dr. Stone's writing. Dr. Stone's commentary on the eyes identifies them as the positive poles of the Fire Principle, "to give external direction for the internal impulses."[96] More recent research has provided more information on this. Observing the eyes shows which part of the brain is activated,[97] how the person processes information, and the level of stress present.

"Sanpaku" is a Japanese term meaning "three whites," a condition in which white is visible below the iris (eye is rolled up, a Yin condition) or above the iris (eye is rolled down, a Yang condition). Either of these shows serious imbalance; extreme Sanpaku indicates danger to life (Yin being danger to self, Yang being danger to others). Sanpaku also changes with age, as the eye moves from Yang to Yin position (Yang at the start in newborns, Yin at the end in death).

Flickering or twitches of the eyes, and poor eyesight, suggest imbalance (excess or deficiency) of Yang energy. If on the right, it indicates stress relating to applying force and creativity to a situation and, more remotely, to Father. If on the left, it suggests stress relating to receiving creative energy or authority, and Mother.

---

96. Stone, Polarity Therapy Vol. I, Book 1, p. 77.

97. References for eye movement's relation to brain activity include: Robbins, Dennisons, Stokes and Whiteside. Reading the eyes is a major specialty in bodyreading, giving quick and accurate information about unconscious or hidden feelings and brain function. This area is well worth detailed exploration for energy-based health practitioners.

The field of Hypnotism has great understanding in this area. In many ways, hypnotism, generally looked down on by conventional psychology, is a grass roots psychology of great insight and knowledge and a source for such recent systems as NLP.

Body Reading for the Torso

"Reading" the language of the torso repeats the basic approach described for the face. However the torso also has additional variables including posture, breathing and expressive movements. Comparable ways of body reading exist for the face, but they are very subtle. With the torso, they become more obvious.

One of the best ways to access this information is to mimic the person being studied.

> If one assumes the bodily attitude of another person, one can sense the meaning, have the feeling of, that body expression.[98]

Twenty years later this technique would become known as "matching" in NLP, used for diagnosis and also as a way of influencing people.

The general guiding concept of looking at the right side for Yang indicators, and the left for Yin, continues to apply. In the torso, which hip is higher? Usually, the high hip indicates the side which has greater stress. Similarly, which shoulder is lower? Look along the diaphragm area for signs of contraction, swelling or rigidity. Look for scars left by accidents or surgeries. Which side are they on?

The idea of horizontal zones for each element, and of elements being associated with specific emotions, can be applied again: look at each horizontal zone and characterize its appearance with a few words. Is it expanded or contracted? What is the tone of skin and muscles? Are there unusual marks or distortions? Are there scars or injuries?

Then, refer to the "25 Combinations" chart to know what emotion relates to the area. With this information, formulate a hypothesis which combines the descriptive words with the relevant emotions, possibly also in terms of Yang (right side) or Yin (left side). You are now using the simplest level of body reading!

For example, a caved in chest (air) can reflect sunken hopes and lost desire. A rigid or swollen solar plexus (fire) can indicate withheld or chronically present anger. A swollen pelvis (water) can suggest excessive enmeshment and holding on. Tightened buttocks with locked knees, and tight walk (earth) could reflect chronic anxiety or fear.

After learning these basic ideas for torso body reading, combine them with the earlier discussion of the face. A good way to do this is to look in a mirror at your own face. Look for right/left differences. Which side is more contracted? Then, look at the horizontal bands of air, fire, water and earth: are any of these disproportionately large (expanded) or small (contracted)? Are there any marks or distortions?

With your observations for the face complete, look at the torso. Follow the same sequence, looking for left/right comparisons first, then horizontal zones. Do you notice any correlations between face and torso?

Body reading for the torso requires a more inclusive, general perspective, observing the overall body. This contrasts with the specific focus used with the face. In addition to the left/right and horizontal zone analysis described for the face, the whole person is considered. Robbins identifies eight main areas to watch in body reading:[99] breathing, eye movement, lower lip size, posture, muscle tone, pupil

98. Feldenkrais, Body and Mature Behavior, p. 93.

99. Robbins, Unlimited Power, p. 328.

dilation, skin color/reflection, and voice. Our experience has tended to emphasize four of these: breathing, eye movement, posture, and voice are easily available, accurate signals well worth study. We also add hand gestures to the list in the following introduction to these specialized subjects.

Breathing indicates the measure of participation in life, and whether a person is "holding back" (over- or under- expansion, a Yang imbalance) or "holding on" (over- or under- contraction, a Yin imbalance). Some successful therapies,

including Reichian psychiatry, Re-birthing, and Kundalini Yoga, begin and in some cases dwell entirely on the expansion and balancing of breath.

Posture is a major area. The unique upright stance of man allows a delicate blending of gravitational response and subtle "moving toward" vs. "moving away from" positioning, which expresses a person's psychological attitude. This is developed with great detail by Feldenkrais and Keleman. The use of the arms and hands, the carriage of the shoulders, spine and pelvis, the style of gait, and postural

Foot-Torso Relationships

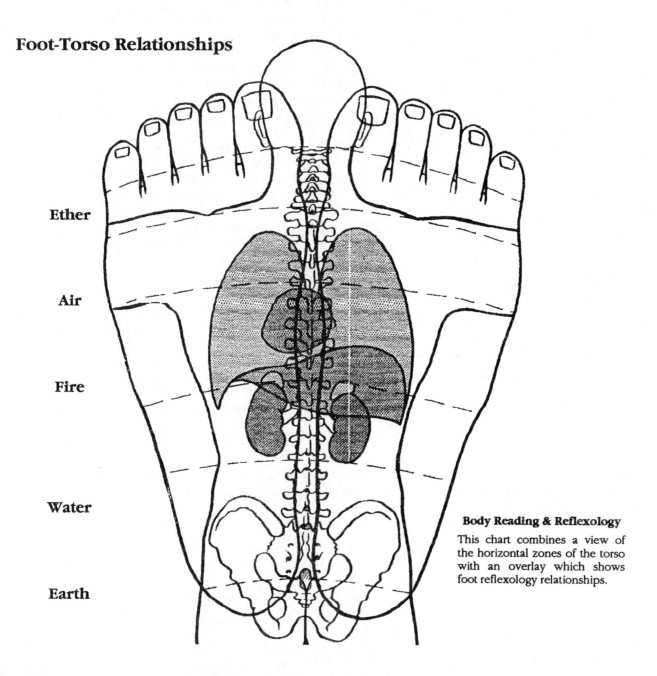

Ether

Air

Fire

Water

Earth

Body Reading & Reflexology

This chart combines a view of the horizontal zones of the torso with an overlay which shows foot reflexology relationships.

response to stimulation of various kinds can all be interpreted valuably.

Lowen classifies posture in two general categories which mesh perfectly with Polarity theory. He characterizes mankind as having two general styles of motivation, aggression (to push, Yang) and longing (to pull, Yin). He found a direct reflection in the spine: those too insecure to act (Yang imbalance) had locked knees and rigid pelvis; those unable to receive life's pressures with successful adaptation and emotional processing (Yin imbalance) had rounded shoulders and a slumping neck, the "dowager's hump."[100]

This idea has been developed further by Keleman. Building on the theme of the duality of pulsation (expansion and contraction, or Yang and Yin) he shows a continuum of postural change from resistance to exhaustion, from youthful ambition to elderly fatigue.

Hand placement is an important part of postural body reading. The hands will move naturally to the zones whose emotions are activated, either to suppress or release expression. When the hands are crossed over the solar plexus, a diaphragm stress (fire/anger) is indicated; when touching the hips (water), enmeshment/clinging or abandonment; when touching the mouth, sexuality and clinging; when at the throat, expression or grief, etc. Often you can intuitively gain insight into the activated element by replicating the posture, especially with the hands.

Voice is similar to eyes. You can differentiate qualities of sound by tone and loudness. Lower tones indicate lower elements, greater loudness suggesting more Yang. Furthermore, important cues for identifying elements involved can be found in pitch, speed and timbre: Beaulieu and Robbins, among others, offer detail in this area.

Lowen emphasizes the therapeutic significance of voice quality:

> If a person is to recover his full potential for self-expression, it is important he gain the full use of his voice in all its registers and in all its nuances of feeling.[101]

Many other levels are possible; we recommend using the references cited to pursue the subject.[102]

As we have seen, the assignment of emotional qualities to specific body areas is one of the great contributions of Dr. Stone to body reading. This idea of identifying the emotion and therefore the mental process behind illnesses according to the location of the problem has also been advanced by others. Louise Hay's Heal Your Body, which gives very specific identifications, is a notable example.

---

100. Lowen, BioEnergetics, pp. 236, 250, 299.

101. *Ibid.,* p. 271.
102. For psychological bodyreading, recommended sources are: Stokes and Whiteside (Under the Code and One Brain, LaBorde (Influencing with Integrity), Hay (Heal Your Body) and Dychtwald (Bodymind). 150.

Body Reading for the Feet

The following material on body reading for the feet is somewhat removed from Dr. Stone. There are Polarity references supporting some of this section's conclusions (identifying the toes as relating to specific chakras, identifying specific emotions relating to those chakras, and linking Yang or masculine energy with the right foot, and Yin, or feminine energy, with the left). But the larger psychological interpretations presented here are not found directly in Dr. Stone's writing.

We offer these ideas in a spirit of experimentation, for practitioners to use and validate for themselves. There is no scientific data to support these theories, and no research underway. Rather than diagnosis, we seek self-understanding. If these ideas stimulate steps in that direction, our purpose is served.

Our theory has three parts:

1. That the shape of the toe indicates the chronic condition of the corresponding energy center.

2. That the energy center, as exhibited by the shape of the toe, can be analyzed directly in terms of its etheric manifestation, or emotion.

3. That the left and right feet reflect a person's sensory experience of Yin and Yang energies, and that these energies generally reflect the blueprint contribution of mother and father, respectively.

1. The shape of the toe indicates the chronic condition of the corresponding energy center.

Correspondences are depicted by Dr. Stone[103] showing earth, water, fire, air, and ether centers represented by toes in order from small to large.

In this context, "shape" means tone (circulation, flexibility, presence of callous or bunion), alignment (location, direction, whether one toe is parallel to other toes), and symmetry (size and shape compared to other toes). "Chronic" in this situation refers to long-term family patterns inherited both genetically and emotionally.

These living current areas divide the body into five zones or fields of receptivity, like the use of the five senses over the five fingers and toes on each side of the body, over which they actually flow. This is a vertical classification of areas of response of the five energy currents operating in the body.[104]

The bones and the joints of the fingers and toes often give a hint in diagnosis, where everything else is obscure and indefinite, and the patient merely exists and suffers. This is nature's own finger of diagnosis and indication, and not mere theory. It reveals the disrupted relationship of the extremities on the surface with the centers of energy within, in the particular region specified by the finger or toe.[105]

Precipitation occurs most often here [the foot] because of its great distance from the invigorating center.[106]

2. The energy center, as expressed by the shape of the toe, can be analyzed directly in terms of its etheric manifestation, or emotion.

The body suffers as an innocent bystander, not as the causative factor. But it gets all the blame because effects and

---

103. Stone <u>Polarity Therapy Vol. I</u>, Book 3, p. 37. The arrangement is repeated concisely in the chart on pages 9 and 127 of Book 2 of the same volume.

104. Stone, <u>Polarity Therapy, Vol. II</u>, p. 33.

105. Stone, <u>Polarity Therapy, Vol. I</u>, Book 3, p. 39.

106. *Ibid.*, p. 38.

end products accumulate there as precipitates of highly emotional chemical action.[107]

The emotions are identified by Dr. Stone in his "Enquiry into the Gross Body" charts,[108] summarized on page 105. For our purposes, we focus on the center line of the illustration, in which an etheric component for each chakra is identified.

These emotions and chakras are: Earth/Fear, Water/Attachment, Fire/Anger, Air/Desire, and Ether/Grief. This linkage of emotions and physical centers has enormous implications, for it supplies the seeker of self-understanding with a way to translate that which is obvious and physical, into that which is hidden and subtle. This is the "missing link" between physiology and psychology.

One of the points of genius about Polarity Therapy is this linkage. The Polarity Practitioner can be giving a session, touching a certain area, and observe the activation of the appropriate emotions.

With the knowledge contained in this chart, these emotions make sense, and can be processed in specific ways. Old feelings can be freed from their deep storage in the tissues, brought into consciousness, and comprehended as family patterns, deeply-held attitudes and emotional reactions. This comprehension is a liberating experience of tremendous significance, for in understanding do we gain access to the blueprint and power to change our lives.

Without defusion of past causors, no present time correction lasts longer than the next stressor.[109]

Facing old emotional traumas, bravely experiencing denied or forgotten pain, maturely comprehending what happened, forgiving those who have created harm, and letting go, is a sure avenue to profound health improvement.

3. The left and right feet reflect a person's sensory experience of Yin and Yang energies, and these energies generally reflect the blueprint contribution of mother and father, respectively.

This statement requires explanation at every stage of the sentence.

This life pattern began by the energy current flow in the male spermatozoon and the female ovum center of vitelline jelly substance, like a thread in a shuttle which travels forward and backward to weave the most wonderful fabric of life, called the human body! The pattern of the body was supplied by the mental and vital energy of the parents, according to their kind and stature. Of course, heritage goes back much further than that, but this is the general rule.[110]

The idea that left and right feet are considered to reflect Yin and Yang energies for the front, or sensory side of the body is illustrated by Dr. Stone in several places.[111] Waves of electromagnetic current have specific direction, flowing down and out of the front of the right foot, and up and in the front of the left foot.

We are concerned with the sensory side (the front side of the body) because of its significance in processing emotions. The "five pointed star" is the field which receives the impulses from above, where

---

107. *Ibid.*, p. 35. This seven-page section is highly recommended as a discussion of bodyreading and bodywork.
108. Stone, Polarity Therapy, Vol.II, p. 222-223
109. Stokes and Whiteside, One Brain, p. 5.

110. Stone, Polarity Therapy, Vol. I, Book 1, p. 9. The essay here (pp. 4-32) is highly recommended.
111. *Ibid.*, Book 2, pp. 10-14.

"sensory tension and emotional frustration" are recorded and stored.

Yin and Yang

The words Yin and Yang in this context refer to the ideas eloquently summarized in the I Ching.[112] It is important to note that Dr. Stone did not elaborate deeply on emotions or family patterns in his therapy, and as we move into this area, we are no longer fully supported by his writings. His use of the words Yin and Yang focused primarily on the electromagnetic attributes of the basic polarity relationship of all of nature. Here we add a much wider range of psychological interpretation.

Generally, Yang refers to outgoing experience, our impulse to be, to act and to do in the world. It is manifested in breath as inhalation and (usually) in brain function by the left hemisphere activities. We all must act on our impulses, and ultimately face the challenge of being responsible (or able to respond) to the results of those actions. Yang also refers to the masculine aspect of experience, which is steady, logical, aggressively goal-oriented. Qualities of Yang are represented by the sperm, its purest manifestation. Yang is also the centrifugal direction of involutionary movement: flowing outward from its source, Yang is the soul's pathway into the material world.

Complementarily, Yin refers to the incoming experience, our receiving of impulses from outside ourselves. It is manifested in breath as exhalation, in blood flow as veins, and (usually) in brain function by the right hemisphere activities. We all struggle to deal with external events, and we all must ultimately face the challenge of accepting what comes to us. Yin also refers to the feminine aspect of experience, for men or women, which is cyclic, intuitive, absorbing, pulling. Qualities of Yin are represented by the egg, its purest manifestation. Yin is also the centripetal direction of evolutionary movement: having landed in matter, consciousness travels the Yin pathway back toward spirit.

Linkage of Yang/right side with father and Yin/left side with mother is hinted in Dr. Stone's writings, and is clearly expressed elsewhere.

> We associate the left side of the body (which is controlled primarily by the right side of the brain) with feelings, emotions, and the relations to the mother. The right side is associated with the father, reason, thinking, logic.[113]

These ideas of Yin and Yang have a tremendous universality, and are useful for psychological inquiry.[114] In the Orient, it is said that there are only four dis-eases, too much or too little of the two basic modes of energy flow. In the dysfunctional relationships model of modern psychology, these four are found as character types: the Tyrant (too much Yang), Wimp (too little Yang), Doormat (too much Yin) and Critic (too little Yin). Relationships tend to represent magnetic equality, with "too much" or "too little" being inevitably, magnetically drawn to each other in appropriate but destructive, painful and unstable relationships.

---

112. Wilhelm. trans., I Ching, pp. 3-15. This describes the extension of the ideas of Yin and Yang into many aspects of human experience.

The principles of Yin and Yang are: 1) All things have two aspects, a Yin aspect and a Yang aspect; 2) A Yin or Yang aspect can be further divided into Yin and Yang; 3) Yin and Yang mutually create each other; 4) Yin and Yang control each other; and, 5) Yin and Yang transform into each other.
--Kaptchuk, The Web That Has No Weaver, p. 7-12

---

113. Kurtz and Prestera, The Body Reveals, p. 47. See also pp. 97-100.

114. For more on the psychological applications of Yang and Yin, see "Man and Woman" a two-part video lecture by Anna Chitty. (see Bibliography).

Toe Reading

Assuming that our three basic premises are understood and accepted for testing, how do we apply them? We begin with two abstract illustrations. The top foot shows an ideal arrangement, in which the toes are in relative proportion and pointing straight to the front. The foot below has the smallest toe out of line, on the left foot. According to our theory, this suggests chronic fear (the emotion corresponding to the earth chakra) in the Yin aspect of experience.

The Polarity "detective" of self-understanding would use these "clues" to formulate a hypothetical solution: that this person's stress has to do with fear and can be traced in childhood to receptivity and/or experience of Mother. With this initial general clue, the detective can then proceed to an informed search for specific information: bodywork focusing on the earth element, self-discovery of family patterns relating to fear, recollection of childhood events with mother, etc.

To carry the discussion to one more level, the next examples are photographs. Both pictures are of institutionalized mental patients, in whom we can assume severe stress has caused functional break-down. According to Dr. Stone's theory, the flow of energy through the system has become so blocked that normal function is no longer possible.

Looking at the feet in the first picture, we see that the smallest toe on the right foot is severely curved under (similar to the drawing above). Meanwhile, on the left, the fourth and third toes are severely distorted, and the left foot generally has more stress than the right. Also, the toenails of the big toe seem to be stressed on both sides.

Attempting to formulate a hypothetical analysis from this evidence, we might say that the individual has severe trauma with his mother (or with his experience of his own Yin energy), including excessive (suggested by elongation) enmeshment

Toe Reading

The alignment of the toes is a valuable way to understand the flow of energy in the body. See which toes are distorted, and analyze the distortion in the context of the whole foot. In this example, the left Yin foot shows chronic disruption in the Earth center. This suggests energy blockage relating to Yin (mother, receiving) experience and the emotion of fear or anxiety.

Each emotion has a Yin and Yang expression. In the case of Fear, a Yin expression would be oversensitivity and tendency to take on anxiety or other people's fear. A Yang expression of fear would be unrealistic fearlessness (bravado) or generating fearful experience in others.

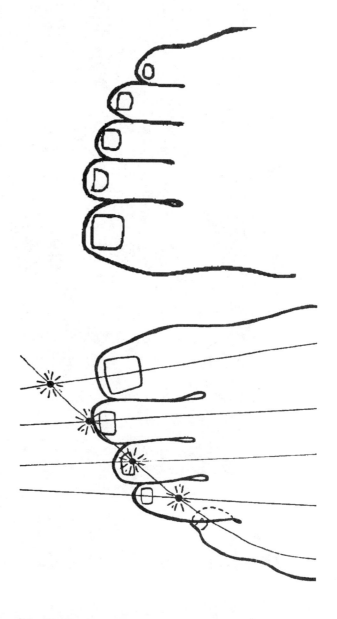

and extreme anger. The anger (third toe) has the additional characteristic of being lifted up from ground level, suggesting that the person's experience of that anger is greatly disassociated from conscious practicality. In Bioenergetics, this would be called "ungrounded." We would expect the related emotions to be deeply hidden or denied with this degree of distortion.

On the right side, fear in the context of father (either fear of father or a reflection of father's fears, or fear relating to the patient's own outgoing Yang energy) is indicated. The poor tone of the toenail on the big toe suggests poor capabilities of expression (at the throat center) and grief.

Response in this case could include movements and bodywork for the pelvis and diaphragm, especially on the left side. During bodywork, the practitioner would be alert for emerging emotions, and would assist in the placement of these in a meaningful context for the individual, using the clues available if they were continually val-

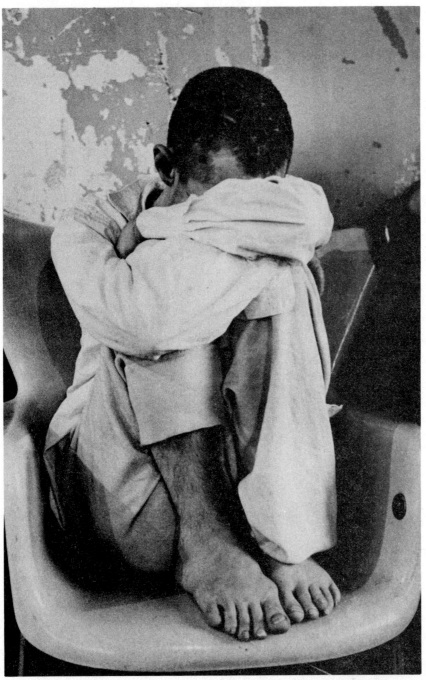

Toe Reading Example #1
This photograph of an institutionalized mental patient gives a good view of the feet. The shape of the toes suggests severe attachment and anger with mother, and severe fear with father.

Magnum Photo

idated by the emerging process.

The second picture offers a less usable example. We see only the right foot, with its great distortion of third, fourth, and fifth toes. The fourth seems to be the most misaligned, suggesting stress relating to attachment ("holding on," "abandonment" or "clinging") on the Yang, or father's, side. Again, its uplifted position indicates disassociation from practical awareness. It is combined with severe fear on one side and anger on the other. Our hypothesis would assume that this individual had major trauma with his father. The specific emotions indicated are those relating to the water center; these include enmeshment, sexuality, isolation, dependence and others (see elements guide, p. 133).

Polarity practitioners often look at the toes as they begin a session, and seek understanding of the person as they proceed. As we have said, this approach has repeatedly been useful, being both accurate and directly to the point, a short cut to self-discovery. Our goal is to help in the discovery and comprehension of the energy block, so that the underlying causes may be understood and removed by conscious choice of the person, and so that the inhibited energy center can be released to a more natural free flow of current.

The inclusion of psychology in physical medicine is inevitable, as the atomic era proceeds. It would be well within Dr. Stone's predictions to reach a time when, along with the allopathic treatment saving patients from their symptoms, the practitioner of the healing arts would routinely do more, by looking for the subtle causes of the problems.

The practitioner would alert the patient to the fact that something was not working in his or her life, and nudge them gently back on to the path of self-discovery, in hopes of identifying unworkable mental attitudes, indigestible emotional experiences, and destructive physical habits. The patient, in his pain, thus acquires an opportunity for increased personal responsibility and growth in self-understanding.

Getting the flu, therefore, is like getting a news update.[115]

115. Chopra, Quantum Healing, p. 260.

Toe Reading Example #2

The second photograph, of another hospitalized mental patient, provides a more limited view, with only the right Yang side visible. Here the water toe is most distorted, suggesting extreme stress relating to attachment with his father.

Magnum Photo

Finally, this discussion would not be complete without mention of limitation. The wholistic approach to health has in the past been guilty of oversimplifying the cause and treatment of disease. Pelletier cautions eloquently against the "Calvinist" attitude that people have "defects" which are to "blame" for their problems.[116]

> Books on holistic health like to say that sick people "need" their sickness. Mainstream psychiatry points its own finger when it says that chronic diseases stand symbolically for self-punishment, revenge, or a deep feeling of worthlessness. I will not argue these insights except to suggest that they may be harmful to the healing process rather than helpful. It is hard enough for any of us to face up to our emotional fallibility even at the best of times. Can we really be expected to reform when we are ill?[117]

We can never know the whole story behind illness. As Dr. Stone said, "heritage goes back much further than that," and we cannot know all of the variables in a person.

> Each incarnating soul or entity brings with it a design of life, of its own, by which it differs from others.[118]

In addition to the knowable contributions of parents, culture, environment, and other forces, there is always a major unknown factor carried from previous forgotten experience. The concept of re-incarnation, of previous lifetimes leading to the present, is inevitable and well-supported by many sources.[119]

A middle ground is recommended, acknowledging "Whatever works, works!" and constantly seeking greater self-knowledge, tempering body reading with a humble realization that full understanding is impossible. We seek a balance between the idea of personal responsibility for disease, which presses for self-improvement, and acceptance of our limits in either knowing or being able to control our circumstances. Like polarized energy, either side is incomplete without the other. It is misleading, deluding and frustrating to hint that perfect, comprehensive knowledge can ever be gained, for it is beyond human vision and capability.

> Polarity Therapy is not based on the illusion that one can achieve a state of constant relaxation and an end to all conflicts. It is rather based on the fact that most people are capable of using their energies more effectively.[120]

This search for self knowledge can only be a middle way, combining responsible action (balanced yang) and discriminating acceptance (balanced yin), and a certain comfort with the limitation of the knowledge available. This attitude is consistent with the scientific basis for the Polarity model, best expressed as Heisenberg's Uncertainty Principle (we can know a particle's direction or velocity, but not both), which transformed the study of physics at the turn of the century.

In this context, it is quite fitting that Dr. Stone walked away from his blossoming inquiry into esoteric health, the worldly passion of his entire life, to devote his last eight years in virtual seclusion, meditating on spiritual matters.

> Unlimited possibilities are not suited to man; if they existed, his life would dissolve in the boundless.[121]

Thus his final teaching is to keep our worldly efforts in perspective. Ultimately, the entire truth is not to be known, and the personal inner quest for higher understanding is more important anyway.

---

116. Pelletier, <u>Mind as Healer, Mind as Slayer</u>, p. 10-11.

117. Chopra, <u>Quantum Healing</u>, p. 158.

118. Stone, <u>Polarity Therapy, Vol. I</u>. Book 1, p. 9.

119. An excellent analysis of reincarnation from a modern health science perspective is Gerber's <u>Vibrational Medicine</u>, pp. 161 ff. and pp. 484 ff.

120. Arroyo, <u>Astrology, Psychology and the Four Elements</u>, p. 182.

121. Wilhelm, trans., <u>The I Ching</u>, p. 232.

Part Four

Essays

The Journey of the Soul

Polarity Therapy is profound in its rich blending of health and philosophy. In ancient times, the concerns of the scientist and philosopher were unified: in Dr. Stone's writing, the two move effortlessly together.

The essential questions at the heart of philosophical inquiry are, "What is humanity?" Why are we here? What is consciousness, and life? Dr. Stone's answers to these questions constitute "the Journey of the Soul," which is presented at the very beginning of his written work and forms the foundation for all that follows.

Here is a summary of the Journey of the Soul, in Dr. Stone's words.

> ...The soul which inhabits this body is a unit of consciousness from another sphere, of much finer essences... Each incarnating soul or entity brings with it a design of life, of its own, by which it differs from others...[122]

The soul...steps down its energy and becomes a slave of the mind, and expresses itself through the senses. The senses relate to the mind as units to the whole...seeking experience in multiplicity and outward expenditure of energy...

In matter, it is action for the sake of action; namely, the sensations, the enjoyment of the senses, the reactions, the accumulation of things, and personal honor, pride and self-aggrandizement through possessions and power...[but] Every pleasure in this world, indulged in as such, has its resulting sorrow-- if not immediately, at some time in the future. The same principle is still active when a child insists on touching a hot stove; it must experience the sensation and the resulting pain.[123]

Our energies are constantly going outward, seeking in things the thrills and satisfactions which are not there. It is a mirage. Only the very highest universal source really has what we seek and crave. So, after maturity of years, after aeons of

---

122. Stone, <u>Polarity Therapy Vol. I</u>, Book 1, p. 9.
123. *Ibid.*, p. 31

The Journey of the Soul

This metaphorical painting depicts the plight of the soul, torn between materialism and its source. The Involutionary Yang experience links the soul to the mind (the Chariot), which is in turn pulled by the senses (the animals). The Evolutionary Yin experience turns the soul's attention back toward its "True Home."

Further symbolism is given here for the five elements in their manifestation as negative emotions: Horse, Ether, Stiff-necked Pride; Pig, Air, Greed; Crocodile,

Fire, Anger; Vulture, Water, Attachment to lifeless things; Snake, Earth, Fear.

The symbolism of the Sun as the true home, or God, is based on the Sanskrit term *Ha* which means sun, the primal Yang creative force. *Tha* means moon in Sanskrit, making *Hatha Yoga* literally "Union of Sun and Moon" or Union of Yang and Yin. This is a great definition for Polarity, again indicating the origin of Dr. Stone's work in ancient wisdom.

wanderings and sufferings, the soul finally is convinced of this fact and, like the 'Prodigal Son', remembers his Father's house and all its abundance. He then rises up within himself, turns his energy and longings of the soul inwards, and comes back home to his Universal Source...[124]

Dr. Stone thus describes life as a school, with a centrifugal force propelling units of consciousness out from a primordial source, into the dense world of experience (involution), until through painful experience the deepest lessons are learned, providing the motivation for a centripetal return to the center (evolution).

> The purpose is for the experience of souls embodied in forms and placed in outer space of matter and resistance in order to gain awareness through perception and action, for the fulfillment of consciousness.[125]

> Man alone stands at the top of the ladder of all Creation. He alone is endowed with all the faculties necessary to understand his Source, his Being, and his relationship to Nature. Writings of the Ancients became sacred because they endeavored to reveal to man some hints about his Source, his marvelous pent-up energies and soul powers, and how to use them wisely in Nature, how to transcend the ego and thereby find his way to his REAL HOME.[126]

This world is the School of Life. We come to gain experience, and have these bodies for that purpose. Through painful "burning of fingers" we learn to transcend the ego (our illusory confusion of true self with senses, body and mind) and seek deeper meaning. Thus the art of Polarity Therapy becomes the art of self-realization, which ultimately is the same as the quest for God-realization. A health system merges seamlessly into a profound spiritual understanding and world view which unifies the beliefs of the world's major religions.

--JC

124. *Ibid.*, p. 29.
125. Stone, Polarity Therapy Vol. I, Book 3, p. 11.
126. Stone, Health Building, p. 23.

How Involution and Evolution create the Emotions

The mind, feelings and body are linked in a chain of cause and effect, constantly cycling from the subtle to the dense, from the mind to the body, and back. As we have discussed, the many manifestations of this cycle are reflections of the larger cosmic cycle of involution and evolution, by which a soul travels into creation and ultimately returns to its Source.

Motor and Sensory

Dr. Stone used the words "motor" and "sensory" to describe these two sides. The motor function is the movement from blueprint through motivation into materialization. The sensory function is the movement from materialization through feelings back to blueprint.

The feedback from the sensory function is the only way for the motor function to know if its pattern is successful. Without the moon, the Sun cannot know itself. If the feedback is painful, the next impulse of the motor current will be adapted to seek a more successful result.

For a simple example, analyze the act of eating. The blueprint (mind) is pre-programmed to create actions to satisfy the need. Based on sensory input, edible material is perceived. A motor impulse is generated, causing the hand to reach out to satisfy the need. A sensory return message then tells whether the motor action was successful. If the food was too hot, the sensory message protects the person from being burned. The next motor response will be adapted appropriately.

The situation is similar, but more complex, for emotional issues. All children are "programmed" with basic etheric "needs" which are real and valid for all children. The motor currents will initiate action to fulfill those needs, and the sensory currents will guide adaptation by giving feedback on those actions.

Using the Polarity model of the Five Elements, the basic emotional necessities are the needs for security (earth), belonging (water), warmth (fire), hope (air), and expression (ether). All of these are given and received to varying degrees through parental love for the child. Pia Mellody has given a very useful five innate qualities of the child which fit nicely: the child is (and has a right to be) vulnerable (earth), dependent (water), imperfect (fire), immature (air) and valuable (ether)[127]

The young child spontaneously initiates motor activity to have these needs met, manifesting the five innate qualities as it does. The nature of these actions is a function of the child's blueprint, which combines traits from that family with traits common to all others of that sex.

Immediately after conception, even before birth, sensory messages begin to flow to the child. The game has begun for this lifetime. Motor actions go out, sensory feedback comes back in a continuous loop of action and reaction

Search for Love

In the child's search for love in the five elemental categories, inevitable frustrations and traumas occur. Perhaps the parents do not feel secure themselves, so the sensory feedback indicates danger. Perhaps the child's innate qualities are denied, due to parental inability to function in a mature way.

Feedback alerts the new mind to the problem. New motor actions attempt to resolve the problem, or adapt in such a way as to extract a garbled, limited form of love, "making the best of the situation."

Adapted strategies soon become habits, for unpredictability is more stressful than limited love. Strategies which lead to love set the stage for successful emotional navigation later in life. Adapted strategies which are unsuccessful in gaining love set the stage for lives of pain. Mellody specifically identifies the types of adaptation which result from frustration of each of the five original motives, complete with

---

127. Mellody, Facing Codependence, p. 113.

the adult dysfunctional symptoms that inevitably result. The symptoms are problems with: boundaries (earth); needs (water); knowing and expressing one's reality (fire); moderation (air); self-esteem (ether).

Once the adaptation is established, new situations are not analyzed on their own merits, but rather from the skewed perspective of a faulty blueprint. Our judgement does not mature past this point in time of childhood emotional injury.

Only by changing the blueprint, a difficult task later in life, can these patterns of pain be transformed. Accessing and re-programing these subconscious blueprint-level mental patterns is the goal of emotional therapy.

Energy Block

Adaptation also interrupts the cycle of involution and evolution. In the presence of pain, we block the reception of sensory feedback or withhold the expression of motor action. This can occur at four points in the cycle: the involutionary side can withhold action or ignore feedback, while the evolutionary side can block the receiving of action or distort the feedback. These problems are locked physically in the body as energy blocks.

The greatest challenge in healing the emotions is overcoming the momentum of habitual patterns. As part of pain-management, we deny its presence. Because we are involved in dysfunctional patterns, we cannot see them. Thus the first priority is to become aware of how we are feeling, and accept the reality of those feelings. This is the road to the blueprint, from which lasting changes can be made.

Thus the therapeutic process is parallel to the larger "Journey of the Soul" process. Just as the soul eventually awakens to its plight of separation from its source, the healing of emotional problems requires an awakening to their presence. From the pain of dysfunctional family histories, we become motivated to start the quest for self-understanding, and ultimately for God-understanding.

--JC

Integrating Chinese and Polarity Systems

The question is sometimes asked, how does the Chinese energy anatomy and therapy model fit with the Polarity model? The two systems seem to be different in some respects, although the underlying theories are generally quite similar. They are thought to share a common origin in very ancient times, although the history is not known.

The success of acupuncture is a testament to the insight of ancient Chinese practitioners, and an "indigestible thought" for the Newtonian western medical model. Kinesiology deserves appreciation for advancing this ancient wisdom into the modern scene, and today's Polarity practitioner can benefit greatly from information presented in the many Kinesiology systems.

How can we compare the two ancient systems theoretically? Why does acupuncture work, from a Polarity perspective? Dr. Stone considered the systems identical:

> ...the old Ayurvedic Medicine and Acupuncture ascribed three modes of motion to energy in the three dimensions of space, and called them the three "Gunas" - "Satwa" the neuter, "Rajas" the positive, and "Tamas" the negative mode of motion. The Chinese called them the "Qi" (neuter), the "Yang" (positive) and the "Yin" (negative) poles of action. These became the Air, Fire and Water elements [Principles] of the Hermetic philosophers, who obtained this information from the Orient.

> ...Acupuncture classifies all organs as either positive or negative, with many qualifications and points of contact for inserting the gold (positive) needle for disbursing and distributing excess energy; or the negative pole, the silver needle, for toning areas as specific spots. The balancing of the two extremes made a blend in which the neuter "Qi" energy could flow

again and link these poles to the Life Current of the Universal Essence, by tuning in; even as male and female are united in the child, the ever-becoming Youth of Life.

Acupuncture balances the two currents in their function and polarity with each other by means of needles, so they will flow in and out of the form freely in normal action and expression, called Health or Well-being. When there is no obstruction to the current energy flow, there is no pain or stagnation in the circulation.

WHAT THE NEEDLES CAN DO, THE HANDS CAN DO BETTER, with a battery of consciousness behind them plus intelligence for direction of currents. The right hand is the positive sun action, radiating, disbursing, outgoing golden energy. The left hand is the negative cooling moon energy, toning, soothing and inhibiting or concentrating the current for sedimentation and use.[128]

While this gives a general sense of similarity, several points of interest remain. How do the acupuncture meridians (the Chinese system energy current mappings) make sense from a Polarity perspective? A possible answer is given in Gerber's Vibrational Medicine.[129] This summarizes research (by Kim Bong Han of Korea and Pierre de Vernejoul of France) tracking the movement of radioactive isotopes injected into acupuncture points.

The patterns which emerge indicate the existence of a microductal system which parallels but precedes (is created earlier in the embryo) vascular and lymphatic ductal systems.

This system seems to lay out energy pathways to shape the creation of tissues, and to be closely linked with autonomic

---

128. Stone, Polarity Therapy Vol. II, pp. 208-209.
129. Gerber, Vibrational Medicine, pp. 122 ff.

nervous system function.

In Polarity terminology, these functions (creation of tissues and autonomic nervous system) are theoretically the action of the Fire Principle, the Yang involutionary side of the energy equation. Thus stimulation or sedation of meridian points with needles, heat or touch may be energy balancing which is tracking the Fire Principle. A complementary hypothesis can be made about the other great arm of Chinese medicine, herbalism, being a treatment based on the Yin energy or Water Principle. In Polarity bodywork, the Fire Principle is the basis for many techniques, especially contacts involving the Interlaced Triangles, umbilicus, back and diaphragm.

Another topic of interest here is the relationship of the Chinese "Five Elements" to the Polarity Five Elements. Are these terms referring to the same phenomena, and how do they match up? Kaptchuk's The Web That Has No Weaver: Understanding Chinese Medicine offers a possible explanation.

First, the Chinese "Five Elements" are properly translated "Five Phases."

> The Theory of the Five Phases is an attempt to classify phenomena in terms of five quintessential processes, represented by the emblems Wood, Fire, Earth, Metal and Water...The Five Phases are not in any way ultimate constituents of matter.[130]

These phases correspond to the natural cycle of growth and decay exemplified in the seasons. From this general beginning based on Yang (Spring and Summer), Yin (Fall and Winter) and Qi (Transition), Kaptchuk describes how the Five Phases idea became rigid, losing some of its usefulness in modern Chinese medicine. Interpretations have varied from age to age and practitioner to practitioner.

To the degree that equivalents can be drawn to Polarity, the following seems to apply:

Polarity	Chinese
Ether	Earth
Air	Wood
Fire	Fire
Water	Metal
Earth	Water

The sequential unfolding of the Chinese Five Phases is very similar to the sequential densities of the Polarity Five Elements. However, there are also differences: for example, the Chinese Five Phases are identified with organs and functions which do not always seem to fit the corresponding Polarity descriptions. For this reason, the equation of the two systems does not seem to hold up completely. The whole context in which these originated and are applied is so different that it does not seem valuable to pursue the equation too deeply. Rather, each system of "Elements" should be appreciated on its own merits.

If anything, the interest in comparison is better focused on the Chinese Qi/Yang/Yin and Polarity Air/Fire/Water Principles, which are the cores of both systems and virtually identical, as we saw in the passage from Dr. Stone. As Kaptchuk describes the resemblance:

> Similarities to the Chinese model are found even in non-bipolar systems, such as the Hindu Ayurvedic system. For example, pitha [the Fire Principle]... resembles China's Fire [Yang]; vata [the Air Principle]...resembles China's Qi, and kapha [the Water Principle]...very much resembles China's Yin...When I worked in an Ayurvedic Hospital in India years ago, I found that my Chinese medical background enabled me in a short time to predict the categories that Ayurvedic physicians would use to describe their patients.[131]

--JC

---

130. Kaptchuk, The Web That Has No Weaver, p. 344. The relevant discussions are on pp. 199 ff. and 343 ff.
131. *Ibid*., pp. 199-200.

Yin and Yang and the Life Lesson

The Polarity model gives a useful perspective on the meaning of gender. Why is one person a man (and thus inevitably challenged biologically by Yang experience, in addition to Yin experience which will arise to varying degrees), and another a woman (and thus inevitably challenged biologically by Yin experience, in addition to Yang experience which will arise to varying degrees)? Is this accidental? Such questions penetrate to the deepest levels of human inquiry, to the "Journey of the Soul," subject matter that Dr. Stone considered the very essence of Polarity Therapy. Polarity Therapy is exceptional in its ability to venture into this realm of human inquiry.

Dr. Stone explains human life as a quest for knowledge and experience. The fact of gender fits in with this quest. A student returning to college after vacation, does not choose courses that are already known, but rather those with new challenges.

Similarly, the soul seeks fields of action in experience which represent new challenge. In traditional Japanese folklore, it is said that "the sex of the child is the challenge of the parents." A child will be born into a male body if the progress of the soul requires Yang lessons (possibly having dealt previously and successfully with Yin challenges). The sould will choose parents whose emotional issues and stress relate to Yang experiences like responsibility and creativity, parents who are creating a field of action in which the appropriate Yang challenges will be certain to manifest.

Thus the fact of gender is a matter to be appreciated, not minimized. All experience, from smallest to largest dimension, follows from the fundamental event of gender identity. The qualities of sperm and egg manifest throughout our experience, bringing us the lessons of life.

The attraction and repulsion of Yang and Yin is an expression of the essential nature of energy, culminating in intercourse and conception and providing the family matrix for the raising of children. The magnetic emotional force of sexual attraction and the miraculous dynamics of conception are perhaps the most remarkable demonstrations of the workings of energy in human experience.

It is a measure of the grand illusion of life that so much controversy has arisen on issues of sexual identity and role. Dr. Stone emphasized that both sexes are on the same spiritual path:

> WOMEN, AS WELL AS MEN, have the same right and footing in both processes [involution and evolution].[121]

Deeper issues await us: we can see this body, male or female, as a meaningful temporary vehicle for the learning of certain lessons, and go on to the search for understanding of what our individual lessons are and how we can successfully learn them.

> This gross body, I cannot be. Why? I am seeing it. It is an object for my sight. I am the seer. It is separate and I am separate.[122]

---

132. Stone, Polarity Therapy, Vol. I, Book 1, p. 40.. This passage includes a denunciation of an earlier era's sexism (p. 39): "A great injustice was done to womanhood by the literal interpretation of the story of the 'Garden of Eden.' WOMAN, AS A PERSON, WAS NOT THE CAUSE OF MAN'S FALL INTO MATTER."

133. *Ibid.*, p. 40.

The Three Principles of Polarity and Three Dimensions of Edu-K

We can understand energy systems easier by looking at the body as an energetic three dimensional figure moving through time and space. These three dimensions of height, width and depth can be analyzed in terms of posture, movement and energy circuits. This study is central to both Polarity Therapy and to Edu-K, the effective brain-integration therapy developed by Paul Dennison.

Back-Front

This first dimension or direction of action has three possibilities: moving out or expanding, moving in or contracting, and stillness or maintaining sameness. As we move forward, we go out to meet situations and people. As we move back, we are more within ourselves and less accessible to outside influences. We may use the inward movement to digest and process experience. In the middle or neutral space we have the opportunity to move in or out, and take in or give out.

When we are functioning optimally, all these modes are accessible to us and we can choose whichever is appropriate at any given moment. Our posture both in general and at each moment reflects our status of outward and inward, back and forward. This dimension also reflects the communication between the back and front brains, connecting the past with the present, the visual experience with expression.

In the Dennisons' Educational Kinesiology, this understanding of the back/front dimension is called 'Focus' and has to do with our ability to focus on things outside ourselves while maintaining our own integrity. We might evaluate our ability to focus by seeing whether we can look at a book, TV show or another person and learn from them while keeping ourselves in perspective. When our energies are out of balance in this dimension, we may be over- or under-focused, "too out" or "too in."

In a state of over-focus we deplete ourselves and lose our sense of self as we become engrossed in something outside ourselves. Posturally, this would appear as a forward head and stooped shoulders. In a state of under-focus, we are unable to focus on things because we are so much inside ourselves that it is too much of a strain to allow the energy to go out. Posturally, we would see this in a "holding back" stance. This dimension has to do with comprehension or understanding. Understanding comes from the ability to interact with something outside ourselves and bring it within in a meaningful and balanced context.

This dimension may be compared to the Fire Principle in Polarity, in which concentric spirals radiate outward from the umbilical or solar plexus area. This has to do with the ability to produce heat and warmth and to put our fiery creativity into expression in interaction with other people and situations. It also relates to our ability to take in and digest experience. The eyes are very much part of the fire. We feel that fire when someone else's anger or warmth is directed toward us through their eyes. We use the fire of the eyes to take in and digest visual cues and written words. This relates to our ability to focus, to allow that fire of the eyes to look outside and in.

Top-Bottom

In the second dimension, we look at the energies that move up and down. As these energies flow, it is a link between our foundation and our manifestation, our reflex and cognition, our denser and finer energies, between the upper and lower centers of the brain. We constantly balance higher aspirations and practical limitation. The term "grounded" has frequently been used to describe this relationship: ungrounded meaning disassociation from feelings or unrealistic attitudes, over-grounded meaning lacking a higher vision of potential achievement.

In the Dennisons' work, this dimension is called Centering and the word that is associated with it is "organization." This dimension reflects how the body organizes its flow through life and whether events throw us off center or we maintain our center.

In Dr. Stone's work, these longitudinal currents relate to the Water Principle. As the currents flow downward into the denser areas of the body, they may crystallize and be blocked in their return upward. In the drawing of the energy man (p. 13), these currents are represented by the lines moving through the fingers and toes. These are similar in flow to the longitudinal nature of acupuncture meridians.

Left-Right

The third dimension is left to right or side to side. This dimension reflects the communication between the two sides of the brain hemispheres, yin and yang, male and female, receptive and outgoing, analytic and feeling. It deals with fine quickly moving energy, as quick as the changing of our minds.

In Educational Kinesiology this dimension is named Laterality and deals with the idea of "communication." This dimension represents our ability to cross the midline of vision, hearing, thought, etc. and use the information of both sides to respond in an integrated or whole brain fashion. This is especially important for reading and writing skills. People commonly experience stress and a lack of integration for crossing the midline. Those with severe difficulties are often diagnosed as dyslexic. Through the Dennisons' pioneering work with integration of the brain hemispheres, much progress has been made in working with dyslexia.

In Polarity Therapy, this is the Satvic ("Satva" means truth) or Air Principle. It is represented by the side-to-side current spinning transversely about the body.

Dimensions and Exercises

In working with exercise and balance, we approach all three dimensions or principles in the type of movement we do and the type of touch we use.

The back-front dimension or fiery Rajas principle is stimulated by rocking movements and fiery sounds. The Edu-K "focus" aspect as seen in postural cues is released by all Brain Gym "lengthening" exercises which release the "tendon guard reflex" holding pattern and allow the body to once again participate with the outer and inner worlds.

The up-down Tamas or water currents are affected in Polarity by bringing them closely together to build on each other and by deep releasing touch, especially on the feet. These currents are also balanced with movements and contacts that connect longitudinal lines and meridians of the body. In Edu-K, all Button contacts are used to balance this "Centering" system by affecting meridian flow. A significant "exercise" which greatly affects this dimension is drinking water. Without the appropriate amount of water in the body for ionization and chemical processing, the electrochemistry cannot function correctly.

The side to side Satva or air currents are balanced in Polarity by gentle touch and side to side movement, followed by pauses which bring stillness and midline balance to the center. In Edu-K the issue of "Crossing the midline" is often addressed by exercises which take the mind and body from one side to the other using the figure eight shape.

We sometimes choose exercises by using the image of the three dimensions to get a feel for our current state. The following chart gives an understanding of emotional/mental states relating each dimension and a "menu" of appropriate exercises for balancing each. Wonderful self-help sessions can be developed based on this approach.

--MLM

Symptoms and Menus for Brain Integration

Dimension	Switched Off	Switched On	Menu
LEFT-RIGHT **Laterality** **Satva** **Communication**	Struggling, polarized, oppositional, win-lose, unable to communicate, feelings and thoughts in conflict, words and feelings unable to integrate, inner and outer don't match, hard on self or indulgent, "coming against a wall," lack of coordination	Effortless effort, both sides, flexibility of mind, alternatives, win-win, inner communication, outer communication, inner harmony, outer-inner consonance, coordination	Polarity: Scissors Kick, Pierre Ha, Side To Side Ha Breath Brain Gym Midline Movements: Cross Crawl, Lazy 8's, Belly Breathing, Sacral Rock, Shoulder Shrug Neck Rolls, Dennison Laterality Repatterning
TOP-BOTTOM **Centering** **Tamas** **Organization**	Off center, pushover, stubborn, frozen, stuck, scattered, shattered, unable to manifest ideals in a grounded way, easily thrown off, disorganized	Centered, stable, sense of integrity, balance (inner and outer), organization, stability with movement, flexibility with grounding, ideals manifest in daily activities and decisions	Polarity: Pyramid, Squat, Rowing, Diaphragm Press, Jaw as pelvic reflex Brain Gym: Brain Buttons, Earth Buttons, Balance Buttons, Space Buttons, Thinking Cap
BACK-FRONT **Focus** **Rajas** **Participation**	Pulled back, withdrawn, dependent, lost in tasks or other people, puts others ahead of self, overfocused, underfocused, can't remember, can't integrate information, can't receive or give, unable to understand, parroting, unmotivated, needy, don't attend to own needs	Participating, have a sense of self, understanding, memory comprehension, stepping forward, receiving and giving, expressive, able to be with self and another task or person simultaneously, balanced perspective or focus	Polarity: Motor Balance, Sciatic Ha, Lion Roar, Wise Man of Old, Humming, Pyramid, Squat, Diaphragm Press Brain Gym: Lengthening, The Owl, Foot Flex, Arm Activation, Hamstring and Psoas Lengthening
DEEPENING ATTITUDES **Peace**	Agitated, confused, unclear, physical discomfort, reactive, energy drain, upset, depressed, overwhelmed	Calm, peaceful, clarity, feel good, capable, compassionate, energetic	Polarity: Sensory Balance, Satvic 5 pointed star. Brain Gym: Deepening attitudes- Cook's Hook-Ups, Positive Points

Terminology Guide To Principles

The Three Principles concept is a vast, universal idea. It is found in ancient and modern sources from both East and West, including science, philosophy and religion. This table summarizes the uses of the idea in many of these fields.

Field	Fire	Water	Air
Electrical charge	+	-	0
Direction	Out	In	Neutral
Pulsation phase	Centrifugal	Centripetal	Transitional
	Involutionary	Evolutionary	
Oriental	Yang	Yin	Balance, Qi
Ayurveda	Pingala	Ida	Sushumna
Sanskrit	Rajas	Tamas	Satva
Current Movement	Umbilical	Bi-Polar	Transverse
	Back to Front	Top to Bottom	Side to side
	Steady, rhythmic	Cyclic, changing	Stillness
	Push, Time	Pull, Space	
Brain/Body Dimension	Back-Front	Top to Bottom	Left-Right
	Focusing	Centering	Laterality
Body Zone	Top	Below, Outside	Middle, Inside
	Right, top, back	Left, bottom, front	Transitional zones
	Motor	Sensory	Diaphragm, Joints
Embryo	Mesoderm	Endoderm	Ectoderm
Developmental phase	Action/Expansion	Reaction/Contraction	Blueprint
Quality	Light, Hot	Dark, Cold	"No thing"
Breath	Inhale	Exhale	Rest, transition
Physiology	Feelings & Motives	Body	Mind
Nervous system	Sympathetic	Cerebro-Spinal	Parasympathetic
	"Fight or Flight"	Creates action	"Rest & Repose"
	Thoraco-Lumbar	Extremities	Cranio-Sacral
Blood Vessels	Arteries	Veins	
Muscles	Flexion	Extension	Rest
Gender, Essence	Male, sperm	Female, egg	
Brain area	Usually Left, Logic	Usually Right, Reflex	Midlines
	Intellect, Either/Or	Intuition, Both/And	
Relationship role	Creative, Directing	Receptive, Yielding	Neutral
Challenge	Responsibility, Doing	Contentment, Being	
Imbalance archetype	Tyrant, wimp	Doormat, Critic	
Yoga	Ha (Sun)	Tha (Moon)	
Astrology	Cardinal	Mutable	Fixed
Time	Beginning, Day	End, Night	Transitions
Seasons	Spring, Summer	Fall, Winter	Transitions
Temperature	Hot	Cold	
Bodywork	Stimulates	Changes	Soothes, balances
Star pattern	Interlaced Triangles	5 pointed	
Religious archetypes	Father	Son	Holy Ghost
	Vishnu	Shiva	Brahma
	Creator	Destroyer	Sustainer
Lifestyle protection	Avoid promiscuity	Vegetarian diet	Avoid intoxicants

Terminology Guide to the Elements

The Five Elements are a way to describe many aspects of experience and personality. This table gives words for qualities of each energy center. Qualities are linked in chronic patterns of healing (center column) or disease (side columns).

Element Emotion	Primary Quality	Focus on:	Balanced Neutral	Too Much Expanded	Too Little Contracted
ETHER Grief/Joy	Self-esteem	Achievement "I am"	Self-esteeming Accountable Longing Humble Making Choices	Arrogant Better than Shameless Tyrant	Worthless Less than Shamed Doormat/Victim
AIR Desire, Integrity	Moderation	Appearances "I want"	Honest Content Moderate	Pumped up Speedy Impatient Creating illusions Supermature Greedy, Dissatisfied	Tuned down Immobile Depressed Jealous Superimmature Hopeless
FIRE Power, Motivation	Self- knowledge	Power: "I care"	Warm Responsible Respectful Enthusiastic Forgiving	Raging at others Blaming Resentful Explosive Controlling others Judging Won't allow others' reality	Raging at self Blaming self Apathetic Imploding Controlled by others Doesn't know own reality or does know but won't tell
WATER Attachment Growth	Self-care	People "I need"	Changing Accepting Receptive Compassionate Nurturing	Isolated Antidependent Compulsive Passionate Charming Sex-addicted	Enmeshed Dependent Needy Possessive Despairing Love-addicted
EARTH	Self- protection	Material "I have"	Protecting Supporting Respecting Grounded Stable Able to let go Accepting Limits	Walls against involvement Invulnerable Paranoid Defensive Self-concealing Hypervigilant	No boundaries Too vulnerable Self-doubting Overly sensitive Defensive Resistance Frozen Anxious

What is Stress?

Stress is commonly considered one of the great maladies of modern society. We have created lifestyles and environments that constantly "stress" our entire being. Ancient stresses of the struggle for survival have been replaced with more complex pressures of time, money, and a thousand other tensions.

Hans Selye, author and pioneer stress researcher, found stress difficult to describe. His simple definition was, "the non-specific response of the body to any demand made upon it." The demand, called a "stressor," is neither negative nor positive but simply requires a response. Even the most delightful changes in our lives can be stressful for us. In this age of rapid growth and change, we are continually challenged to adapt with equanimity and balance. Many of our stressors come from our need for stimulation and growth; and we would not do without them, for they enliven and challenge us. Others we need to change, for they will hurt us in the long run. Energy exercises help release tension, but we must remember that the ability to discriminate between "positive" and "negative" stressors, and to seek ways to reduce negative influences, precedes exercise as a stress management strategy.

As we meet daily stresses, many of us have chosen to ignore or over-ride the body's natural feedback to us. The use of alcohol, caffeine, nicotine, painkillers and other drugs is symptomatic of the stresses of our modern lifestyle and our difficulty in managing them.

This book is about "personal responsibility." It teaches methods to take stresses in our lives and process them, to use our personal energy to enliven and grow rather than contract and suffer.

Where do stresses affect our bodies? It can be anywhere. There are many conditions currently considered to be stress related: heart disease, stroke, asthma, ulcers, migraine headaches, colitis, rheumatoid arthritis, depression, etc. All people are more prone to disease when they have been under stress so we could consider all disease to be stress related. When we experience stress, we might feel neck and shoulder tension, back ache, headache, fatigue, over-reactivity, tightness in the chest, depression, poor concentration, or chronic anxiety.

The body responds to stress by "calling in the guard." The initial response is called the alarm reaction or fight or flight response. The sympathetic nervous system activates and the body sets off hormonal activities which send messages to get ready for quick action. Blood pressure, heart rate, respiration, sweat and muscle tension increase while non-essential processes related to the digestive, urinary and reproductive systems are cut back. Though the breathing rate increases, the breath itself becomes shallower and we feel the state of stress in our body as the tension and shallowness of breath. We may also experience heart palpitation, weakness, knots in the stomach or other symptoms. Ideally, we respond in some way that ends the stress. Then we can relax and allow our body to readjust.

In some cases however, the stress persists and a second stage of response occurs called the resistance reaction. This allows the body to continue its readied state after the initial alarm reaction has dissipated. The blood chemistry returns to nearly normal, but blood pressure remains high due to blood volume increase from water retention. In most problems, this is the highest stage we reach before we return to normal.

However, when this stage is not successful the body will move to the stage of exhaustion. Cells become depleted as they use more and more potassium. They function less effectively and finally start to die. A strong long-term resistance reaction wears on the body, particularly the heart, blood vessels and adrenal cortex. The body may not be able to meet the heavy demands or may suddenly fail with the strain. Our ability to handle stressors is largely determined by our general health and the baseline from which we operate.

Obviously we wish to prevent this exhaustion. We cannot necessarily change the factors creating stress, but we can change our responses to them, and we can create a foundation level of vitality and general health that can meet the stresses we are exposed to.

Different people carry their stresses differently. We all tend to have a "vulnerable spot" where we feel things first as our body begins to feel pressure. We can use our own connection with the feeling of discomfort in this area as an automatic alarm system telling us to take a stress release break. This feedback function is a natural value of (and reason for) pain.

We tend to have certain common tightening responses to stress. The tendon guard reflex is our natural primitive defense. You can picture this when you imagine a lizard freezing in place when startled. In our bodies, we similarly freeze and lock the back. The knees become rigid and we tighten up the underside of the foot, the muscles in the back of the calves and thighs and up the spine when we feel threatened. In many activities we work with the muscles involved in this reflex and help them to release their tension.

-- MLM

Exercises in a Chair

Exercise is for everyone. Youthful people in good health can easily do the exercises in this book, but the unwell, overweight and elderly can have difficulty. Don't be discouraged! If the obstacles are greater (and the beginning will be the hardest), the potential for change is also greater. There is always a way to exercise.

This list is for people of limited exercise capability. All these can be done while seated in a chair, with little effort.

Breathing is emphasized even more than usual. With each position take time to breathe deeply and fully, emphasizing the exhale. This does not mean hyperventilation, but rather deep and relaxed breathing with plenty of rest as needed.

These exercises are listed in a series which can be done in sequence, omitting any which are too difficult or time consuming. This sequence is not fixed: experiment with other orders or do just the favorite or most appropriate postures.

In the Beginning

Going Deeper

At the End

Exercises for Pregnancy

This list gives exercises which are particularly valuable during pregnancy. Generally, only a few of the exercises in this book are contraindicated for pregnancy. As a rule, avoid exercises which are painful (such as deep pressure on the feet or calves) or which require extreme exertion (such as rowing with great resistance, and woodchopper). The Up and Down Ha Breath should not be done rapidly or with any downward force.

Attitudes are emphasized during pregnancy. We advocate a peaceful, low-pressure lifestyle during this time especially. We believe that the baby "sees" and "hears" everything that happens while in the womb. Security is a top priority. Talking to the baby (make it feel wanted), enjoying soft music and natural scenery, and optimistic, positive thoughts are valuable during this time.

Exercise	Page
Squat	54
Pyramid	52
Rocking Perineal	61
Sacral Rock	63
Cliffhanger	23
Diaphragm exercises (be gentle!)	32
Buttons series	74
Cook's Hook Ups	69
Positive Points	77
Seated Scissors Kick	60
Humming	85
Five Pointed Star Butterfly	51

In addition, the following are brief descriptions of useful exercises specifically for pregnancy. These are well-known in birth classes.

Pelvic Tuck: On all fours, alternately flex and release the pelvis.
Partial Inversion: Lying head down on a slanted surface relieves gravity pressure.
Kegels: Tighten and relax internal muscles of pelvic floor.

Glossary of Terms

Activation: An exercise technique which uses muscle pressure against light resistance to relax the muscle. Similar to isometric exercise, but more gentle and for relaxation more than strength building.

Air Element: The second element and level of materialization, the gases. Centered in the chest.

Air Principle: The neutral blueprint from which action and reaction are generated.

Ayurveda: The traditional medicine of northern India, one of the primary sources for Polarity Therapy.

Bi-Polar Current: The movement of the Water Principle, from top to bottom and back. Also called Long-line or Longitudinal current.

Bioenergetics: A therapeutic system created by Alexander Lowen.

Breathing: An exercise technique in which the breath is consciously controlled and observed.

Centrifugal treatment: In bodywork, treatment from the inside out and/or the top down, emphasizing involutionary function.

Centripetal treatment: In bodywork, treatment from the outside in and/or the bottom up, emphasizing evolutionary function.

CranioSacral Therapy: A therapeutic system based on understanding the qualities, roles and relationships of cranium, spinal system and sacrum. The Upledger Institute in Florida is a principal teacher of CS Therapy.

Diaphragm: The large dome-shaped muscle in the solar plexus. See p. 32.

Differentiation: An exercise technique in which the movements of muscles are isolated from habitual groups, for relaxation and self-discovery.

Earth Element: The fifth element and level of materialization, solids. Centered in the pelvic floor.

Elements, Five: See Five Elements

Energy: A general term for the primal force which creates, sustains, and destroys all phenomena.

Energy Balancing: A term for working with subtle fields and pathways to restore the natural flow of current in the body.

Ether Element: The subtlest level of materialization, the space in which the lower four elements are created. A reflection of the Air Principle. Centered at the throat.

Fire Element: The third level element and level of materialization, heat. Centered in the solar plexus.

Fire Principle: The involutionary, active, Yang side of the duality of phenomena.

Five Elements: The second (after the Three Principles) level of differentiation applied to phenomena, referring to the increasing density of manifestation as spirit moves into matter. They can be thought of as the space, gas, heat, liquids and solids of all existence.

Five Pointed Star: The geometric pattern of the Yin Water Principle.

Hallucis tendon: A tendon which attaches the big toe to the lower leg, used in energy balancing bodywork. Its main access point is on the inside of the ankle.

Interlaced Triangles: The geometric pattern of the Yang Fire Principle.

Kinesiology: A natural biofeedback system using muscles as indicators of underlying energy movement. Systems using kinesiology include Touch for Health, Edu-K, Hyperton-x, PHP (Professional Health Provider) and One Brain.

Lengthening: An exercise technique in which the range of potential motion of a muscle is increased.

Longitudinal Current: The movement of the Water Principle, from top to bottom and back. Also called Long-line or Bi-polar current.

Martial Arts: A general term for the physical disciplines of the far East, including T'ai Ch'i and others. These were based on Polarity ideas and had the goals of self-understanding and living in harmony with nature.

Meridians: Energy current circuits in Chinese acupuncture, thought to trace the pathway of the Fire Principle.

Motor: The functions of the Yang, Fire Principle

Pannetier, Pierre: (1914-1984) One of Dr. Stone's best known Polarity Therapy students and a successful teacher of Polarity in America.

Polarity: The idea of two interdependent forces. It is the foundation of several energy-based health systems, Eastern philosophy, and modern physical science.

Prana: A Sanskrit term for the subtle life force of energy which rides on the air.

Pressure: An exercise technique involving touch, for energy balancing, tissue release, or easing tension.

Principles, Three: See Three Principles.

Rajas: A Sanskrit term for the positive, Yang Fire Principle.

Reflexology: The concept that different parts of the body are linked by invisible connections, being "reflections" of each other.

Satva: Sanskrit term for the neutral Air Principle.

Sensory: The functions of the Yin, Water Principle

Six Pointed Star: See Interlaced Triangles, which is the preferred term.

Stillpoint: In CranioSacral Therapy, a healing moment when the body relaxes and self-adjusts. The term refers specifically to a pause in the cranial pulsation or rhythm.

Tamas: A Sanskrit term for the negative, Yin, Water Principle.

Three Principles: The first and most basic differentiation applied to primal Energy. They can be thought of as the beginning, the middle and the end of any event, or as going out, coming back, and stillness. See the table on page 132.

Transverse Current: The movement of the Air Principle, from side to side in a spiral shape.

Umbilical Current: The movement of the Fire Principle, a spiral radiating out from the Umbilicus. Also called the Spiral current.

Water Element: The fourth element and level of materialization, liquids. Centered in the pelvis.

Water Principle: The evolutionary, reactive, Yin side of the duality of phenomena.

Wu-Wei: Literally, "effortless effort" of Oriental physical discipline systems.

Yang: The Chinese term for the active, involutionary side of any manifestation of energy.

Yin: The Chinese term for the reactive, evolutionary side of any manifestation of energy.

Yoga: Literally, Union. Ancient Indian systems of self-discipline and self realization, and a source for Polarity Therapy.

Part Five
Lists & Indexes

Exercises Listed in Alphabetical Order

140

Energy Exercises

Rebounding	98	72	Water	Water
Roar	87	60	Ether, Fire	Fire
Rocking Cliff	21	2	Air	Fire
Rocking V	29	9	Air, Ether	Fire
Rowing	64	38	All	Fire
Sacral Rock	63	37	Water	Fire
Satvic 5 Pointed Star Butterfly	79	51	Ether	Fire
Satvic 6 Pointed Star Balance	77	50	Water, Earth	Water
Sciatic Ha Breath	42	19	Fire	Fire
Scissors Kick	59	33	Water	Fire
Seated Scissors Kick	60	34	Water	Fire
Sensory Balance Posture	66	39	Ether	Air
Shoulder reflexes	19	1	Air	Fire
Shoulder Shrug Neck Roll	25	4	Air, Ether	Fire
Shoulder Tapping	26	5	Air	Fire
Side to Side Ha Breath	45	22	Fire	Air, Fire
Skin Brushing	96	69	Earth	Water
Space Buttons	75	45	Ether	Fire
Squat	54	32	All	Air
Sympathetic Balance	80	53	Ether	Fire
Taoist Arch	31	10	Air	Water
Tennis Ball Head Cradle	82	55	Ether	Fire
Thinking Cap	82	54		
Thymus Thump	84	57	Air	Air
Up and Down Ha Breath	40	18	Fire	All
Valve Tapping	97	71	Earth	Water
Watch your Breath	93	66	Air	All
Wise Man of Old	68	41	Ether	Air
Woodchopper	46	23	Fire	Water, Fire

Exercises Listed by Primary Element

Listing of exercises by the Element primarily affected is an indefinite categorization, because it implies that the elements can be simply separated, when in fact they are all interrelated. Nevertheless, the following list is offered as an introductory approach.

Number	Exercise	Page	Element	Principle
31	Pyramid	52	All	All
32	Squat	54	All	Air
35	Light Rocking Perineal	61	All	Air
38	Rowing	64	All	Fire
54	Ear Reflexes	82	All	Air
56	Fountain of Love	83	All	Fire
63	Dennison Laterality Repatterning	89	All	All
68	Box	95	All	Water
8	Head Lift	28	Ether	Air
39	Sensory Balance Posture	66	Ether	Air
41	Wise Man of Old	68	Ether	Air
42	Cook's Hook Ups	69	Ether	Air
44	Earth Buttons	75	Ether	Water
45	Space Buttons	75	Ether	Fire
46	Brain Buttons	76	Ether	Air
47	Brain Energy Buttons	76	Ether	All
49	Positive Points	77	Ether	Water
51	Satvic 5 Pointed Star Balance	79	Ether	Fire
53	Sympathetic Balance	80	Ether	Fire
55	Tennis Ball Head Cradle	82	Ether	Fire
58	Humming	85	Ether	Air
59	Ha!	86	Ether	Fire
61	Ah	87	Ether	Water

Exercises Listed by Principle

Listing the exercises according to the Three Principles is even less well-defined than the preceding elemental list. Generally the Air Principle (Neutral, Satva) is soothing and balancing, the Fire Principle (Yang, Rajas) is stimulating and moving, and the Water Principle (Yin, Tamas) is changing and eliminative. An exercise with stillness will be involving the Air Principle. An exercise with movement, muscular action or strong sound will involve the Fire Principle. An exercise which connects top and bottom, facilitates elimination or letting go, or causes change involves the Water Principle. Obviously, many postures combine movement with balancing, or balancing with changing. This list is an entry-level categorization with the overall caveat that this kind of categorization is limited in its value.

Number	Exercise	Page	Principle	Element
48	Balance Buttons	76	Air	Ether Fire
46	Brain Buttons	76	Air	Ether
52	Bridge Reflex	80	Air	Air, Ether
3	Cliffhanger	23	Air	Air
42	Cook's Hook Ups	69	Air	Ether
54	Ear Reflexes	82	Air	All
8	Head Lift	28	Air	Ether
58	Humming	85	Air	Ether
35	Light Rocking Perineal	61	Air	All
39	Sensory Balance Posture	66	Air	Ether
32	Squat	54	Air	All
57	Thymus Thump	84	Air	Air
41	Wise Man of Old	68	Air	Ether
21	Pierre Ha Breath	43	Air, Fire	Fire
22	Side to Side Ha Breath	45	Air, Fire	Fire
67	Alternate Nostril Breathing	94	All	Air
65	Belly Breathing	93	All	Air
47	Brain Energy Buttons	76	All	Ether
63	Dennison Laterality Repatterning	89	All	All
64	Inhale 2, Hold 8, Exhale 4	93	All	Air
31	Pyramid	52	All	All
18	Up and Down Ha Breath	40	All	Fire
66	Watch your Breath	93	All	Air
20	Arch Pull Ha Breath	43	Fire	Fire
7	Arm Activation	27	Fire	Air
26	Back Curl	48	Fire	Fire
24	Back Reflexes	47	Fire	Fire
27	Clock	49	Fire	Fire
14	Diaphragm Activation	36	Fire	Fire
56	Fountain of Love	83	Fire	All
25	Gluteal Activation	48	Fire	Fire
59	Ha!	86	Fire	Ether
43	Jelly Roll	74	Fire	Fire
40	Motor Balance Position	67	Fire	Fire
6	Owl	26	Fire	Ether, Air
60	Roar	87	Fire	Ether, Fire
2	Rocking Cliff	21	Fire	Air
9	Rocking V	29	Fire	Air, Ether
38	Rowing	64	Fire	All
37	Sacral Rock	63	Fire	Water
51	Satvic 5 Pointed Star Butterfly	79	Fire	Ether

19	Sciatic Ha Breath	42	Fire	Fire
33	Scissors Kick	59	Fire	Water
34	Seated Scissors Kick	60	Fire	Water
1	Shoulder reflexes	19	Fire	Air
4	Shoulder Shrug Neck Roll	25	Fire	Air, Ether
5	Shoulder Tapping	26	Fire	Air
45	Space Buttons	75	Fire	Ether
53	Sympathetic Balance	80	Fire	Ether
55	Tennis Ball Head Cradle	82	Fire	Ether
15	Diaphragm Pres Leg Life	36	Fire, Air	Fire
13	Diaphragm Press	35	Fire, Air	Fire
11	Diaphragm Reflexes	33	Fire, Air	Fire
17	Lion Roar	38	Fire, Air	Fire
61	Ah	87	Water	Ether
68	Box	95	Water	All
30	Butterfly Activation	51	Water	Water
75	Calf Lengthening- Gastrocnemius	100	Water	Fire, Earth
74	Calf Lengthening- Soleus	100	Water	Fire, Earth
70	Colon Reflexes	97	Water	Earth
44	Earth Buttons	75	Water	Ether
36	Foot Flex	62	Water	Water
76	Hamstring Lengthening	101	Water	Fire, Earth
73	Inner Thigh Lengthening	99	Water	Fire
62	Lazy Eights for Eyes	89	Water	Ether
16	Organ Drain	38	Water	Fire
29	Pelvic Reflexes	50	Water	Water
49	Positive Points	77	Water	Ether
77	Psoas Lengthening	101	Water	Water
72	Rebounding	98	Water	Water
50	Satvic 6 Pointed Star Balance	77	Water	Water, Earth
69	Skin Brushing	96	Water	Earth
10	Taoist Arch	31	Water	Air
71	Valve Tapping	97	Water	Earth
12	Calf Reflex	34	Water, Air	Fire
23	Woodchopper	46	Water, Fire	Fire
28	Pelvic Lift	49	Water, Fire	Water

Index of Illustrations- Alphabetical Order

Index of References

The following is a list of all authors and references cited in this book. Citations of the works of Dr. Randolph Stone are excluded, being too numerous to meaningfully recount here.

Author, Pages

Arroyo, Stephen 122
Bach-y-Rita, Eileen 49
Barhydt, Hamilton 26, 36, 50, 74, 76, 77, 93
Beaulieu, John 84, 85, 115
Berkson, Devaki 21, 22, 32, 39, 46, 49, 58, 60
Busa, Sam 22
Caspari, Elizabeth 84
Capra, Fritjof 3, 5, 9, 86
Chitty, Anna 118
Chopra, Deepak 3, 4, 84, 103, 106, 121, 122
Cook, Wayne 69, 70
Cousins, Norman 33, 72, 87, 106
Dennison, Paul 26, 27, 36, 51, 63, 69, 70, 74, 76, 77, 82, 89, 92, 112, 129
Diamond, John 31, 32, 34, 84
Dychtwald, Ken 33, 47, 84, 106, 115
Fast, Julius 103, 104
Feldenkrais, Moshe 18, 33, 49, 50, 103, 113
Francis, John 24, 30, 35, 37, 39, 42, 45, 46, 51, 54, 58, 60, 67, 68, 82
Gach, Michael 21, 32, 51, 83
Gerber, Richard 106, 122
Govinda, Lama Anagarika 86
Gordon, Richard. 5, 73
Gray, Robert 96
Hay, Louise 72, 115
Horwitz, Ted & Himmelman, Susan 106
Jensen, Bernard 96
Joudry, Patricia 85

Juhan, Deann 72, 106
Kaptchuk, Ted 78, 118, 127
Keleman, Stanley 9, 115
Kurtz, Ron & Prestera, Hector 92, 106, 111, 118
Kushi, Michio 78, 112
LaBords, Jeanne 115
Lowen, Alexander iv, 24, 31, 32, 49, 93, 95, 103, 104, 115
MacDougall 94
Mahoney, Frank 21, 33, 36, 63
Mellody, Pia 127
Menuhin, Yehudi 85
Muromota, Naboru 78
Pannetier, Pierre 1, 43
Pelletier, Kenneth 107, 122
Reich, Wilhelm 31
Robbins, John 94
Robbins, Tony 6, 93, 112, 113, 115
Seidman, Maruti 24, 30, 42, 54, 60
Siegel, Alan 24, 35, 58, 63
Siegel, Bernie 72
Selye, Hans 134
Sills, Franklyn 6, 42, 54, 58, 72
Stokes & Whiteside 27, 70, 73, 82, 107, 112, 117
Thie, John 4, 71, 77, 82, 104
Trager, Milton 57
Upledger, John 70, 82, 83
Welles, William 96
Wilhelm, Richard (trans.) 118, 122
Zukav, Gary 9

Bibliography

Arroyo, Stephen, Astrology, Psychology and the Four Elements (CRCS, Reno, 1975)

Bach-y-Rita, Eileen, "Feldenkrais at Home" (Cassette Series, Bach-y-Rita, Mill Valley CA, 1985)

Barhydt, Hamilton & Elizabeth, Self-Help for Stress and Pain (Loving Life, Auburn CA, 1989)

Beaulieu, John, Music & Sound in the Healing Arts (Station Hill Press, Barrytown NY, 1987)

Berkson, Devaki, The Foot Book (Barnes & Noble, NY, 1977)

Capra, Fritjof, The Tao of Physics (Shambala, Berkeley, 1975)

Chitty, Anna, "Man and Woman" (Murrieta Foundation, Murrieta CA, 1988)

Chopra, Deepak, Quantum Healing (Bantam, New York, 1989)

Cook, Wayne and Wanda, Universal Truths (Wanda Cook, Prescott AZ, 1988)

Cousins, Norman, Head First (Dutton, New Yor, 1989)

Dennisons, Paul & Gail, Brain Gym (Edu-Kinesthetics, Glendale, 1986)

Dennisons, Paul & Gail, Edu-K for Kids (Edu-Kinesthetics, Glendale, 1987)

Dennisons, Paul & Gail, Personalized Whole Brain Integration (Edu-Kinesthetics, Glendale, 1985)

Dennison, Paul, Switching On (Edu-Kinesthetics, Glendale, 1981)

Diamond, John, Your Body Doesn't Lie (Warner, New York, 1979)

Dychtwald, Ken, Bodymind (Tarcher, Los Angeles, 1976)

Fast, Julius, Body Language (Pocket Books, NY, 1970)

Feldenkrais, Moshe, Body & Mature Behavior (International Universities Press, NY, 1973)

Feldenkrais, Moshe, The Master Moves (Meta, Cupertino, 1984)

Francis, John, Polarity Self-Help Exercises (APTA, Boston, 1989)

Gach, Michael, Accu-Yoga (Japan Publication, NY, 1981)

Gerber, Richard, Vibrational Medicine (Bear & Co., Santa Fe, 1988)

Gordon, Richard, Your Healing Hands (Wingbow, Berkeley, 1984)

Govinda, Lama, Foundations of Tibetan Mysticism (Rider & Co., London, 1960)

Gray, Robert, The Colon Health Handbook (Emerald, Reno, 1986)

Hay, Louise, Heal Your Body (Hay House, Santa Monica, 1984)

Horwitz, Ted, Tai Chi Ch'uan (Chicago Review Press, Chicago, 1976)

Jensen, Bernard, Tissue Cleaning Through Bowel Management (Jensen, Escondido CA, 1981)

Joudry, Patricia, Sound Therapy for the Walkman (Steele & Steele, St. Denis, Saskatchewan, 1984)

Juhan, Deane, Job's Body (Station Hill Press, Barrytown NY, 1987)

Kaptchuk, Michael, The Web That Has No Weaver (Congdon & Weed, NY, 1983)

Keleman, Stanley Emotional Anatomy (Center Press, Berkeley, 1985)

Kurtz, Ron. & Prestera, Hector, The Body Reveals (Harper & Row, San FRancisco, 1976)

Kurtz, Ron, Hakomi Therapy (Kurtz, Ashland, 1989)

Kushi, Michio, The Book of Macrobiotics (Japan Publications, Tokyo and New York, 1977)

Lowen, Alexander, Bioenergetics (Penguin, New York, 1975)

Lowens, A. and Leslie, The Way to Vibrant Health (Harper Colophon, NY, 1977)

MacDougall, John A. and Mary A., The MacDougall Plan, (New Century, New York, 1983)

Mahoney, Frank, Hyperton-X (Hyperton-X, El Segundo CA, 1988)

Mellody, Pia, Facing Codependence (Harper & Row, San Francisco, 1989)

Muramoto, Naboru, Healing Ourselves (Avon, New York, 1973)

Pelletier, Kenneth, Mind as Healer, Mind as Slayer (Delta/Dell, New York, 1977)

Robbins, John, <u>Diet for a New America</u> (Stillpoint, Walpole, 1987)

Robbins, Tony, <u>Unlimited Power</u> (Fawcett Columbine, New York, 1986)

Seidman, Maruti, <u>A Guide to Polarity Therapy</u> (Newcastle, No. Hollywood, 1986)

Siegel, Alan, <u>Polarity Therapy</u> (Prism Press, Dorset England, 1987)

Sills, Franklyn, <u>The Polarity Process</u> (Element Books, Dorset, 1989)

Stokes & Whiteside, <u>Louder Than Words</u> (Three in One Concepts, Burbank, 1988)

Stokes & Whiteside, <u>One Brain</u> (Three in One Concepts, Burbank, 1987)

Stone, Randolph, <u>Health Building</u> (CRCS, Sebastopol, 1986)

Stone, Randolph, <u>Mystic Bible</u> (Radha Soami Satsang Beas, Delhi, 1977)

Stone, Randolph, <u>Polarity Therapy Vol. I and Vol. II</u> (CRCS, Sebastopol, 1986 and 1987)

Thie, John, <u>Touch for Health</u> (DeVorss & Co, Marina del Rey, 1979)

Upledger, J. & Vredevoogd, <u>CranioSacral Therapy II</u> (Eastland Press, Seattle, 1987)

Upledger, John, <u>CranioSacral Therapy I</u> (Eastland Press, Seattle, 1983)

Welles, William, "The Hidden Crime of the Porcelain Throne" (Welles, San Diego, 1988). For information on Dr. Welles' products to assist Squatting: W. Welles, D.C., 4295 Gestner St., Ste 3A, San Diego, CA 92117 (619) 458-9210.

Wilhelm, Richard, trans., <u>The I Ching</u> (Princeton Univ. Press, Princeton, 1971

Zukav, Gary, <u>The Dancing Wu Li Masters</u> (Bantam, NY, 1980)

References for Face Reading

Narayan S. Khalsa, Ph.D., has adopted an Ayurvedic perspective for comprehensive analysis of the face. His article "What's in a Face? (Unpublished, 1985) cites the following references:

Bellak, L. and Baker, S.S., <u>Reading Faces</u>, Holt, Rinehart & Winston, New York, 1980.

Shen, P. and Wilson, J., <u>Face Fortunes: The Ancient Chinese Art of Feature Reading</u>, Perigree Books, New York, 1982.

Kushi, M., <u>Oriental Diagnosis: What Your Face Reveals</u>, Sunwheel Publications, London, 1978.

Mar, T.T., <u>Face Reading</u>, Signet Books, New York, 1974.

Rinn, W.E., "The Neuropsychology of Facial Expression," *APA Journal*, 1984.

Stokes, G. and Whiteside, D. <u>Under the Code</u>, The Body/Mind Connection, 1979.

Trotter, R.J., "The Sign of Music Read in the Face," *Psychology Today*, March 1985, New York.

Ekman, P. and Friesen, W.V., <u>Unmasking the Face: A Guide to Recognizing Emotions from Facial Expressions</u>, Prentice Hall, Englewood Cliffs, NJ, 1975.

Ekman, P. and Friesen, W.V., <u>Facial Action Coding System: Investigator's</u> Guide, Consulting Psychologists Press, Palo Alto, 1978.

Whiteside, D. and Stokes, G., "Louder than Words: The Structure Equals Function Connection," 1980.

Whiteside, R.L., <u>Facial Language</u>, Pocket Books, New York, 1975.

Young, L., <u>Secrets of the Face: The Chinese Art of Reading Character through Facial Structure and Features,</u> Little, Brown & Co., Boston, 1984.

Zajonc, R.B., "Emotion and Facial Efference: A Theory Reclaimed," *Science*, V. 228, 1984, pp. 15-21.

Energy Exercises

ORDER FORM

Ship to:

Name: _____

Address: _____

City: _____

State: _____ Zip: _____

Telephone: _____

# Copies	Per Copy	Total
	$17.95	
Shipping		$3.00
Tax (CO orders only)		
Total		

Payment: Check or Money Order, payable to Polarity Press

Send completed form to:

**Polarity Press
2410 Jasper Ct.
Boulder, CO 80304
(303) 443-9847**

Ask about volume purchase discounts

Other Polarity Therapy Products available from Polarity Press

Send for a free descriptive brochure!

POLARITY CHARTS
$8
$35 per set of 5

These charts are black and white reproductions of charts in this book, on heavy 18" x 28" paper. These are an invaluable aid for teaching the Energy approach to Health.

Charts available:

Chart	Page
Wireless Anatomy	13
Energy Zones	15
25 Combinations	105
5 & 6 Pointed Stars	77
Weaving the Body	110

MURRIETA HOT SPRINGS VEGETARIAN COOKBOOK
$9.95

Dr. Stone taught how diet could be used for specific health benefits, and created two diet plans for cleansing and maintenance programs. These are the "Purifying" and "Health Building" diets. This 232 page, well-illustrated cookbook has delicious recipes for Purifying and Health Building diets, each clearly marked for easy reference. It also includes many "Gourmet" recipes, a special section on "Spa Cuisine" for weight loss dining, and an educational section on the Polarity approach to diet.

ENERGY EXERCISES VIDEO
$29.95

This one hour film by Anna Chitty gives easy-to-follow instructions for the "Polarity Yoga" exercises presented in this book.

MURRIETA POLARITEA
$3.00 per box
$30 per case of 12
Specify Bags or Loose

This delicious, healthful tea comes from Dr. Stone's own formula as described in Health Building. It is a soothing, slightly-sweet blend of five herbs all known for their benefit to the digestive system: peppermint, fennel, flax, licorice and fenugreek.

PSYCHOLOGY OF YIN AND YANG VIDEOS
$29.95 each (two titles)

These one hour films by Anna Chitty show how the Polarity Therapy concepts of Yang and Yin can be applied to mental patterns and relationships. Part One gives an overview of the essential personality qualities of Yang and Yin. Part Two tells how each has a particular language and set of needs in relationships.

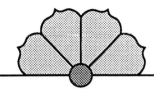

Energy Exercises

ORDER FORM

Ship to:

Name: _____

Address: _____

City: _____

State: _____ Zip: _____

Telephone: _____

# Copies	Per Copy	Total
	$17.95	
Shipping	$3.00	
Tax (CO orders only)		
Total		

Payment: Check or Money Order, payable to Polarity Press

Send completed form to:

**Polarity Press
2410 Jasper Ct.
Boulder, CO 80304
(303) 443-9847**

Ask about volume purchase discounts

Other Polarity Therapy Products available from Polarity Press
Send for a free descriptive brochure!

POLARITY CHARTS
$8
$35 per set of 5

These charts are black and white reproductions of charts in this book, on heavy 18" x 28" paper. These are an invaluable aid for teaching the Energy approach to Health.

Charts available:

Chart	Page
Wireless Anatomy	13
Energy Zones	15
25 Combinations	105
5 & 6 Pointed Stars	77
Weaving the Body	110

MURRIETA HOT SPRINGS VEGETARIAN COOKBOOK
$9.95

Dr. Stone taught how diet could be used for specific health benefits, and created two diet plans for cleansing and maintenance programs. These are the "Purifying" and "Health Building" diets. This 232 page, well-illustrated cookbook has delicious recipes for Purifying and Health Building diets, each clearly marked for easy reference. It also includes many "Gourmet" recipes, a special section on "Spa Cuisine" for weight loss dining, and an educational section on the Polarity approach to diet.

ENERGY EXERCISES VIDEO
$29.95

This one hour film by Anna Chitty gives easy-to-follow instructions for the "Polarity Yoga" exercises presented in this book.

MURRIETA POLARITEA
$3.00 per box
$30 per case of 12
Specify Bags or Loose

This delicious, healthful tea comes from Dr. Stone's own formula as described in Health Building. It is a soothing, slightly-sweet blend of five herbs all known for their benefit to the digestive system: peppermint, fennel, flax, licorice and fenugreek.

PSYCHOLOGY OF YIN AND YANG VIDEOS
$29.95 each (two titles)

These one hour films by Anna Chitty show how the Polarity Therapy concepts of Yang and Yin can be applied to mental patterns and relationships. Part One gives an overview of the essential personality qualities of Yang and Yin. Part Two tells how each has a particular language and set of needs in relationships.